Eccentric Islands

Eccentric Islands

Travels Real and Imaginary

/e

BILL HOLM

MILKWEED EDITIONS

Published 2000 by Milkweed Editions
Printed in the United States of America
Jacket design by Wink
Front cover photo by Terry G. Lacy
Map illustrations by Matt Kania
Author photo by Einar Oleson
Interior design by Elizabeth Cleveland
Music deciphering and notation (Finale 3.0) on pp. 256–57 by Jim Phillips
The text of this book is set in Chaparral.
00 01 02 03 04   5 4 3 2
First Edition

Milkweed Editions, a nonprofit publisher, gratefully acknowledges support from the Elmer L. and Eleanor J. Andersen Foundation; James Ford Bell Foundation; Bush Foundation; General Mills Foundation; Honeywell Foundation; Jerome Foundation; McKnight Foundation; Minnesota State Arts Board through an appropriation by the Minnesota State Legislature; Norwest Foundation on behalf of Norwest Bank Minnesota; Lawrence and Elizabeth Ann O'Shaughnessy Charitable Income Trust in honor of Lawrence M. O'Shaughnessy; Oswald Family Foundation; Ritz Foundation on behalf of Mr. and Mrs. E. J. Phelps Jr.; John and Beverly Rollwagen Fund of the Minneapolis Foundation; St. Paul Companies, Inc.; Star Tribune Foundation; Target Foundation on behalf of Dayton's, Mervyn's California and Target Stores; U.S. Bancorp Piper Jaffray Foundation on behalf of U.S. Bancorp Piper Jaffray; and generous individuals.

Library of Congress Cataloging-in-Publication Data

Holm, Bill, 1943–
    Eccentric islands : travels real and imaginary / Bill Holm. — 1st ed.
        p. cm.
    ISBN 1-57131-245-5
        1. Holm, Bill, 1943—Journeys. 2. Voyages and travels. 3. Islands. I. Title.

G530.H638 H66 2000
910.4—dc21

                                                                    00-023180

I dedicate this book to two old friends who thought it ought to be written and who goaded and charmed its lazy author to write it.

To Emilie Buchwald, publisher, editor, and counselor, who graces the sometimes shabby world of book publishing with intelligence, generosity, and stubborn persistence. My whole life as a writer owes her a great debt.

To Wincie Jóhannsdóttir, who has shown me the life inside Iceland for over twenty years and, after too long an absence, needled me into coming back to discover how much I love this peculiar place and how much it has taught me.

Eccentric Islands

Pronunciation Note

In most books the odd letters in the Icelandic alphabet are simply translated to awkward English equivalents. In this book I mean to restore the honorable peculiarities of real Icelandic orthography. To that end the reader should recognize these three letters:

þ, ð, æ

Thorn—þ—and eth—ð—represent the two English sounds of *th* in "thin" and "wither" respectively. The Icelandic word for "that"—það—is pronounced *thath*, the initial *th* unvoiced and the terminal *th* voiced. The two letters simply describe two different sounds you make with your mouth but spell sloppily. These two letters and this sound distinction existed in Anglo-Saxon. We need them back. Æ is pronounced exactly as the English diphthong in "eye." Ö is similar in sound to the German umlaut. Á is pronounced *ow* as in "pow-wow."

Icelandic words and names are *always* stressed *heavily* on the first syllable. There are *no* exceptions to the rule. *R*s are trilled with as much violence and ferocity as you can muster.

There are more rules but these are all you need to begin enjoying the grand noise of these words in your mouth.

Eccentric Islands

ॐ *Call Me Island*

CALL ME ISLAND. Or call me Holm. Same thing. It's one way to start, though like so many other human starts—or human books—it's not original. We stand on the shoulders of our ancestors no matter how many machines we invent. Only our memory and our metaphors carry us forward, not our money, not our gadgets, not our opinions.

"No man is an island," said John Donne in a sermon, but I am. Holm—an Old Norse masculine noun, whose forms are *Hólmi* or *Hólmur*—means small island or inshore island, in some dictionaries islet, the diminutive form of island. Island itself comes from Old Norse too: *ey,* traced back from the old hypothetical proto-Indo-European *Ea,* "river" (thus all water), grappled to "land." You know what land means; its form has not changed. Thus an island is a tract of land surrounded by water, but smaller than a continent.

Then what is the size of a continent you ask? How many galaxies between here and infinity? How many thimbles full of water in the Pacific? How many boxelder bugs in your own tree? An island is whatever we call an island. Or whatever I call an island. I am one and thus have rights and prerogatives in this matter.

I call Iceland island, as well as Mujeres, Madagascar, Moloka'i, and Mallard. In Arizona, locals call the Chiricahua Mountains "sky islands." An astronomer might call earth an island in space. Or the Milky Way an archipelago.

Island is both thing and metaphor. Without the weight of things, metaphors turn vapid, sour, empty, fly off into space and connect with nothing. Eugene McCarthy, both poet and public man, thought the Vietnam War one consequence of Washington's weakened metaphors. How else to explain that triumph of folly in American history? Islands are good to think on if a man would express himself neatly. They are generally made of rock and whatever garnishes nature or human ingenuity provide to decorate them. In going for the bottom of things, keep plunging until you strike the hard and intractable.

Some islands start as things in search of metaphor, but others begin in metaphors that grapple things into their space. Call them "sign" islands, spiritual facts gone backward to natural facts, as our island philosopher Emerson would have it. Islands of age, death, pain, prison, experiment, magic, isolation, even the island of music, thus the invisible. Don't sink under the weight of your prejudice against the invisible.

Many years ago a rich merchant built a grand house on the shore of Lake Phalen on the northeast side of Saint Paul, Minnesota. A small island in the lake that blocked his view of sunset irritated him, so he decided to rearrange nature. He bought the island, then hired a crew to remove it. They did— tree, rock, weed, grass, dirt, everything, boat to truck to dump. The island ceased to exist except as ghost, rumor, or example. It was—it is—invisible. Was the man pleased? No one can remember his name, only the story. Is he dead? Probably.

Since he is now invisible, has he, like his pesky island, ceased to exist too? Not so long as somebody remembers the story, whether it is true or not. Call it "The Disappeared Island." Let the name stick.

Farms in Iceland mostly huddle along the coast. The tail end of the gulf stream means warmth (the fjords seldom freeze in winter) and food: seabirds, eggs gathered on cliffs, seals, sharks, fish, washed-up whale carcasses, and that most precious of all commodities in a treeless place: driftwood. The sea is an easier highway to the outside world than the roads over harsh interior lava deserts. An Icelander grows up with salt in his nose and the boom of surf in his ear. The whole economic life of modern Iceland depends on the sea, the fish harvest. Farms, offices, shops, crafts are only hobbies subsidized by the Atlantic Ocean that keeps (as it has always kept) the whole country afloat in the world of commerce. Move Iceland to the interior of a continent and it would be uninhabited in ten years, or less. To be an island is to be alive. Civilization—here at least—floats on saltwater.

The vast majority of nineteenth-century Icelandic immigrants to the New World settled not just away from the sea, but as far equidistant from saltwater as it is possible (aside from central Siberia) to be on this planet. Nor have we started inquiring of our new poverty-stricken immigrants their preferences in climate, landscape, and (perish the word) lifestyle. They go now, as they went then, where there is empty space, and where it is possible to eat and stay alive. My great-grandfather came to western Minnesota near the South Dakota border, an area undisturbed by tidal irregularities, and took a farm. There, in Swede Prairie Township in Yellow Medicine County, he found himself at least eighteen hundred miles (or three thousand kilometers) from salt water in any direction. He might better have chosen Rugby, North Dakota, the geographical belly button of the North American continent, but he at least came within a few hundred miles of it. No sharks would swim close to his property (his home district in northeast Iceland was famous for the quality of its rotten shark meat—a great Icelandic delicacy), nor would kelp clutter his ditches. His farm, bought in 1885 from the railroad, sat atop a slight swelling on the prairie. In a place with low geographical standards, and not a real mountain for a thousand miles in any direction, he called it a hill. The nearest creek was three miles away, but it froze in November, dried up in August, and even in good years contained only bullheads and mud carp. So Jóhannes Sveinsson and his son Sveinn Jóhannesson (my grandfather) changed their names to "island" so that they could become citizens of a country that insisted, tediously, on the same last name for an entire family. Icelanders, who still use patronymics, don't pay much attention to last names except as a means of tracking down who was in whose bed on any given winter night.

Sometime in the 1890s Sveinn Jóhannesson became Swan J. Island, and a century later, I am William Jon Island. It's a satisfactory name, and I'll keep it. Evidently LeRoi Jones thought Imamu Amiri Baraka a blacker name than Jones. He was wrong. Jones is a fine black name, and he contributed to the honor of its history with his books. That's what it means to be an American, to take an inconsequential—even comic—name and domesticate it. We all bear the wrong names. Holm is the Old Norse equivalent of Jones or Smith or John Doe, a trifle, a commonplace, an anachronism, a puff of air. Why shouldn't a man, three thousand miles from his real home, thinking in the wrong language, looking out at a horizon of grass thousands of miles from large water, call himself "Island" and be done with it? I hope old Swan laughed when he signed his new name for the first time, maybe at a bank that loaned him a little island money to buy slabs of air-dried board-hard ocean fish at the Icelandic grocery store in Minneota.

Islands seduce us because sometimes the universe seems too big. We want to shrink it a little so that we can examine it, see what it is made from, and what is our just place in it. An island is a microcosm. We cannot count the trees, the animals, the humans, much less the insects or the orchids or even so modest a planet as the one we inhabit, but we imagine that the creatures on islands are countable, and sometimes they are.

Think of the thousand cartoons you have seen—in the *New Yorker* or a multitude of other places—of the marooned human or pair of humans (in whatever combination of sexes) on some microscopic tropical atoll, a little sand, one palm tree, one rock, the vastness of the sea. Humor and pathos live together in these scenes. Here at last, we think, life is cut down to the bone so that we can see what stuff it is made of. If two men, they are The Odd Couple; if man and woman, they will find the roots of the old sex wars and quarrel, as they might on a street in New York; if only one, there is a message in a bottle, generally with cheerless news. Do we love this cartoon scene because we imagine we can discover the bedrock of human nature inside it?

Our great American conscience nagger, Henry Thoreau, was not, in the geographical sense, an island man, but in the spiritual sense, he was never anything else. Walden Pond was his desert island, his plunge to spiritual bedrock, his downsizing of the universe in order to get a better look at it. "I wanted to live deep and suck out all the marrow of life, to live so sturdily and Spartan-like as to put to rout all that was not life, to cut a broad swath and shave close, to drive life into a corner, and reduce it to its lowest terms, and, if it proved to be mean, why then to get the whole and

genuine meanness of it, and publish its meanness to the world;
or if it were sublime, to know it by experience, and be able to give
a true account of it in my next excursion." Concord was too big,
so he rowed to his island in the woods, where the world was more
countable and visible, but where the invisible might peek out
now and then from behind the vastness of its mask to surrender
a nugget or two of wisdom.

I'm not sure I was looking for wisdom when I invented islands
on the prairie as a boy. Like most children, I longed for a private
world with boundaries unassailable by adults, or even by other
children. Maybe only children like me discover the essential isolate quality inside human beings before others, but I'd guess that
all humans discover it in the course of an average life; pain, disease, failure, betrayal, death, all have proved themselves adequate
instructors.

My father's island was his hilltop farm from which he could
survey the roof peaks of his neighbors' barns and the twenty-
mile-distant line of glacial hills that rose southwest of his house.
My island was not his island, despite the fact that we shared a
name. The farm seemed to me a bottomless pit with its practical
labor, animal smells, grain dust, whirling eternal winds, barbed-
wire boundaries. I discovered the imagination early, then fed it
with books, music, and daydreaming till it grew to the usual monstrous human size. I lived in a private mental world, sure that no
other human being on the face of the earth had any remote notion of the strange goings-on inside my head, or what singular
oddities gave me pleasure. I found my comrades among the dead:
Poe, Hawthorne, Shakespeare, Icelandic sagas in literature; the

fiercer and stranger books of the Bible: Job, Ecclesiastes, the
Song of Solomon; the romance of the Arctic: Fridtjof Nansen,
Vilhjalmur Stefansson, Robert Peary, and Frederick Cook, the
search for the lost Franklin expedition. I savored the gothic and
the horrible: Frankenstein, Dracula, stories of zombies, of corpses
risen from their coffins for revenge, mischief, self-assertion.

Though I think I was a friendly enough boy in my functions on
the surface of life, I was always convinced at bottom of my utter
disconnection from humanity. Who else longed for violin music,
dogsleds mushing over frozen ice floes, old heavy leather-bound
books, eerie scratchings on night windows from inhabitants of
the next world? I would look in the mirror at my pink, soft, fleshy
head, crowned with a mop of bright red hair, adorned with thick
black plastic glasses and think: there is someone else trapped
inside this body—another life, another possibility. The universe
has made some mistake here.

So in the brief subarctic Minnesota summer after the box-
elders and cottonwoods leafed out and the legions of insects
hatched, I would journey out with my equipage to furnish and
fortify my private island. It was not a long trip. Trees were scarce
on the prairie and aside from farm groves and river courses grew
one or two at a time in odd places, along fence lines or in the
middle of fields, where the birds had shat out or the wind had
scattered as if by random chance, a seed that actually amounted
to something and grew up to be a real tree. A fine old cottonwood
sat on a little island of grass in the middle of the field just west of
the house. You passed through a grove of Chinese elms and box-
elders to arrive at the field's edge and there it stood, as if out to
sea—either corn, wheat, alfalfa, oats, or flax. An ambitious farmer
might have cut down the tree to reap another bushel or two and
to avoid plowing around this impediment to agricultural progress,

but my father was willing to circle it and leave nature well enough
alone. His character did not resemble that of the rich merchant
island owner on Lake Phalen. I furnished my island always with
food, (I was and remain a happy eater), bottles of water, books,
paper, and pens. I used fallen branches and pulled up weeds and
farm scrap to make the island invisible to prying eyes, though
my father could always follow my progress from his tractor seat.
Such are the illusions of youth in its pursuit of a private world.

The illusion of island life always looked best in years when
my father planted the hilltop with flax. Flax is the loveliest of all
crops on the northern prairie. When it flowers, the field turns
into a sea of bright blue blossoms, pitching and rolling in that
omnipresent prairie wind. Now my island of green grass with its
single tree had the look of a real tropical island. I don't think I
ever pretended to canoe through the flax to arrive there, but
I might have with some justice. My imagination wasn't as big as
I thought. Corn provided the best cover. When it arrived at its
stately mature height, the island turned invisible even to my
father. Had I been able to invent secret and terrible rites, I could
have practiced them undisturbed, at least until my mother summoned me for a meal. Even the imagination doesn't like missing
dinner. It must be fed too—sometimes with pork chops and
rhubarb pie.

What did I do on my namesake island? I practiced geography,
naming and mapping it, charting its chief natural features, its
cities, industries, resources. I did what young liars do: I made it
up. I imagined invaders and the means I might use to repel them.
I populated the island with large, plump nerdy boys who, astonishingly, shared my odd tastes. I had scintillating and witty conversations with them. Puberty hadn't arrived in my island days,
so I probably didn't imagine colonies of beautiful black-haired

women, but I confess to having done so since. Thoreau had his
flute at Walden, but I had my black plastic tonette on Holm's
Holm, so I composed and wrote down whole symphonies—one
tune—and labeled them, like my hero Beethoven, with opus
numbers: Grand Symphony for Tonette in D Minor by William J.
Holm, Opus 12, 1953. I began to assemble my collected poems,
though I think I was a little premature in that. I folded, then
bound them either with Scotch tape or string. I don't remember
assembling Festschrifts in honor of my upcoming Nobel Prize,
but I might have. Isolation breeds grandiosity in human character. If no one can see what you're at, you may as well be extraordinary. It doesn't cost any more than Lutheran modesty.

I drove by Holm's Holm last summer, but found it gone. The
tree must by now have died, or the new farmer cut it down when
he sensibly reshaped the hilltop field in terraces to prevent the
downward slide of topsoil, a conservation practice my father
never discovered. But, of course, the island goes on existing where
it always existed: in my mind's eye, the same ocean that holds
Crusoe's island, Dr. Moreau's, Lilliput, Laputa, Brobdingnag, and
Treasure. Like Thoreau, I wanted to drive life into a corner, to see
what it was made of. The big world seemed too strange, too hos-
tile, too unsuited to my nature, but we all discover, as we age, that
in at least one sense, our interior islands grow even larger. We
find that we are, in fact, connected, that John Donne may have
been no fool when he said we are not islands—entirely. Those
connections may not always please us, and we may sometimes
long to return to the private and fortified island surrounded by
flax. We may even conspire to remove the other islands that we
imagine get in the way of our vision. The idea of this book will be
that islands are necessary for us to be able to think about what
is true at the bottom of our own character; we need to reduce the

world for a while to count it and understand it. But finally no island is without fine threads traveling mostly invisibly under the ocean floor to every other island, that we are, like it or not, part of the gang, and the gang, like it or not, had better get used to that fact. You can safely take all this sound advice from me: call me island and I will answer, though probably to other names as well. Walt Whitman thought we were all continents, even planets, each and every one of us, and that might be true too.

Isla Mujeres

Yucatán

Cancún

Isla Mujeres

Isla Cancún

Cozumel

✒ Isla Mujeres
Island of Women

I MAY BE AN ISLAND MAN, but I am, most certainly, not a beach man. The most tedious places on the planet are the artificial colonies of tourists assembled—usually in poor though dependably warm countries—for fun in the sun: condos, time-shares, duty-free shopping, happy hours, gift shops with cutesy stuff peddled by colorful natives, tireless street hawkers, sunset harbor cruises with canapès and muzak, Big Macs just like home, queen-size beds, potable water, surfboards for rent, rum drinks with tiny pink umbrellas stuck in them, natives who have miraculously learned enough English to respond to commands if addressed loudly and slowly enough, super bargains and sun, sun, sun. Fie on it all! But it's only a travel agent away, and Minnesotans, numb from the first four or five months of frost and gloom, and facing several more, think often of such dismal escapes. Such places are generally cheap and offer at least the possibility of a little thawing for both body and soul.

I once flew from Minneapolis to Cancún in February. Cancún must certainly be among the worst of a bad lot of such places, a completely invented hunk of Miami-style resorts carved out of Yucatán jungle next to a crowded, noisy, rather nasty dormitory town for the locals who do the grunt work for the international tourist hotels. You have landed at Erewhon when you arrive. You don't have to worry about being in Mexico, an actual foreign country afflicted with dirt, poverty, corruption, a real culture, a fascinating history, and a foreign language. None of the ghosts of the old Mayan priests and intelligentsia will rise with their bones rattling to trouble your sunburned sleep. Rest easy and have another strawberry margarita.

I did not stay in Cancún—either strip or town. I had been warned. Six old friends departed the Arctic at minus-twenty-eight degrees, stepped off the plane four hours later at eighty degrees, and took a fast taxi to the Puerto Juárez ferry dock. For a few pesos, we joined the locals on a creaky boat for the forty-five-minute ride to Isla Mujeres, the Island of Women. Caribbean swells are mild and gentle (except, presumably, in hurricanes), not much like the big Atlantic rollers. From the ferry dock we walked a few blocks down the street to a cheap and sleepy hotel smothered in bougainvillea and twenty other unidentifiable tropical flowering bushes and plants, stripped off parkas, mufflers, sweaters, mittens, shirts, underwear, long pants, wool socks, pac boots, and the other protective layers in the arctic survival and defense gear, and lay down to nap with a warm breeze laving our uncovered, naked, pale, half-frozen bodies, entertained by speedy green geckos scurrying across the ceiling and up and down the walls, and serenaded by the crying of tropical birds, and the not-too-distant boom of the Caribbean.

Why the Island of Women? In one way, all islands are female, surrounded by female water. John Fowles, in his book, *Islands,* says, "The domain of the siren has been where sea and land meet; and it is even less for nothing that the siren is female, not male." Islands are secret places where the unconscious grows conscious, where possibilities mushroom, where imagination never rests. "All isolation . . . is erotic. Crusoes, unless their natures run that way, do not really hope for *Man* Fridays. . . . Puritans, from Homer on, have always suspected islands, and wished their addicts the fate allotted Odysseus and his men." That fate, as you remember, was to be lured by sirens, drugged by lotuses, turned to swine by Circe, and to spend twenty years getting home from that favorite male hobby—war. All the great island dangers were represented by women, culminated by the waiting Penelope, besieged by suitors, weaving and unweaving a tapestry at her loom.

Histories give us two speculations about the name of Isla Mujeres, one more likely to be true than the other. Did Spanish buccaneers leave their lovers here while they were off at sea, practicing looting, pillage, and mayhem? Probably not. In 1517 a Spanish ship blown into harbor by high winds discovered a Mayan temple on the south tip of the island, adorned with clay statues of women. The next year, the indefatigable Cortés stopped here long enough to destroy the statues. He knew island eros when he saw it and wanted us to have no part of it—another Puritan helping his fellow humans along the road to virtue. Almost certainly the statues were connected to the worship of the Mayan goddess of fertility, Ixchel, whose primary sacred site was Cozumel, the next island south. Thank God for vigilant Spaniards or there's no telling to what erotic depths the hemisphere might by now have sunk.

Four hundred and eighty years after the statues—maybe naked!—disappeared, Isla Mujeres is a sleepy shrimp-fishing and tourist island. It's five miles long and skinny—sometimes only a city block or two wide—so that from any small height you can often see the Caribbean on both sides. It points northwest and southeast. The inner (western) shore is calm and gentle, with white sand and a shallow slope out to open water, but the east side faces open sea and is grandly rough and roiling, no place for beaches, thank God! It could take you as much as five minutes to stroll from one coast to the other if you dawdled.

Islands this size are not for the claustrophobic. No place to drive, two hours walk from end to end, water water everywhere, the same faces day after day, the unstoppable whanging of the incoming tide on the immovable rock. But Old Island himself, who is nervous in narrow canyons, discontent in deep woods, and terrified of caves, likes this watery confinement. The horizon is far away, and the heavy breathing of the sea calms the interior jumpiness of daily machine-age America. Sea noise seems an eternal ground bass, a Chaconne on its way to being composed, the bottom of a Lutheran chorale, the string bass laying out the changes for a jazzman. So the six old friends from Minnesota snooze away to recover from their long plane trip, lulled by the music, thawed by the wind, protected by guardian geckos.

In a proper resort there is nothing to do; in a perfect one there would be nothing to buy. At the center of Isla Mujeres, as in every other Mexican village, sits the square, dominated by a big stuccoed Catholic church and ringed by the town hall, a few cafés, shops, a monument to something or other, benches to rest on, flowering bushes, a few trees for shade, and a patch of grass. And a basketball court. The square provided the only nightlife in a splendidly uneventful week. At this distance from the equator, sunset and sunrise are even and dependable. Day is torpid and muggy, hammocks hang in deep shade, blinds are drawn; but when the sun disappears, a wind comes up from the sea, and bodies emerge from hiding. One night we heard clapping and laughter, saw floodlights over the square, so we all strolled down to have a look. Half the island seemed assembled for a basketball game, crowding around the court. The descendants of the Mayans are not shaped like seven-foot, lean, mean pro-basketball stars, but they played with enthusiasm and a sense of fun. Parents, grand-parents, teenage girls, little children milled around applauding all the baskets. It was hard to tell which side was which—no blood-thirsty competition here, most shots missed. The local ice cream store, behind the court, did a brisk business selling homemade mango, papaya, pineapple, and pistachio ice cream cones. Most chins were adorned with small orange driblets of double dip mango. The Caribbean applauded every few seconds, the stars looked bright and benevolent. The priest, in clerical garb, stood at the open door of his church; forbidden by Mexican law from appearing in the street in his working clothes, he clapped from a safe distance. Now this is resort nightlife! After a slightly sweaty hour, the crowd dispersed into the night, the basketball stars hand in hand with their girlfriends, old grandma taking the arm of old grandpa. Norman Rockwell in the tropics.

The other memorable tourist event was the bullfight. Who could resist the macho swagger, the high drama, the throbbing duende of this most Latin of all entertainment? The walled bull-ring sat next to the town cemetery with its gaily decorated graves, here all above ground—Isla Mujeres is, of course, at sea level. On this Sunday afternoon the crowd looks as if it came fresh from church to the bullring, all the little girls with their black hair tied up with pink or red ribbons, fancy gaily colored flouncy dresses, fathers in crisp new Levi's with big silver belt buckles, mothers fresh from the beauty parlor, the smell of hair spray and perfume trailing after. The ticket taker charges a few pesos and we're in, assembled next to the locals on tiers of bleachers, a chattering of excited Spanish, canned mariachi bullfight music. The action be-gins. A few sleepy, flea-bit, over-the-hill bulls (probably steers), ready for the bovine nursing home, stumble lethargically into the ring, driven by the bullfighters: dwarves in orange-, pink-, red-brocade matador costumes carrying cattle prods and red blankets. It's the Abbot and Costello bullfight! Or the Three Stooges. High drama parodied as low comedy—the mini-matadors whacking the somnolent old bulls to get them to their feet for a slow-motion charge. The crowd loves it. This good-humored farce provokes them to giggles, squeals, guffaws. The pink-ribboned little girls love it most of all, their black eyes wide with delight, their braids vibrating. What would Hemingway think of this? Or Garcia Lorca? Blood, danger, death remodeled to humor, sweetness, pleasure. Maybe there's something to Fowles's idea of the femininity of islands, of island eros. Here on Isla Mujeres you have basketball without competitiveness—no Vince-Lombardi's-winning-is-everything mindset—and comic bullfights to amuse children. If women would agree to remodel the defense department in this style, it ought to be turned over to them immediately.

If you hate the beach, the only other entertainment on Isla Mujeres is to walk from the beach end of the island to the Mayan ruins on the other, five flat placid miles. It takes two or three hours at a proper Walt Whitman loiterer's amble. No sense in hurrying; there's only one road out, one road back. You can't get lost. Roadside soda peddlers and makeshift barbecue cafés—four poles, plastic sheeting, a simple open grill on coals, the smell of roasting chicken basted with chilies and limes—will keep you from starvation. If you walk on the west side you pass through a real Mexican village, no tourists here, poorer houses, sleeping skinny dogs, cooking smells, the always audible open sea a block or two away, just over the sand dunes. At the end of the road, a rise to a narrow rocky point, the sea thrashing all around you now, a few broken pillars, part of a stone wall, a stone floor, a sign in

Spanish and English describing what once stood here till Cortés practiced God's will on the statues and occasional hurricanes helped finish the job. Not a soul here but the six now-thawed Minnesotans. The Caribbean is the only water I have ever seen that resembles its postcard photographs; it really is that color, a rich warm turquoise. Such water, until you have seen it, exists only in the imagination.

A few miles to the south across that rolling sheet of turquoise, stands the real Cancún strip: a skyline of hotel after big hotel, a stream of traffic, a few sailboats. Imagine thousands more thawing tourists sitting at the white tables with pink umbrellas in their drinks staring out across open water at us—though these ghost ruins are surely invisible from the veranda of the Hotel Deluxo. Here are two worlds nose to nose, island to continent, yin to yang, maybe female to male, too? Did the old Mayans think of this when they built their temple of women here? We will never be able to ask them, since the conquistadors and the missionary priests murdered every literate Mayan and burned most of their books. So we are left to wonder. But maybe that's the real job of humans who come to islands: not to demand answers but to think hard on questions.

I like this island. You would not like it. You should almost certainly forget you ever heard it mentioned, and you should stay away from it. Much better hotels in Cancún—all with good room service. I seem to remember huge stone women in the middle of a Swede Prairie cornfield.

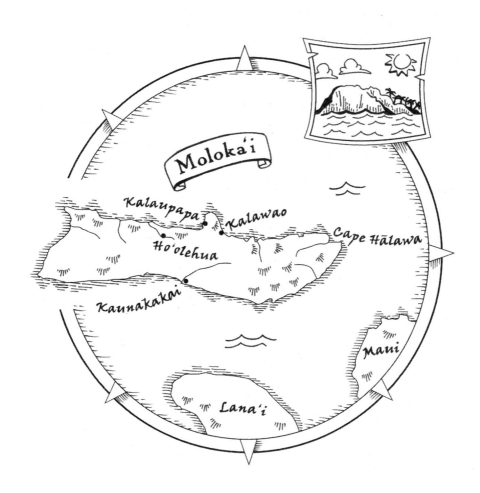

ᔡ Molokaʻi
Island of Lepers

IN MY SMALL TOWN SECRETS DISAPPEARED. Retarded children vanished into the upstairs bedrooms of farmhouses, where someone carried food to them. They did not emerge in the presence of company, even neighbors having morning coffee. I remember hearing (probably by mistake) four children mentioned on a neighboring farm. "Who besides Burt and Elmer and Mabel?" I asked. "Never mind. Their brother stays upstairs, it's not your business." Pregnant, unmarried girls were not mentioned once they had been safely transported to the anonymity of Minneapolis to give birth. Most never came back, though sometimes the babies appeared in other houses, virgin births dropped by a prairie stork. When depression or any form of madness visited a house, someone disappeared (often a woman) who was described as resting because of "nerves." I spent my boyhood blissfully unaware of how many neighbors had experienced shock treatments. Some diseases prompted rich stories (details of diarrhea, flatulence, pustular swellings, and multiple stitches were much loved) but I never heard the word tuberculosis, though I even had an aunt dying of it. Suicide? Silence. The gay uncle? More silence. Prison? Nobody we knew. Maybe there was a mysterious island somewhere in Lake Superior where they all went: the sacred idiots, the swollen bellies, the straitjackets, the hemorrhaging lungs, the limp-wristed, the jailbirds, all having tea together far away from us.

The other sure path to disappearance (if you were Lutheran) was to marry a Catholic and *Turn*. I capitalize the previous verb deliberately, because of its weight. To *Turn* meant exile from your family, your former life. Often, having *Turned,* you were instructed never to darken the door of your father's house, and often, for the rest of your life, you didn't. Presumably the same shunning worked its magic in Catholic families too. Sell your children's souls to the priest? Out. Insult the Holy Father and the true church? Out. In Minneota this religious war assumed at least one comic aspect because of the town's ethnic peculiarities: half Scandinavian, mostly Icelandic and Norwegian, and half Flemish-speaking Belgians. Belgians were the dark repositories of unreformed apostasy. The Belgians presumably got similar warnings about godless Icelanders. This succeeded (in my case at any rate) in making Belgians the most supremely attractive people on earth. I still fall in love with that black hair, those pale hands fingering rosaries.

I was nevertheless fascinated by the pious literature in my Belgian neighbors' houses: missals, saints' lives, heroic tales of martyred missionaries—all heavy with the stamps of the *Censor Liborum*. It must have been while snooping in some such book or pamphlet that I discovered the story of Father Damien of Moloka'i. I assumed at the time that Damien showed up so often because of Belgian ethnic pride—he was a native son of Flemish-speaking peasants—but I've since come to understand that the power of his biography moves almost anyone who takes the trouble to know it, even—saints be praised!—protestants and freethinkers.

Father Damien was born Joseph de Veuster on January 3, 1840, outside the small town of Tremeloo, Belgium, the seventh of eight children of a Flemish-speaking farmer. The family, like Minneota Belgians, were practioners both of hard physical work and of devout Catholicism. They offered up four children to religious vocations. Two of Joseph's older sisters and a younger joined an order of nuns, and his older brother Pamphile had become a priest in the congregation of the Order of the Sacred Hearts of Jesus and Mary and of the Perpetual Adoration of the Blessed Sacraments of the Altar (or "Sacred Hearts" for short). Joseph liked farmwork, but as he became a teenager loved God more, so he pestered his father to be able to join his older brother Pamphile in the monastery at nearby Louvain. In 1860 he succeeded, first intending, since he was an unenthusiastic scholar, to become a monk, but, his imagination fueled with the possibility of missionary work in distant and exotic places—the wild west of America or the tropical south seas, he put his peasant's shoulder to the hard job of studying the Latin, Greek, and theology necessary for the priesthood. Just short of ordination in 1863, he got his wish. His brother Pamphile had been slotted to go to Hawaii, but came down with typhus and couldn't travel. The order sent Joseph—now almost Father Damien—instead. He was twenty-three.

Sixteen days before boarding the ship to Honolulu, on October 7, 1863, Damien took his next-to-last vows before ordination. Gavan Daws describes them in his biography of Damien, *Holy Man:* "For this ceremony of transition, the Sacred Hearts chose to borrow from the funeral rites of the Church: candlelight, smell of incense, touch of holy water, sound of chanted prayer, solemn silence, and the insistent, overmastering presence of death. . . . Damien prostrated himself before the altar and was covered with a black mortuary pall. Lying dead to the world of

his past . . . [he] rose reborn . . . consecrated to the service of God."
Death was a prescient metaphor in light of what was to happen
to him.

In the pre-Panama Canal, pre-diesel-engine, pre-Concorde
days of 1863, the twelve-thousand-mile trip from Bremerhaven
to Honolulu took 148 days, from October 23, 1863, to March 19,
1864. The ship docked at no ports. In January the R. W. Wood
rounded Cape Horn, where, twenty years before, twenty-four
Sacred Hearts missionaries (including a bishop) drowned in a vio-
lent storm. After reciting the Office of the Dead in memory of
them, Damien experienced a ten-day gale in the heaviest seas on
earth. Day after day the ship pitched and rolled south toward
Antarctica. Finally the sky cleared, the sea settled, and the three-
masted schooner continued north to Hawaii without further
incident.

After ordination in Hawaii, Damien was assigned first to an
enormous rural district on the Big Island. His widely scattered
parish required him to walk or ride for days at a time, scale cliffs,
traverse lava deserts, sleep in the open air, and celebrate his
masses under trees next to the thatched hovels of his poor parishioners. His Belgian-peasant constitution stood him in good
stead in this wild place. He liked physical work, carpentry, rough
travel, and simple food. Gradually he learned the Hawaiian language well and began to feel real affection for native Hawaiians,
both for their character and culture—and for their souls.

Even by modern standards of distance, Hawaii is a long way from
anywhere else, twenty-five hundred miles from the nearest landmass. Look at a globe. Somewhere in the middle of the vastness
of the Pacific sits this tiny arc of islands, eight big enough to
count. Trace your finger toward Japan or San Francisco or the

Mexican Baja coast or move north toward the Aleutians and the Bering Sea. Water, all water with wind moving over it, for thousands of miles, roads only for whales. Geologically, Hawaii, like Iceland, is a youngster, the tops of a chain of undersea volcanoes that still, on the Big Island at least, erupt continually, gradually increasing Hawaiian real estate. Hawaii seems to have been settled at about the same time as Iceland, a little over a thousand years ago. Canoes from Samoa, the Marquesas, somewhere in Polynesia, somehow managed to navigate that enormous emptiness of ocean to find these pristine islands. No snakes (or any reptiles), few insects, no predators, almost no fauna at all, rich tropical vegetation, none of it poisonous, none of it armed with spikes or thorns, a sea rich with fish, a mild and equable climate cooled by trade winds, watered by sometimes massive rainfalls. Here they settled to make a prosperous culture, which, if not exactly peaceful and harmonious, at least caused no harm to neighbors—who were far away. This peace lasted eight- or nine-hundred odd years until 1778 when Captain James Cook arrived on an exploring expedition for the British Navy. According to the best historical estimates, the Hawaiian population was at least 300,000 when Cook and subsequent expeditions arrived, bearing whiskey, gunpowder, syphilis, smallpox, measles, whooping cough, cholera, and probably bubonic plague, which thinned the native numbers to 135,000 in 1820, 85,000 in 1850, and 40,000 in 1890. In their island isolation the Hawaiians had built up no immunity to European diseases and died in hordes. What gifts humans give one another in their ignorance!

By the time Damien began his priesthood among the Hawaiians, missionaries had been at work for forty-four years. The first, in 1820, were Calvinist New Englanders. The natives' nakedness, sexual openness, and reluctance to practice the moral virtue of hard labor, appalled the stern Puritans, who, in addition to Bibles, immediately began shipping corsets, wool suits, high-necked black dresses, top hats, and leather boots to civilize the happily naked Hawaiians. Mark Twain noted with delight the natives' pleasure in these fancy duds, but their reluctance (in a climate that seldom strayed under seventy degrees) to get the point, showing up for Presbyterian hellfire preaching adorned only with white gloves and top hats. Even here at the ends of the earth, the pious Calvinists were plagued by the arrival of the Papist menace in 1827 when the Sacred Hearts order began their missioning. The protestants succeeded in having them banished in 1831, but, supported and fortified by the gunboats of the French Navy, the Sacred Hearts returned to stay in 1836. For the better part of the century the American Puritans, the British Anglicans, and the French Papists duked it out to gather in the souls of the Hawaiians. Since the Americans and the English quickly began acquiring vast property and setting up sugar plantations, the soul wars inevitably melded with the money-and-politics wars.

Gavan Daws, Damien's biographer, reminds us that "the Bible and leprosy made their way to the islands within a few decades of one another" so that an epidemic was in full swing by the time Damien arrived in the islands. The Hawaiians called this most ancient and horrible affliction *Ma'i Pākē*, the "Chinese Disease," just as the English called syphilis the "French Disease," and the French called it "the Italian disease." The ancient Egyptians, who knew it well, called it "death before death." In the same year, 1873, that Damien began his life as the lepers' priest, a Norwegian bacteriologist, Gerhard Henrik Armauer Hansen, finally succeeded in isolating and identifying the leprosy bacillus. But the Norwegians were not afraid to give the disease a Norwegian name; they renamed leprosy Hansen's disease. Whatever its name, the disease remained, until halfway through the twentieth century—contagious, incurable, inexorable in its horrors, and finally fatal, a primitive human nightmare that was all too real. The Book of Leviticus gives divine orders for the treatment of lepers: "And the leper in whom the plague is, his clothes shall be rent, and the hair of his head shall go loose, and he shall cover his upper lip, and shall cry unclean, unclean. All the days wherein the plague is in him he shall be unclean; he is unclean; he shall dwell alone; without the camp shall his dwelling be."

Leprosy arrived in Europe after the Roman invasion of Egypt and expanded along with the empire, as far away as Germany and Ireland by 550 A.D. John Farrow's pious biography, *Damien the Leper,* tells us that by the twelfth and thirteenth centuries "at least a quarter of northern Europe's population were lepers. England was the most sorely affected, for there the disease met a rich soil in which to flourish. Personal sanitation and cleanliness were in a lamentable state." So much for filthy Hawaiian savages, or leprosy as an affliction of the dark peoples, or, as the Puritan missionaries of Honolulu thought, the last stage of syphilis, thus the visitation of the vengeful hand of a just god to punish sexual license.

Medical science, witchcraft, and prayer all proved equally useless at stemming the epidemic in Hawaii, so the government—and missionaries—reverted to the ancient defense: isolation and quarantine for the unclean. The leper was a criminal to be taken by force if necessary from his house and family. Here is the exact wording of the public announcement:

ALL LEPERS ARE REQUIRED TO REPORT THEMSELVES TO THE GOVERNMENT HEALTH AUTHORITIES WITHIN FOURTEEN DAYS FROM THIS DATE FOR INSPECTION AND FINAL BANISHMENT TO MOLOKAI.

No beating around the bush in that sentence. Hawaiians, not surprisingly, sometimes resisted with heroic defiance and had to be
tracked by police after they had holed up—armed—in isolated
valleys. Their pet name for the board of health was the board of
death, and for Kalawao, the leper town, "*Ka Lua Kupapaʻu,* corpse
pit, tomb."

The medieval church would have understood the Hawaiian
name well, for in their eyes the leper was already dead. After ex-
amination by a physician the leper was relieved of his possessions,
taken from his family, then "turned over to the ecclesiastical authorities who usually arrived shortly after midnight to remind
him that his plight was a punishment from God and that there
could be no escape." He was then taken in solemn procession into
the church where he found his family garbed in mourning clothes
waiting to celebrate his requiem mass. The sermon referred to
him in the past tense. Instead of a coffin, "a canopy of black cloth
was erected near the altar and in its dark shadow the leper was
placed." After the mass the procession continued to the graveyard, "where beside a freshly dug pit the leper again knelt while
the officiating priest threw a handful of earth over him as a final
sign that in the eyes of his fellowmen he was dead." He was given
"the possessions of his banishment . . . : a black cowl, a wicker
basket, special gloves, a barrel and a long stick upon which there
was a rattle." "Unclean, unclean," cries the leper, rattling his stick,
till finally, fingers and toes rotted to stumps, body bloated with
pustulating sores, face fallen off the bones of the skull, he dies in
a ditch where the dogs and pigs can eat him.

My gorge rises, your gorge, dear reader, rises, but I did not
make up any of these fine details for your moral edification or
spiritual satisfaction. I found them in John Farrow's biography,
and he found them in histories of leprosy in the middle ages, and

those historians found them in daily life and ecclesiastical records
and legal codes. Human beings, when afraid for their lives, do
not function at their best. They do not often rise to the occasion.
More likely, fear sinks them into a bestial cruelty and deliberate
ignorance. It is then that they want islands with high cliffs and
unruly seas and no boat docks. They want the objects of their
fear invisible and far away and they want it done now—in fourteen days or sooner. Can you hear the rattle, can you see the
black cowl lurching toward you on rotted feet?

The epidemic continued flourishing in Europe, but the medieval
monastic orders redeemed themselves by opening hundreds of
"lazar houses," essentially leprosariums, where Saint Benedict's
lovely rule was at least theoretically practiced: "All guests who
come shall be received as though they were Christ." Lepers were
fed, washed, prayed for, and finally buried with dignity. Europe
itself was cleansed of leprosy by yet another disease—this one
from rats: the Black Plague. In addition to cleaning out a third
to a half of the regular population, it almost completely extermi-
nated the lepers, whose weakened bodies offered no resistance
to it. Nature sometimes conspires to save us in the oddest ways.
One historian, Michel Foucault, speculates that the now empty
multitude of lazar houses were reopened as insane asylums, always, as Dean Swift ironically assured us, a useful addition to a
civilization.

European leprosy survived only in odd, out-of-the-way corners
like rural Norway and Iceland. Clearly it is not a tropical disease
for the dark-skinned or the godless if it carried on among the
blondest-of-the-blond, thoroughly reformed, pious Lutherans.
Hallgrímur Pétursson, the greatest Icelandic poet of the seventeenth century and author of the *Passíusálmar* (Passion Hymns),
the most famous book of religious poems in Icelandic literature,

was, in addition, a magician, a Lutheran priest, and a leper, not
necessarily in that order. But finally a leper. He died of it in 1674
and is still honored by Icelanders for his courage and fortitude
in the face of that awful fate. Among the Minneota secrets I've
unearthed as an adult is the curious rumor that a great uncle of
mine died of leprosy in Þingeyarsysla, a county in the far north
of Iceland, hardly over a century ago. Had he been a Hawaiian instead of an Icelander, a Catholic instead of a Lutheran, a man of
the tropics rather than the Arctic, he might have found himself
one of Father Damien's parishioners at Kalawao. I like to imagine
it, a leprous Icelandic farmer taking in his swollen lips the sacred
host from the leprous hands of a Belgian priest. The thought
cheers me up a little about humanity.

Most modern tourists to Hawaii are less interested in the history of leprosy or the relics of a long dead leprous priest than in
golf, sun, frolicking in the surf, and sweet frothy rum cocktails in
frosted glasses with plastic accoutrements. Airlines, for only fifteen dollars, provide you with a single flower lei when you land at
Honolulu airport to put you in a festive mood for your sun-fun.
Probably, your travel agent has consigned you to Waīkikī, the
beach strip on the edge of Honolulu, sardine-can stuffed with
high-rise resort hotels full of tens of thousands of your fellow
pasty-skinned midwesterners and middle-class Japanese ladies
warding off the tropical sun with brightly colored umbrellas.
Have a pūpū platter and a Tropical Surprise daiquiri, get a little
sunburn on the packed white beach, then check your tee times.
It's still winter in Minnesota and you've got fun to attend to.
In seven days the airport van will transport you and your now
wilted lei to the charter plane, for the long flight over the endless
Pacific back to snow and galoshes. If boredom overwhelms you by
the third day, I recommend a stroll in downtown Honolulu, a real

town with businesses, offices, seedy cafés, bums, hot dog peddlers, old ladies shopping, and a real harbor smelling of fish and diesel fumes. In front of the old city hall stands a heroic statue of Kamehameha the Great, unifier of the Hawaiian kingdom, black bronze with spear, a gilt helmet, and a fierce countenance. Stroll past the tamarind and banyan trees to the fountain in front of the modern state capitol of Hawaii (admitted to the union in 1959, the fiftieth star in the flag); here stands not a heroic statue but a grotesque lump of misshapen black bronze. Is it human? It wears a battered priest's hat. Its vast boots are too large for human feet. The face seems diseased, full of lumpy protrusions. The expression is pained. The hands, like the feet, seem swelled to twice human size, the figures gnarled as if the bronze itself were suffering. Something like a bronze shroud covers the back of the grotesque form. But around the neck of this decidedly un-heroic statue hangs a garden of leis, forty, fifty, maybe more. Did this statue fly to Honolulu so many times?

This is Father Damien de Veuster, leper priest of Kalawao, a statue by the contemporary Spanish sculptress Marisol Escobar, based on the famous photograph taken only a few weeks before Damien's death in 1889. It is probably the classiest statue in front of any of the fifty state capitols. It doesn't take much imagination to adorn a public building with a grandiose bronze of some stuffy general, tycoon, politician, explorer, but this statue shows the face of real heroism—and love. The fifty leis around Damien's bronze neck come not from the Legislative Committee on Public Beautification, but from ordinary Hawaiians who still honor his memory, and have, in fact, beaten the Catholic Church to the punch to sanctify him themselves. The Church beatified him—second base in the sanctification process—in 1996. It would offer great amusement to those who quarreled with him or attacked him while he was alive, or newly dead (and their numbers were legion, though not among the lepers), that he is here already Saint Damien. Saints are not easy people.

Leprosy, like communism, witchcraft, heresy, and AIDS, arrived in Hawaii not only as an epidemic disease but as an epidemic outburst of almost psychotic fear, the same effect it has had on humans for the last two millennia. The board of health, the monarchy, and the business and protestant missionary communities all cried in unison: Quarantine! Isolation! Banishment! If they had had rattles and cowls, they would have issued them. They needed a geographical prison, and Moloka'i perfectly suited that need. Only twenty-two miles by sea from O'ahu, it is shaped like a shoe thirty-eight miles long and ten miles wide. Kalaupapa is a four-square-mile volcanic outflow that protrudes from the north coast, lying like a flat green tongue in the rough water. Behind it rises a fifteen-mile-long wall of the highest sea cliffs in the world, two thousand sheer vertical feet. In Hawaiian it is called the *pali*. The northwest coast of Moloka'i is one of the most isolated places on the planet, perhaps not even excepting the Arctic and Antarctic. Only one narrow path leads sixteen-hundred feet down the cliff; heavy surf and strong currents surround the peninsula, no place to land a boat. Perfect! Anyone with suspicious skin became fair game for bounty hunters and officials who harvested them by the dozens. The suspects were allowed a small tin box of possessions, then herded into cages on board the transport ship. When they reached Kalaupapa, they were dumped out from the cages into the open sea—with surf in places rising up ninety feet above the rocks, it was too dangerous to attempt a landing—and left to make their way to shore as best they could. Then the contaminated cages were thrown out to sea after them. The ship's crew stood at attention with loaded rifles to make fast work of anyone who tried to reboard the ship. Many drowned, but what's the difference? They were dead anyway, dead as the medieval lepers celebrating their own requiems. Presumably, in the early days of leprosy hysteria, eczema, psoriasis, acne, birthmarks, or basal-cell skin cancers were enough to seal your fate, but there were also real lepers among those picked up, too sick to build a house or plant a garden or keep themselves alive in any way. The quarantine made them invisible.

How much the human race needs islands at moments like this! South Africa needed Robben Island for Nelson Mandela's twenty-seven-year sentence. France needed Devil's Island for Dreyfus. Britain needed Australia for its convicts, then the convicts needed Tasmania, then Norfolk Island, for their own new generation of convicts. America needed Alcatraz for its mobsters. The czar needed Sakhalin so many versts from the drawing rooms of Moscow and St. Petersburg. All Europe needed Elba, then Saint Helena, to keep Napolean from rising up again to conquer them. Hitler planned to exile all the world's Jews to Madagascar. Take whatever you hate and fear or wish to punish, fling it away, surround it with water. You've solved your problems! Now it is invisible and, like the spirits of the megalithic dead, can never cross over the salty moat to haunt you anymore.

On May 10, 1873, Damien arrived at Kalawao, the lepers' town, from Maui, on a boat with fifty lepers and fifty cattle. He slept his first night and for many weeks afterward under a puhala (pandanus) tree, worked over by the scorpions, fleas, roaches, and centipedes that lived in its fronds. Though a small church had been built, there were no quarters for a priest—nor for sheriff, doctor, or nurse. Kalawao consisted of a few rough thatched shacks built on the ground—no law, no missionaries, little medical equipment, no drugs, no orderly means of distributing what little food

arrived. The lepers existed in close to a state of nature à la
Rousseau, the pure essence of the "poor, bare, forked animal. . . .
the thing itself." Debauchery, drunkenness, murder, theft, all the
joys of chaos and anarchy attended them. The leper's main job
was to remain invisible, as far removed from the haole, non-
Hawaiian culture as they could get. Moloka'i was the island of the
premature dead.

Damien convinced his reluctant bishop to assign him there.
He was cautioned to be prudent in his dealings with the lepers—
in plain language: don't touch or be touched. It was not easy advice for a man of Damien's nature to follow. Gavan Daws says of
him that he "did not stand upon the ceremonies of high Western
civilization. Damien did not mind closeness with Hawaiians. He
would sit on the ground and eat sticky, pasty *poi* out of a family
calabash, something that very few American protestant ministers
would do. . . . He liked Hawaiians for what they were, or rather
for what he took them to be." Every visitor to Kalawao noted the
smell of rotting flesh. Officials toured the island with camphor-
stuffed handkerchiefs strapped around their necks. Damien used
his pipe, smoking strong black tobacco, now and then sharing a
puff or two with his leper guests.

He built a church, he built and repaired houses, he became
a skilled roofer, he laid water pipes and built a reservoir so that
Kalawao might have running water, he planted gardens, he dug
graves, he built coffins, he groomed horses, he tended pigs, he
washed and dressed wounds and sores, he cleared roads. He
pestered his ecclesiastical superiors and the board of health for
money and supplies. He raved and ranted at bureaucratic snivel-
ing in Honolulu. His Belgian-peasant ancestors would have been
proud of him. He was tough, strong, bullheaded, unafraid of dirt
and sweat. He was the first and, for most of his sixteen years,

the only priest to minister to the souls of his dying congregation. He washed and tended and prayed over and buried even the protestants and pagans, leaving the sorting of spiritual categories to God's undoubtedly more capable hands.

He organized choirs and bands. Every visitor to Moloka'i remarked over the beauty of the singing from the lepers' choir. An orchestra was organized with a blind conductor; Damien fashioned many of the flutes and drums from hollowed-out sticks and old cans. The church organist's chords grew smaller as fingers disappeared so Damien crafted an invention of sticks to hold down the bass notes. At night the lepers would come with ukuleles and guitars to serenade Damien as he sat reading by candlelight on his little porch.

He raised money—eventually in amounts sufficient to arouse jealousy and suspicion in Honolulu. He became a nineteenth-century media star, praised in the newspapers of England, France, Belgium, the United States, almost everywhere but Honolulu. The prince of Wales not only praised him but sent a large check.

Meanwhile, back in Honolulu, a month after Damien arrived at Kalawao, forty-eight protestant ministers, members of the Hawaiian Evangelical Association signed a statement that read, in part, as follows: "Our Hawaiian people will become in a very few years, a *nation of lepers*. . . . Do we consider what this means? It means the disorganization and total destruction of civilization, property values, and industry, of our churches, our contributions, our Hawaiian Board and its work of Missions. It means shame, and defeat, and disgraceful overthrow to all that is promising and fair in the nation. We are on the brink of a horrible pit, full of loathsomeness, into which our feet are rapidly sliding." In the next sixteen years, during which Damien remained active at his priestly duties, no white protestant minister ever lived at Kalawao.

Do you feel your gorge rising again, dear reader, at the mention of declining property values? And this from the mouths of presumed Christians? Oh, curse the lepers, what will become of my taxes? My sugar plantations? The rise of moral turpitude? Down what slippery slope to the pit of loathsomeness do you find yourselves sliding, my dear protestants? You have already arrived! It is your house! Your eternal abode! It is your interior Kalawao. Clean though your skin might appear, isn't that a suppurating pustule there on the corner of the soul?

Look at leprosy from the view of a nineteenth-century Hawaiian. In 1778, James Cook, the first haole, arrives uninvited. Within fifty years the population has declined by half from haole diseases. Your land has been parceled out into huge plantations owned by haoles (often missionaries). The old religion is discredited, almost dead. Few foreigners speak even a word of your language. Your myths, songs, habits, pleasures, are preached against and finally made illegal. Bibles and leprosy arrive in your islands simultaneously, gifts from "civilization." Infected with a haole disease, you are tracked down by police and bounty hunters (paid by the head) as if your sores made you a criminal, and you suffer exile for life in a stinking hole condemned to poverty, starvation, rot, loneliness. Worst of all, you are turned into a moral example of the wages of sin and God's vengeance and are viewed as a threat to the progress of the haole economy. Your own culture is deeply physical—to touch and be touched is to be alive, and you have been declared "untouchable" by a leper tradition of fear and contempt stretching back to Bible times. You have fallen into the hands of armed abstractions, vaporous virtue with the safety off and the trigger cocked.

To Damien's credit, and despite whatever spiritual abstractions he represented to his parishioners, he was not afraid to touch and be touched. Maybe it was the farmer in him, the Belgian peasant, who wanted to feel with his hands his own topsoil, his own chickens, his own pigs. He touched the Hawaiians, and they respected him for it. Science being science, touch also probably turned him into a leper by 1884, but he always half expected, even desired it. When he started preaching on Moloka'i in 1873, he addressed his congregation metaphorically as "we lepers." Now, in 1884, metaphor turned fact, as it so often has the habit of doing. By 1889 he was finished. A photographer came to record him on his deathbed, his swollen gnarled hardly human hands lying inert on the bedclothes. No death looks lovely, but this photograph will haunt you till your own deathbed.

That great aficionado and chronicler of islands, Robert Louis Stevenson, narrowly missed meeting Damien. Damien died four days before Good Friday, on April 15, 1889. Stevenson arrived on Moloka'i shortly after and stayed eight days, appalled at the misery and ugliness of life on Kalawao, but alert to the stories of Damien, told both by those who loved and admired him and by those equally numerous who found him an irritant—a bad-tempered and willful saint. Stevenson, by inclination a skeptic, but by centuries of genetics a dour Scots Presbyterian, was no fan either of Catholicism or of missioning, but he was moved both by Damien's courage and feistiness and by the human misery he saw on this charnel house island.

Damien became the instrumentality for Stevenson's most passionate and famous essay. He had traveled on to Sydney by early 1890, still in search of the perfect island on which to humor his terminal tuberculosis, when he saw in a local paper a letter from the Reverend Doctor Charles McEwen Hyde, a leader of the Honolulu New England missionary tribe, to an Australian clergyman, savaging Damien's reputation. Here is the gist:

He was a coarse, dirty man, headstrong and bigoted. He was not sent to Molokai, but went there without orders. . . . He had no hand in the reforms and improvements inaugurated which were the work of our Board of Health. . . . He was not a pure man in his relations with women, and the leprosy of which he died should be attributed to his vices and carelessness. Others have done much for the lepers, our own ministers [who, as you remember, still did not live at Kalawao], the government physicians [who lifted the lepers' rags with a long pole to examine them] . . . but never with the Catholic idea of meriting eternal life [rather, perhaps meriting continued sugar profits and sound real-estate values].

Stevenson's literary gorge rose fast and erupted. On February 25, 1890, he locked himself in a hotel room, coming out six thousand words later with one of the great pieces of English invective. He begins in high dudgeon: "There are duties which come before gratitude, and offences which justly divide friends, far more acquaintances. Your letter to the Reverend H. B. Gage is a document, which, in my sight, if you had filled me with bread when I was starving, if you had sat up to nurse my father when he lay a-dying, would yet absolve me from the bonds of gratitude." From that point he turns up the heat. Hyde has, of course, revealed himself as a pious hypocrite. Stevenson, playing devil's advocate, even admits the possible truth of many of Hyde's charges.

"Damien was *coarse.*
"It is very possible. You make us sorry for the lepers who had only a coarse old peasant for their friend and father. But you, who were so refined, why were you not there, to cheer them with the lights of culture? . . .
"Damien was *dirty.*
"He was. Think of the poor lepers annoyed with this dirty comrade! But the clean Dr. Hyde was at his food in a fine house.

"Damien was *headstrong.*

"I believe you are right again; and I thank God for his strong head and heart. . . .

"Damien *had no hand in the reforms, etc.*

" . . . If ever any man brought reforms, and died to bring them, it was he. There is not a clean cup or towel in the Bishop-Home, but dirty Damien washed it."

He goes on in this vein, pulverizing Hyde with waves of sarcasm. Damien has assumed his real Christian duty while Hyde sits "stretching [his] limbs the while in [his] pleasant parlor on Beretania Street," one of the fine "houses of missionaries [that] are a cause of mocking on the streets of Honolulu."

But it is the accusation of "impurity in his relations with women" that rouses Stevenson to his greatest paroxysm of rage. "How do you know that?" shouts Stevenson, grabbing the courtly Hyde verbally by his well-tailored lapels. "Is this the nature of the conversation in that house on Beretania Street which the cabman envied, driving past?—Racy details of the misconduct of the poor peasant priest, toiling under the cliffs of Molokai?" Stevenson has heard such rumors only once, from a drunk from Honolulu in a bar in Samoa, after which another bar patron ("I doubt if you would care to have him to dinner in Beretania Street.") sprang to his feet. " 'You miserable little ———' (here is a word I dare not print, it would so shock your ears). . . . 'If the story were a thousand times true . . . you are a million times a lower ——— for daring to repeat it.'" Stevenson plunges for the kill: "It was to your 'dear Brother, the Reverend H. B. Gage,' that you chose to communicate the sickening story; and the blue ribbon which adorns your portly bosom forbids me to allow you the extenuating plea that you were drunk when by you it was done." But even supposing the story true: that he "failed in the letter of his priestly oath—he, who was so much better a man than either you or me, who did what we have never dreamed of daring—he too tasted of our common frailty. 'O, Iago, the pity of it!' The least tender should be moved to tears; the most incredulous to prayer. And all that you could do was to pen your letter to the Reverend H. B. Gage!"

In the midst of his fury at Hyde's hypocrisy, Stevenson remembers that "We are not all expected to be Damiens; a man may conceive his duty more narrowly, he may love his comforts better; and none will cast a stone at him for that." But for the pompous Hyde, as for Fortunato in Poe's "Cask of Amontillado," Stevenson mortars the last stone firmly in place: "The man who tried to do what Damien did, is my father, and the father of the man in the Apia bar, and the father of all who love goodness; and he was your father too, if God had given you grace to see it."

In 1890 Stevenson's grand blast was probably legally libelous, but Hyde wisely chose not to pursue the matter. Hyde called him "a Bohemian crank, a negligible person, whose opinion is of no value to anyone." The great irony, of course, is that Stevenson's justly famous essay is the only reason we have ever heard of Hyde. Stevenson had the peculiar literary honor of creating two immortal Hydes, one fictive, one actual, both villains.

I suppose I first heard of Damien when I was eleven or twelve and imagined Moloka'i with its black cliffs, its fierce surf. At that age I had never seen a cliff of any kind—to a western Minnesota farm boy a twenty-foot slope seemed precipitous—nor had I ever traveled to water that made noise and couldn't be seen or even waded across. Still, the imagination makes its own plans, then bides its time. On my first visit to Hawaii, I spent three days in a Waīkikī hotel with a Lutheran college choir. I loathed it, but somehow I knew Moloka'i was only thirty miles away by sea or air. Finally, well past fifty, I made it. An old friend had taken a year's exchange-teaching job at the University of Hawaii, and rented a small house in Kāne'ohe, a working-class suburb across the *pali* from Honolulu. He engineered a poetry reading for me as a lame excuse for a Minnesotan to escape a blizzard or two in February. Following the usual Midwest sequence, we flew out of Minneapolis at minus-twenty-five degrees in a snow-storm and, after the long Pacific journey, landed at Honolulu to eighty degrees at night—with flowers. I liked Kāne'ohe with its run-down gospel churches, pomelo and avocado trees, chickens chasing each other across backyards and stopping traffic to cross the streets, languid skinny cats, junked machinery behind the house, Spam cans, frangipani, and a decidedly un-Scandinavian-looking lot of neighbors who played loud radios and owned socket wrenches and battery chargers. The old war between haoles and kanakas still raged in the newspapers, the Hawaiian-sovereignty movement laboring to restore a little land, dignity, and money to the by now almost decimated survivors of Captain Cook's greeting party. The islands had discovered that golf, beaches, and tourism generated money and bloated the value of real estate to monstrous levels, but left you living in a place that didn't much resemble a real Hawaii so much as a Hawaiian theme park. The last pitched battle for what remained of the "old" Hawaii and its culture seemed to be in progress on Moloka'i, the least golfed and condoed of the islands. Poverty, difficult terrain, thin soil, and probably its haunted historic reputation as the leper charnal house had left it without stoplights, glitzy golf re-sorts (only one), overpriced beach condos for the idle rich, strip malls, native craft shops, and hula nights with rum drinks. So four old friends traveled to see if Damien's ghost still lived in the pandanus fronds.

Moloka'i's airport at Ho'olehua is an unpretentious little building, a runway in the middle of a pasture. We rent an old car to drive
across flat, grassy prairie to Moloka'i's metropolis: Kaunakakai—
three blocks long, flat, with pickups parked in front of hardware
and grocery stores, seedy cafés, store-front churches. It looks like
Minneota in July, with cow-feed and seed-corn hats, work boots
and Levi's, old ladies gossiping, the "local boy" special for break-
fast—fried Spam or a hamburger patty between two scoops of
white rice, topped with eggs over easy, all swimming in a big dol-
lop of brown floury gravy. No rum drinks and pūpū platters here.

For an island the size of a county in Minnesota, a ranch in
Texas, or a medium-sized iceberg fallen off the Ross Ice Shelf,
Moloka'i possesses a complicated and fantastic geography, as if a
whole continent had been squished down, then glued together
into a microcosm of itself. "From the mountains to the prairies,
to the ocean's shining shore" goes the old song, but you don't
need a block of property as vulgarly oversized as North America
to sing it. Moloka'i will do. The western half is dry, rolling prairie
grasslands, now mostly the Moloka'i Ranch—a seventy-thou-
sand-acre chunk still owned by a missionary-descended land
trust. In Hawaii the servants of God laid away their treasures in
the kingdom of real estate, whatever additional treasures they
might have acquired in heaven. For most of the twentieth century the ranch was leased out for pineapple farms, but Dole and
Del Monte found cheaper handier garden patches, so the old half-
empty company town had a melancholy last-picture-show look
about it. For a few miles you might even imagine west Moloka'i
with its tan shivering grass and low hills as transplanted from
western Dakota in late August. But if you open your car window,
you hear the distant noise of the inescapable island fact: boom!
as the big salt surf bangs away at the Moloka'i coast.

Kaunakakai sits at the arch of the foot on the bottom of shoe-shaped Moloka'i, the last gasp of the Midwest look before you drive east out of North Dakota into the tropics. A coral reef surrounds much of the town, extending a half mile out toward Lana'i, so the surf is quiet here, the Pacific like a calm tepid bathtub sloshing lethargically. The beach is littered with broken coral, Spam cans, and wine bottles. We checked into the local motel, the Pauhana, renting a two-room cabana with a deck overlooking the bathtub beach. The clerk warned us of a big dance that night in the bar; the noise would go on into the night—it might keep us awake. Good, we said, and continued to circle Moloka'i in our rental '79 Chevy.

The coast road moves east into another biological world, festoons of flowers and giant ferns, dense tropical forest, old fishponds, small clearings with tiny churches and shacks, the road windy as a slinky, the sea a few yards away, sometimes a hundred feet below. We stop at Saint Joseph's, a one-room wood church built by Damien in 1876. A modest statue stands in the churchyard, adorned (as in Honolulu) with garlands of leis. This was one of his "healthy district" parishes, a long climb from Kalaupapa peninsula, maybe fifteen miles away if you are a crow, but light years if you are a human being. We round the southeast tip of the island; the mountains of Maui come into view, and the road narrows and climbs to a high outlook over the sea and the forbidding northeast coast—the beginning of a wall ten miles long of the highest sea cliffs in the world, plunging even more deeply under the sea. Behind those cliffs stand more steep mountains, all rain gatherers robed with velvety green moss and forest. This is terra incognita; even fanatical hikers and wilderness addicts enter this country cautiously. After over a thousand years of settlement, in some places yours might be the first human foot to touch the earth. The sea along the north *pali* does not look kindly. Even from hundreds of feet up we can hear it snarling, biting at the valley floor far below. This is not North Dakota. The road spirals down to Hālawa valley, the only easily reachable place on this northeast coast. Once a fertile farming settlement, it was wiped out in 1946 by a tidal wave that shrouded its taro fields in salt and washed the farmers' frail shacks into the Pacific. Today it is calm, green, damp, empty, silent except for sea noise. The only way out is the way in.

We drive back to the middle of the shoe, then go north from Kaunakakai, the highway bisecting the island: rolling grasslands to the west, jungles and cliffs to the east. Halfway up the slope to Kalaupapa overlook is Molokaʻi's real golf experience, a nine-hole rough course in the middle of a wooded cow pasture, eight-dollar greens fees on the honor system. It was deserted when we stopped on a sunny February afternoon. Neighborhood holsteins stared placidly over fences as if waiting for putters and drivers.

The road ends in the parking lot for the little state park at the top of the bluff. A two-hundred-yard walk to the left sits Kauleonānāhoa, the Phallic Rock, a ten-foot erect penis in the middle of the woods. According to Hawaiian legend, a husband got caught too ardently admiring a young girl admiring her own reflection in a pool. When the wife found them, she struck the girl. The husband then struck the wife who fell over the cliff and turned to stone. The gods took vengeance on the husband by turning him to stone too—an erect ten-foot rocky penis pointing at the sky. If islands, as John Fowles proposed, are always female, then maybe it's reasonable that they should house a penis or two to hatch new little islands. According to local legend, barren women come to spend the night sleeping next to the stone, leaving Molokaʻi dependably pregnant the next morning.

As we walk into the woods from the parking lot, the noise begins. The path is shaded by eucalyptus and ironwood, both, like
Damien, immigrants to Moloka'i. But what a pungent and lovely
smell! From a few thousand feet up, the sea breathes like a prehistoric animal, watching us from deep underground. The woods
are cool and dark. The breathing below tightens and loudens.
After a few hundred yards, light begins again, and the cliff falls
away in a great sweep. This is the edge of the flat earth; one more
step and you are gone. At first, everything is blue a thousand
miles out to the horizon. What's next from here on the globe?
The Aleutians, Bering Strait, then the ice. What is this music
the great blue sings? Ahhh—ahhh—ahhh—Look down. There,
a green tongue lays on the blue, the pockmark of an old volcanic
crater on its skin, a ring of white spray circling it. Behind the
tongue, the dark perpendicular cliffs march in formation away
to the east till they too disappear into the blue. The path down
the *pali* looks like tiny scratches on a green face. Could a human
being, much less a mule, walk down to that tongue without sliding off to disappear into the blue noise? Could a boat come close
to that white ring of spray without smashing on the rocks? How
would a human being go to that place and how leave? But most
who went in the last century-and-a-third did not leave. They are
still hiding under the skin of the green tongue, their invisible
eyes still scanning the blue, their invisible backs to the green
wall. What are they waiting for? To be raised again at Judgment
Day, their bodies now perfected and glorified, their skin bronzed
and glowing, their ten fingers and ten toes safely reattached to
hands and feet, their tin whistles and oil-can drums replaced by
old and precious violins, silver flutes, guitars with an almost
human voice, an organ with ten keyboards, pipes numberless as
stars. What music do they intend to make now, what joyful noises

to rise above the eternal banging of the sea? Is this the song of the lepers, given notes and form at last, the choir invisible, the choir invincible singing away thousands of years of misery, fear, the meanness and stupidity of authority, whatever human beings can't face so that they invent islands all over the planet to hide that shadow they imagine following after them, waiting to eat them, pull them down into the stomach of death? And yet, as our old leper Walt reminds us, out of these sour dead, this fetid compost, grows the sweet grass that nourishes the milk of the sleepy holsteins on the golf course, that sweetens the bread and wine that Damien offered to every leper, whatever his disease. For every spear of grass was once a catching disease. Your lawn has leprosy—mow it tenderly.

Moloka'i, like every island, is a real place. Its isolation in the Pacific and its volcanic origin make it interesting to scientists. Its poverty and underdevelopment (in twentieth-century terms), coupled with its resurgent nativism, make it interesting to students of politics and sociology. Its use as an isolation ward for lepers makes it interesting to historians, Catholics, and me. But despite all these uses, metaphors, projects that we cast onto it, it is itself, just a place, like Minneota or Milbank or Patagonia or Puyallup. Its islandness makes it a handy instrument for our fear—and our contemplation.

The human race is afraid of so much these days. As technology, prosperity, and too much population have spread out over the planet, our fears have multiplied as the justifications for them have shriveled. We are afraid of food, that what we eat will rise from the plate to choke us if we are not careful. We imagine harm in eggs, pork chops, butter, chickens, tomatoes, chocolate, sugar, salt, flour, beefsteak, coffee, whiskey, oysters, milk, bacon, cheese, bread. Just as all these lovely foods become safer and cleaner than they have ever been in human history we recoil from them in terror, imagining them as secret poisons. We are afraid of being too fat or too thin. As our longevity grows almost at a geometric ratio, compared to any previous age in human history, anywhere, we become more hysterical in the presence of death, sure that by right action and careful planning we can evade it. Just as the prime killers in human history have been almost defeated—starvation, dysentery, pneumonia, childbirth, tuberculosis—we become terrified of new diseases that threaten to carry us off. We are afraid of government, we are afraid of business, we are afraid of religious fanatics, or we are afraid of the godless secularist. We are afraid of abortionists or of anti-abortionists. We are afraid of communists or capitalists, or we are afraid of all these things simultaneously. We are afraid of sex (in any random combination) and we are afraid of celibacy.

Dying is the most normal of human functions. One hundred percent of us will succeed in accomplishing it. Some go early, some late, some of leprosy, some in their sleep at 103. Does it make a difference to us, to the life force, to the mystery that lies under the universe how we accomplish this most human of jobs? Damien was a Christian and a flawed man, maybe a saint, maybe not. But I think, through whatever means, he came to understand the normality of death and to rise above the squeamish fear that paralyzed the real-estate-happy protestants and bureaucrats of Honolulu. Most of us can't bear to think very hard on the triviality of our own fear. It shames us. But unless we try to think on it as hard as Damien did, there will be neither grief nor joy, nor indeed any real life in us at all. To sing, you must spit in the face of fear. When you hear the leper's rattle coming, be ready to kiss.

In 1991 I watched a dear friend die of AIDS in his own house.

He was a doctor, a punctilious prudent man who, because he happened to be gay at the wrong point in human or medical history, acquired a disease as unknown to him as it was to medical science when he got it. He suffered bad luck. He was a victim of ironic coincidence. He was not an emblem or symbol of anything; he was not (as I have heard so many Christian moralists argue) being punished by a vengeful god for his evil lifestyle. How many arguments I read for compulsory testing, identification, quarantine, even exile on the island of AIDS! while I sat in his house trying to keep him company as he sank toward his premature death. I thought often of Moloka'i as I looked out over the water in Seattle from his front window.

One of his great pleasures had been to take his friends sailing in the San Juan Islands in late summer. Whoever could manage it came to join him on his big comfortable doctor's boat, not so much to have strenuous marine adventures as to lounge about at anchor in pretty little coves off small islands like Decatur and Stuart, drinking Bloody Marys, reading spy novels, fussing over elegant gourmet dinners, then sitting up late at night telling stories and philosophizing while the boat rocked gently, seals splashed, and the stars became a mirror of themselves in the sloshy black waters of Puget Sound.

One of those picturesque little islands could be our very own AIDS charnal house! Kalawao East! We could gather up the untouchables of Seattle and dump them in the cold gray waters to swim to shore, let them dig clams and gather rainwater, plant a little garden of rutabagas, cough on each other, practice strange sexual rites. No one would ever have to touch or see them again. They could all compost back into the stony soil, thus sparing western civilization, real-estate values, and public health the danger of their company. Ideas like that cross the minds of many of your neighbors, even—confess it now!—sometimes your own. We are all afraid, and fear does not make us splendid.

I watched the doctor's family come—sternly denying that this man they loved could be a leper; I watched the faces of his medical partners, some of whom had no idea he was gay, collapse in horror when they saw the visible evidence of leprosy on him; I took phone calls from friends who called to apologize for their absence, saying "It's not safe to come." I saw, too, a little Damien consciousness from many others, who came to sing for him, to wash him, to stroke his forehead and calm him. I saw his own black rage as he realized that leprosy was on him and couldn't be bribed out of the house. I saw his world shrink to the size of the bed that sat in the middle of the living room. Out the front window, the expanse of gray water below seemed to flow uphill and into the house till it lapped at the iron legs of the bed, leaving him alone in his island of dying. Hospice workers came and rowed their small boats ashore to change the bedclothes, to cool his fevers, to gently rub his emaciated body. But death is island enough, quarantine enough, exile enough.

Did I name the wrong disease in the last paragraph? AIDS, you correct me. Quite different from leprosy. Is it? Or do we invent new projections of leprosy out of our interior fearfulness generation after generation, meanwhile reassuring and flattering ourselves that we are prudent stewards of public good, that we're thinking hard for us all, for the health of the community. Oddly enough, grand epidemics like leprosy, bubonic plague, syphilis, Spanish influenza, tuberculosis, AIDS are probably good for us as a species biologically if we (to sound the voice of the Honolulu bureaucrat) "examine the big picture." An HIV-resistant mutant gene seems to exist in rising numbers in populations as one moves north in Europe. One speculation is that the bigger and more comprehensive the kill during the Black Death within a given population, the greater the likelihood that the survivors made an immunological leap forward, thus making vast and terrible epidemics an epidemiologic encouragement for the immune system to evolve—a kind of lead gift in the twilight, pure misery for the present, but resulting in a strengthened species for the future.

But no matter such scientific speculation. The evidence is clear and compelling, that like the Japanese with their Burakumin and the Indians with their caste of untouchables, we have always needed the lepers. Someone has to be unclean. Leprosy—or AIDS—becomes thus, not a disease, but a profession, even a vocation in the religious sense. I think Damien understood his own leprosy (and his life among the lepers) in that way, as God's gift to him, the operation of grace.

The Kalaupapa peninsula is now a national historical park, but an odd one. It still houses a handful of old lepers, their disease arrested by sulfate drugs, their contagiousness gone, for whom this island prison has become home. Exiled from their families and communities fifty, sixty, seventy years ago, they have planted what roots remain to them on the planet here at Kalaupapa, and they intend to die here in peace. To visit this now national property, you must ask permission to be a guest in the leper's community, then either walk or ride a mule down the *pali* or fly to a small landing strip at the tip of the peninsula. They will be your tour guides. Standing on that wild overlook above them, I decided not to disturb their peace, but rather to honor them—and Damien—by the absence of my body and the presence of my imagination. The tiny village of scattered houses is almost invisible on the west side of the tongue. Kalawao, on the east side, is now deserted except for graves and ruins, and maybe the ghost of Damien. *Requiescat in pace,* I mumble to the wind and to the vast blueness stretching north to the Bering Sea.

Damien was first buried at Kalawao among his parishioners. Visitors present at his deathbed, or seeing him just after death, were amazed at the changes in his body. Leprosy, evidently, wants only to torture you while you are sentient. Once the last breath expires, the heart stops and the final blood has made its way to the brain, the bodily swellings, discolorations, distortions leave. Soon the hands shrink back to human size, color returns to the skin, the boils close, the swellings recede. You now boast a robustly healthy-looking corpse, as if you had died in your sleep at great age with complete calm. Leprosy has loved you to death, in a firestorm of misery, but now deserts you for a newer, younger lover.

Damien, shrouded inside his redwood coffin, processed, like so many of his leper congregation, from church to grave. His new house was a little stone sarcophagus, mortared slabs of lava half above the ground, then three stone steps down to a bed of straw on a platform where his coffin rested. There it remained until the Belgians in 1936 asked for the return of his bones to Louvain, only a few miles from the de Veuster farm and home of the Sacred Hearts order. He was an honor for Belgium, too. Franklin Roosevelt, then president, ordered an American navy gunboat to escort Damien back—this time not around Cape Horn, but through the new Panama Canal, across the Atlantic to Europe.

Since mumblings of sanctification had already begun for Damien, the Catholic Church sent a devil's advocate to Kalawao to supervise the disentombment, making sure that correct procedures were followed, keeping a skeptical eye peeled for any miracles. I heard the story I am about to tell late one night at Blue Cloud, a Benedictine abbey on the prairies of eastern South Dakota. I retreated there to work on this essay; abbeys are islands of calm and silence far away from the noise and speed of daily life in modern America, good places for writers—or other humans in need of some island privacy and serenity. I think the old monks were a little amused at the presence of a Lutheran apostate scribbling away in an upstairs room—about a beatified priest, a hero of ordinary Catholics all over the world. First, Father Guy loaned me a tape of a magnificent one-character play on Damien's life performed on Hawaiian Public Television. I watched it, kept writing, sang a few psalms with the monks at vespers, ate a Lenten fast supper, went back upstairs to scribble more. At ten o'clock, a late hour in an abbey, the door opened and Father Augustine came in.

"Am I disturbing you?"

"Not at all. I've become stupid and am ready to stop for the night."

"I heard you were writing about Damien. I'm from Hawaii, actually. I was in Honolulu when they moved his bones."

Father Augustine had indeed been in Honolulu, from the mid '20s till the end of World War II. He was a military brat till his vocation found him. He lived twenty miles from Pearl Harbor on December 7, 1941. He remembered Hawaii before it was one vast golf course. He was fifteen when Damien's bones were exhumed, but didn't hear the story of the exhumation until he came later to meet the priest who had acted as devil's advocate.

When they entered Damien's sepulchre for the first time since April 1889, they expected to find only a handful of dried bones. The three steps down into the half hole in the earth where Damien was laid were low and awkward, the coffin bearers and the advocate bent double in the damp darkness. The porous lava stones above the coffin had leaked, presumably for forty-seven years in rainy Kalawao. The coffin rested on straw soup. The dripping had eaten away a hole in the coffin lid over Damien's head. When they bent their lanterns over the hole, they saw not a skull but a fleshed-out head, beard and all, recognizably Damien. The coffin was, of course, still heavy with the unrotted body, and the two parties stumbled a bit as they wrestled it up the stone steps to daylight. When the coffin tipped, the advocate noted the still supple head roll to one side. Perhaps it was Damien shaking his head "No," trying to tell them his body was happy at Kalawao; he belonged to Belgium no more. They had to summon Honolulu to get a man-sized coffin for transport; they had brought only a small box for dry bones. Damien, newly sealed in copper and Hawaiian koa wood, lay in state in the Honolulu cathedral for a week while Hawaiians filed past to bid a respectful Aloha 'Oe! to their beloved leper priest. Father Augustine gave me a yellowed copy of the eulogy preached at Damien's memorial mass in Honolulu on February 3, 1936, by Father Patrick Logan. It ends with a fine rhetorical flourish praising Damien for "the works which are wrought, and our island of Moloka'i, with the spirit of Damien hovering over it, will be no longer the Lonely Isle of sorrow and mourning, but the Friendly Isle of goodwill and resignation—a visible bond between earth and heaven." Then off through the canal to chilly Belgium he went. Believe that story or not; it makes no difference. It was a gift to me and I pass it on to you. Something in that place, that island, that peculiar life seems to me incontrovertibly a bond between one world and another, whether you choose to call them earth and heaven, nature and spirit, island and continent, fearfulness and joy. Yeats said, "Everything exists, everything is true, and the earth is only a little dust under our feet."

After the overlook, the four old friends went back to the Pauhana Hotel, ate a fish in the hotel café (passing up the Spam dinner), then adjourned to the bar for the dance. While the hotel itself is unpretentious as a Super 8 in Grygla, Minnesota, the bar is remarkable. A massive banyan tree grows in the middle of it, providing the only roof. I wrote a little prose poem that night describing this sweet, lively dance:

DANCING IN FEBRUARY: MOLOKAʻI

The band in the Pauhana Hotel on Molokaʻi tunes up on Friday night. The dance floor is open to the sea, full moon above, the shadow of Lanai across the channel, not a single light on the mountain. A mammoth old banyan tree grows in the middle of the bar, spreading out its enormous horizontal branches over the whole hotel as if patting us on the head, saying "It's all right."

The band leads off with country music, Hawaiian style: ukelele plinking, guitar twanging and sliding, "Funny Face, I Love You." A dapper wiry white-haired old Hawaiian changes partners on every song. Fat, thin, old, young, haole, local, he loves them all. A woman is a woman when you're shaking it.

The band works up to old rock and roll, then lets fly. The whole place erupts with dancing—even the sprinkle of pale tourists. What a grand mixture of funny faces: some beautiful, some maybe, some maybe not. They are half this, half that, half some other thing, more halves than add up in the statistic world, but here, tonight, they add up nicely.

It's a happy crew, shaking their hind ends. Nobody wants to punch anybody else, or argue, or brood, tonight anyway. And why not be glad, for the banyan tree and the moon and the shadowy mountains on Lanai and the noisy sea and the ukelele and the cold beer and the beautiful girl and the loud drum?

It occurs to me now that that banyan tree, its gnarled branches like a huge malformed leprous hand, spread over that bar to offer the blessing of nature.

After a while we left, like old Walt in his poem about the learned astronomer, "rising and gliding out . . . / In the mystical moist night-air, and from time to time, / Look'd up in perfect silence at the stars."

We drove back up the middle of the island, past the golf course, past the holsteins, to the Pauhana parking lot. The moon was full, the night sky a blend of pale gray and ice blue. No one brought a flashlight, so we stumbled a little awkwardly into the ironwoods and eucalyptus until some night vision took over. We followed the breathing noise, somehow louder in the moonlight. When we came out of the woods, there it was, the dark tongue lying in the water, the surf now silvery and glowing by moonlight. A few thousand feet below, the scattered lights from the houses of the old lepers flickered like fireflies in the half dark. We stood a long time in silence in that strange light, listening to the sea, looking north. The church may be waiting for a little while to canonize Damien, but I assumed my private authority in the Church of Walt and sanctified that place as Saint Kalaupapa. I pray for it to intercede for me whenever fear takes over inside me. By this intense moonlight, I call this island of the doomed instead the island of the blessed, the island of the human, the island of the big mystery that Walt found growing in the grass on whatever island where you live.

⁄℮ The Piano Island

I TAUGHT LITERATURE FOR A YEAR at a Chinese university just as the tourist boom began taking baby steps toward altering the face of Chinese cities forever with strips of Western-style hotels, glitzy with white marble slabs, oversized chandeliers, potted ferns, imitation Buckingham Palace doormen and bellboys, and an inexhaustible supply of credit-card receptacles to relieve you of hard currency. In 1986, Xi'an had only the Golden Flower, a Japanese-Swedish joint-venture hotel that billed itself as a "miracle in the heart of China." In some ways their blurb didn't exaggerate much. The Golden Flower owned its own generator, thus sparing guests the experience of continual power outages. The menu boasted cheeseburgers and Carlsberg beer, a herring plate, and shots of real Aalborg aquavit to wash it down—all at a tidy price. Sometimes China drove foreigners to need a slab of herring and a shot or two of schnapps—even if it cost half a month's teaching salary.

The hotel lobby was decorated with the usual pretentious froufrou: cascading fountains, revolving colored lights, plastic vegetation, enough marble sheeting to line a tycoon's sarcophagus, and, in the midst of it all, a lit-up wading pool a few feet deep with a round marble island in the middle. But on that island stood the real miracle in the heart of China in 1986: a black

Yamaha six-foot grand, tuned, regulated, and ready for human
fingers. For a few hours every evening an astonishingly beautiful
Chinese girl of modest pianistic accomplishment stepped over
two feet of open water to the piano island to soothe the dining
guests with appropriate selections of light classics: "Für Elise,"
Chopin's sticky E-flat Nocturne, "Claire de Lune," Mozart's
"Turkish March," "The Blue Danube," "Theme from Love Story,"
"Somewhere over the Rainbow," and "Edelweiss," standard
Chinese favorites. In her long glittery white gown, cascades of
black hair falling down her back, a few well-placed strands escap-
ing over her forehead and eyes, her finely turned ankle pushing
her black slippers down on the pedal for just slightly too much
blurry fuzz around the notes, she was exactly what most lonesome schoolteachers far from home might have in mind as a solitary companion on some remote oceanic version of this artificial
island. But not me.

   While not exactly impervious to her loveliness, it was the
piano that roused my real lust. Months without a functional
piano close at hand left me jittery as an alcoholic in Saudi Arabia.
I faced the probable truth that I was a true addict, with no higher
power to save me, to lead me back to a life of keyboardless sobriety; the higher power itself lived inside the piano, hiding its
omnipotent face somewhere under the ivory keys or behind the
hammers. When the strings were set vibrating, the divine came
out to dance the sacred dance in the currents of sound, mis-
strikes, botched tempos, and all. The gods don't care about a few
wrong notes if you strike them with a full heart.

I started trying to play a piano at twelve or thirteen. Since I lived
on a pianoless farm, my first real chance at privacy with a keyboard came when I was bussed in to the Minneota town school

after my one-room rural school closed. The old brick schoolhouse stood just catty-corner down the block from the Icelandic Lutheran church, where I was officially a member. After lunch every day I crossed the street to the church basement with its mostly in-tune "upright grand." My first music instructor was the black hymnal with its sad dour chorales full of blood and guilt, but also full of the most elegant voice leading in the history of music. Without instruction I could intuit the superiority of Johann Sebastian Bach to all his rivals in the tone business. It was apparent first to the hands, then the ear, and finally to the mind—and to the soul, insofar as I understood that as a boy. This was the way a line of music was meant to move, every voice alive with its own melody, grinding dissonance making the skin tickle, then resolving into sweet harmoniousness, the bass moving always in its own contrary direction, the true master of all the other voices, the deep fundamental tune that underlies everything in the universe, the sound of great waves moving in contrary motion to a continent. That church piano, with its yellowed keyboard and floral carved legs, sat on an island too, just as the glossy black Yamaha in the Chinese hotel lobby. When a human being is alone with a piano, an ocean of air rises in the room to seal him off in a private world, even if the island of hammers and strings stands in the middle of a vast prairie. The piano differs from other instruments—say an oboe or trombone or viola—in that, with ten fingers and a damper pedal, you create an imaginary orchestra, or choir, or opera house, or, if you want, Thoreau playing his flute alone next to Walden Pond as the Massachusetts birds sing the sun under its waters. This is the true genius of Liszt's transcriptions of Bach, Beethoven, Schubert, Verdi. You are alone with an interior symphony of a hundred players, or singing "Erlkönig" for yourself, or the whole sextet from *Lucia*. It is the genius of Jelly Roll Morton's piano scores; in "Grandpa's Spells" or the "King Porter Stomp" you've got the whole gang of Red Hot Peppers under hand: drum, clarinet, trombone, trumpet, jug. The left hand keeps the rhythm, the right takes its chorus— hooting clarinet, wailing trumpet, the fist whacks drumbeats in the bass. The piano is a literal one-man band, an orchestra, or opera company. And there you are on your solitary bench, sailed away from the shores of daily life with its demands and distractions, its blathering and nattering, sending bottles of music into the tides of air, all bearing the same message: "Don't rescue me quite yet; I'm just getting to the good part."

This happy illusion of being marooned on the island of music works only so long as nobody rows to shore to remind you that the rest of the world goes on tediously existing. I haunted the church basement over lunch hour even in winter, with the heat off. I sat in my coat, wearing gloves with fingers, thumping away at "Alle Menschen Müssen Sterben" or "Jesu, meine Freude" or "O Traurigkeit" or something equally peppy to warm the blood. The Icelandic minister, Guttormur Guttormsson, came over one day to rescue me from my island. He had been pastor to his Icelandic flock since the end of World War I (this was 1955), and he seemed old as the greenstone bedrock to me with his shiny bald head, omnipresent black suit, thick spectacles, and Icelandic accent. "It's too cold for you to play down here. Come next door and play the piano in the parsonage." Thus ended the island privacy in which I could imagine myself Vladimir Horowitz, Albert Schweitzer, and the Mormon Tabernacle Choir rolled into one, no matter what awful noises my hands made. The consolations for rejoining civilization were considerable: a warm room, a tuned piano, and Rannveig's (Guttormur's wife) cookies and vínarterta. On all sides of the piano rose shelves of Guttormur's books: dictionaries of Greek, Latin, Hebrew, Icelandic, German, Norwegian, theology in three languages, the Icelandic sagas, poetry, history. Guttormur was loved not for his sermons, which were lengthy scholarly discourses delivered in a soft Icelandic burr, but for being a genuinely learned man, the Scandinavian equivalent of Singer's learned rabbis in the Polish shtetl. As I started one day to leave, to resume my afternoon of social studies and pep band, Guttormur entered the room carrying a slim red book. He handed it to me. "You will find this useful. I studied from it many years ago in Winnipeg." I opened the book: *A Treatise on Harmony, with Exercises,* by J. Humfrey Anger, printed in Toronto, 1905. Inside lived the rules that explained why Bach sounded with such splendor. "When the roots move a third, let two of the upper parts take oblique, and the other contrary motion with the bass." Anger's treatise was not what most thirteen-year-olds had in mind for amusement and diversion, but I devoured that book and own it still, with Guttormur's neat signature on the flyleaf: G. Guttormsson, 16 *Águst,* 1910. It is an island book, to be savored in the interior, private world, a luminous world where notes move gravely in their ordered sequences, where fingers obediently strike true, singing together to raise the morning stars.

When Guttormur died in 1956, his widow, Rannveig, called my father. "Come and get the piano. Guttormur wanted Billy to have it." With a few grumbles, my father assembled a moving crew and a pickup truck. I sat in the back of the pickup, playing all the way home, eight gravel miles north of Minneota. Now I occupied a moving island—serenading the air at thirty miles per hour. It was my first piano, and, like a man's first lovemaking and his first drink and his first funeral, it remains monumental in the imagination. Every piano has its own feel under the hands. My hands still remember that one. The piano saved my youth; whenever

the worlds of football, or farming, or the awful premonition that
I might never escape Minneota weighed me down toward despair,
I sailed out to the piano bench with a foot of music and threw
away the life raft. I never learned true technique; though I had
both a good teacher in high school and a splendid teacher in college, who tried to shame me into mastering scales and arpeggios,
to face up to a little discipline, my real joy (and my only real skill)
was to read at the piano. What delight, that Beethoven thirty-
two times made sonatas, Haydn fifty-two times, that Bach started
with forty-eight and went on to a hundred more fugues, that Liszt
tried to transcribe every bar of music written from Palestrina to
Wagner, and that I could read them all forever, over and over, no-
ticing some new detail of genius every time I read them.

Back on the mainland, the gravelly voice of the everyday world
waited for me to finish thumping. It croaked: practice your scales,
get a job, keep your opinions to yourself, fear the commies, do
chores, slim down, try to be more like normal people, save your
money (after you've figured out how to get it), listen to rock 'n
roll, learn to type, believe in the shriveled God of the churches
not the sublime divinity inside Bach. But for a while, I could live
in a world where my only orders were to play *con molto gran espres-
sione, cantando e dolce, appassionato, presto furioso.*

In the lobby of the Golden Flower, the miracle in the heart of
China, thirty years after the Guttormsson piano traveled north
to my father's farmhouse, I am covered with a layer of Chinese
grime (no hot water for a week), not having touched a piano for
a month or two, slavering at the sight of the big black Yamaha,
wondering if I dared. To eat a peach is duck soup, compared to
taking over a piano in a strange hotel lobby.

I did, of course. After the vision of loveliness had folded her music for the night, she lifted her skirt just slightly for the trip back over open water. After a decent interval, I clumped onto the piano island and played: a couple of Joplin rags, the C minor fugue from "Well Tempered Clavier I," half a Mozart sonata, a few Schubert waltzes, and a Chinese pop tune I liked that I had heard on the radio every day for a month. When you are in danger of being evicted from the only decent piano in central Asia for a thousand miles, do not risk playing Arnold Schoenberg or what you remember of the Concord Sonata. The dining patrons on the deluxe American Express tour will not forgive you. Even the hotel clerks seemed to like the music, either that or they were bemused by the fat, pink, scruffy foreigner attacking their Yamaha. Scott Joplin's music has a great power of charming ordinary people across whatever cultural barriers you choose to erect. Its rhythmic vitality and melodic sweetness mask the fact that like a Bach chorale or a Chopin mazurka, it is composed out of stainless steel. It will not fall down in a heap if you play it a thousand times. This makes it a good choice if you are trying to charm strangers into letting you have a proper go at their Yamaha.

I crossed many times to the piano island at the Golden Flower that year. I often brought students with me, who, of course, loved to sing—and knew very well the words to the Chinese pop tune I had learned, a patriotic love ballad about a brave soldier who sheds his blood to save Mother China from the Vietnamese menace. I even learned the tune of "White Haired Girl," an old Cultural Revolution favorite from one of Jiang Qing's approved revolutionary operas, a real Maoist toe tapper full of correct people's sentiment.

The Chinese, like human tribes anywhere, loved music of any kind—so long as it was live and played with a little spirit. They particularly loved pianos, and their almost complete absence from

China at first astounded me. The answer arrived when I became acquainted with recent Chinese history. During the Cultural Revolution, the Red Guards took particular pleasure in the smashing of pianos with axes and hammers. I read one fine story of a piano shoved off the balcony of a fifth-floor apartment. It must have made a remarkable clatter when it landed; one can only hope that any stray human who happened to be walking under it was a counter-revolutionary class enemy or hooligan intellectual who deserved this musical surprise fallen from the heavens.

The Great Proletarian Cultural Revolution was an unsavory brew of Mao's manipulative and cynical political plotting, mixed with the xenophobic nationalism that can be whipped to a fury among any tribe: Chinese, Serb, German, American, Tutsi, Irish—name your own relatives. The piano was transmogrified from a simple musical instrument (and a wonderful gift of human ingenuity) into a symbol of foreign humiliation of China. It played European scales, European sonatas and fugues, European augmented and diminished chords. If you owned one, you probably stole the price of it from the mouths of peasants and workers, and worse yet played on it those oppressors of the proletariat: Beethoven and Liszt, rather than "The Red Sun of Mao Zedong Rises Gloriously over the People's Republic." Oh humans! If science could only miraculously amputate the fanaticism button from the brain, we would be eons ahead in the evolution sweepstakes!

If you could float the Golden Flower piano island to the middle of an ocean, and anchor it securely, you would still not escape human history with all its knotty complications. The piano's tentacles go deep both into the physiology of the brain and the hand and into the history simultaneously of music, technology, and industrial capitalism. Whatever private worlds you imagine as your fingers amble through a Haydn sonata or try to imitate Art

Tatum's improvising on "Willow Weep for Me," you sink your hands deep into the mulch and grime of history. Your island is not a retreat but a bridge.

Start with two facts: first biology, then history. Take your hands off this essay and lay them flat on the table. If you have not worked around farm machinery, you should be able to count ten. Now admire your two thumbs. Move them around a little. Improvise a thumb dance. Notice they are mirror images of each other and swivel independently of the hand. These are your opposable thumbs. They tell you that you are a human being and neither a chimpanzee nor a killer whale, your close relatives. Because of these miraculous thumbs, you can, among other things, play a piano. Russell Sherman, a famous pianist and a wise man, says: "The thumb is the capital, the fingers are the provinces. The fingers pay taxes to the thumb, which in turn diminishes the taxing strain on the fingers by providing a general security system and command center. The thumb is an ultra-benevolent despot except in times of war, when it marshals its retinue of howitzers and torpedoes, of which it has the greatest supply. Then everybody is grateful to have such a strong boss. But otherwise, when the loudest sonorities are the chirping of cicadas or the mating rites of bees with flowers, the thumb becomes the invisible (if not inaudible) branch to the filigree of fingers. . . . The thumb is by birth a beast on the way to becoming an aristocrat." Or to make still another metaphor, here is the entire poem, "Thumb," by Philip Dacey: "The odd, friendless boy raised by four aunts." Your thumbs are your man Friday on your piano island.

Next, look at the old upright piano, which, I hope against hope, still stands in your parlor. Like you, that piano has ancestors; it was not hatched from a miraculous egg. Pythagoras, an island man born on Samos in the sixth century B.C., founded a cult of

number worshippers, mathematicians, astronomers—the first
acousticians and musicologists. The Pythagoreans, as histories
of philosophy tell us, thought that all things are made of numbers. They believed in the magical properties of certain numbers,
among them: ten—the fingers. Both musical tones and the move-
ments of the planets were assigned numbers; these numbers
together made "the music of the spheres—the celestial dance."
Though the Pythagoreans were not likely the first humans to discover that by stretching a string over a hollow box and plucking
it, one could invent music, they were the first to imagine the
overtone series, that by stopping the string at various points you
could make various pitches, all of them contained in the fundamental tone, and that those pitches rose out of the fundamental
in an exact mathematical progression. Strike the lowest C on the
upright in your parlor. The whole scale of twelve notes rises up
in a predictable column out of it, first the fifth, then the twelfth,
until the notes disappear out of your hearing, and bother only
your dog, whose ears are more acute and sensitive to music than
yours. All music, by implication, rises from that fundamental
tone. If next you nail more strings of various lengths to your hollow box, you don't have to wait for the mathematics of the overtone series to imply music. You can make tunes yourself with
your hands by plucking, bowing with a horse's tail, or striking
with a stone tied to a stick. If next you want to damp the strings
to stop them from vibrating when they have reached their proper
pitch (or number if you are a Pythagorean), then wind some moss
or bark—or if you have it, cloth—between the strings. After a
few hundred years, you may as well invent a board with keys—
a little wooden seesaw—that will strike or pluck the strings for
you. Then you can make harmony—whole chords—or play two
or three tunes together. Now you have made counterpoint. Keep

adding strings to the bottom and top of your contraption and soon you will have enough of the overtone series under your hands to invent the music of Johann Sebastian Bach or, to give it its other name, the music of the spheres, the celestial harmony, the dancing of the whole universe. Most wonderful of all is this fact: though your dog can hear more than you, he cannot make music with his paws; the universe in its infinite wisdom gave you your opposable thumbs—or mathematics or astronomy. Considered from this angle, it is not such a bad deal to be a human being.

In my old house floats an archipelago of keyboards: clavichord, harpsichord, a 1922 Raudenbush upright, made in North Saint Paul, and finally a black Yamaha six-foot grand, a first cousin of the Golden Flower piano. I sail from one to another whenever I please, dropping anchor on the bench or stool after I have provisioned myself with some piles of music that interest me.

The clavichord and harpsichord, historically grandpa and grandma to the other two, are, in my case, children of the sixties. When I entered graduate school in Lawrence, Kansas, in 1965, I found myself both broke—a normal state for graduate students in those days—and bereft of a piano for the first time since the ministerial upright made its voyage north of Minneota. *The Nation* advertised do-it-yourself harpsichord kits for $150, made by Wallace Zuckerman. A musical cousin of mine had already built one, but who would put mine together? I couldn't pound a straight nail into a two-by-four or saw a board at a respectable right angle. But in the sixties, odd saviors surfaced in American life. I made the acquaintance of a marvelous eccentric Kansan, whose various professions included building geodesic domes (on Buckminster Fuller's model), cultivating discrete gardens of hallucinogenic pleasures, and assembling harpsichord kits. I hired him for a modest sum, and thirty-three odd years later, my plain-Jane

workingman's model Zuckerman single-manual harpsichord with
lute stop still plays Bach fugues, Scarlatti sonatas, William Byrd's
pavans and galliards and "Carmen's Whistles." It was an intelligent twentieth-century adaptation of an old machine, suitable for
and affordable by ordinary citizens. Thus, unlike smart bombs,
cell phones, and e-mail, it represents true technological progress.
The harpsichord, certainly the most mechanical of keyboard instruments, makes its noise by plucking the stretched strings. In
the seventeenth and eighteenth centuries the strings were made
of gut; the jacks, which held the pluckers, of ox bone or ivory; the
pluckers themselves sharpened goose quills; the springs, which
held the pluckers in place, of hog bristles; and the dampers, which
stopped the string from sounding, of leather. The entirely wood
case housed a sound board of thin spruce, the most resonant
wood, garnished with a painted rose. Thus every time you played
a minuet or a fandango, you had under your fingers a whole farm
with a woodlot. Now the jacks and plectra (pluckers) are made of
Delrin, a plastic invented for artificial heart valves. It does not
warp easily. This is progress.

I bought the clavichord, also a Zuckerman kit, for $150 the
next year. This is the true ancestor of the piano, the strings not
plucked but struck and pressed on the end of a little seesaw by
brass tangents. It is the smallest, simplest, quietest, and certainly the most expressive of all keyboards. Since your finger remains in control of the vibrating string once you have pressed
the tangent upward, you can, like a violinist, make a vibrato—
called by the Germans *Bebung*. On only this keyboard can the
hands truly make song, rather than create the illusion of singing.
But the song, though penetrating and soulful, is very soft. The
humming of your refrigerator, much less the snarl of your lawn
mower, will drown it out. The French and the English did not like

the clavichord. The Germans loved it and, like Bach's son Karl, moved themselves to tears and trembling while improvising on it. The Italians liked it too, though they always tucked it away in a tiny private alcove of their houses where at most one person could listen. They called this private corner for the clavichord *paradiso,* paradise. The clavichord is probably the true island instrument, but better on a freshwater island in a calm lake. Heavy surf would overwhelm it.

In the sixties perhaps a half-dozen small handwork companies made kits for assembling into antique keyboards. This was capitalism at its noblest: using modest but intelligent technology to make something lovely and useful with history inside it. Owning these simple instruments—which compelled you to tune and repair them yourself—connected you to Bach, Cabezon, Byrd, Sweelinck, back to Pythagoras himself; furthermore, you constructed and maintained them with the most sophisticated trained professional help: your own brain and hands. The Harpsichord Makers of America were the first professional organization to oppose the continuation of the Vietnam War and to endorse Eugene McCarthy for President. As I always suspected, keyboards were useful not only for the aesthetic, but for the ethical lives of human beings as well.

The piano is a third thing. If we are to understand clearly what it is, and why it is wonderful, we must first understand what it is not; to do that requires getting our metaphors straight—and maybe for a while pretending that we are not Americans who have been driving cars, buying digital contraptions, watching television, or checking our voice mail for twenty-five years and imagining that we are normal, that gadgets are part of Jehovah's grand plan for our eternal happiness. To do this, take "progress"—either word or idea, immediately out of your frontal lobe and set it in an empty glass next to the false teeth. Don't throw it out yet. You may have need of it later in an altered form.

The clavichord and the harpsichord are perfectly achieved machines for making music. Vast piles of very great music exist for both that cannot be as well played or understood apart from their peculiar qualities. The thin textures and emotional outbursts of Karl Philipp Emanuel Bach come clear best on a clavichord; Couperin's elegant dances and character pieces need the bite and clarity of a harpsichord. But like human beings, these two noble instruments are not comprehensive. The soulful clavichord makes too little sound to be of much use in public. It cannot even be recorded accurately. The harpsichord speaks in a loud clear voice and can entertain a large audience, but it cannot sing; it cannot louden and soften except by mechanical means. It does not feel the fatty flesh of your fingers.

Human beings are smart creatures; best of all, they are curious. In 1709 Bartolomeo Cristofori of Florence invented a Rube Goldberg contraption in which one hammer is lifted to strike another hammer, which then strikes a string. Simultaneously, a leather damper rises to stifle the sounding string. The mechanism of hammers sinks back, ready for the next strike. The right engineering name for this ingenious system is the escapement mechanism. It means that a loud strike makes a loud tone, a soft strike a soft one. Cristofori doubled the number of struck strings and added another contraption to move the hammers to the side so they struck only a single string—*una corda*. Thus a third machine for the keyboard was born, louder than the clavichord, more expressive and responsive than the harpsichord. If this was not an invention quite of the magnitude of the wheel, fire, and the second law of thermodynamics, the human race nevertheless had good cause for gratitude at Cristofori's ingenuity.

A German, Gottfried Silbermann, also began manufacturing pianofortes (soft louds), trying to refine Cristofori's mechanism. By 1747 Frederick the Great of Prussia had invested in fifteen of these new-fangled instruments. He invited Johann Sebastian Bach, the most famous keyboard virtuoso and composer of learned fugues in his realm, to test these new keyboards in his palace. A dutiful and obedient subject (he was German after all . . .), Bach arrived ready to play. Frederick presented him with an abstruse, chromatic, exceedingly difficult fugue subject, and invited old Bach to improvise a fugue on one of his Silbermann pianos. Bach, rising to the spirit of the game, improvised a three-voice ricercar (a highfalutin name for a "learned" fugue) full of playful chromaticism. Frederick ought to have been sufficiently dazzled by this, but he pressed Bach to perform the impossible: improvise a six-voice fugue on the royal subject. Six-voice fugues are not matters for trifling and Bach probably demurred, but promised that, in the privacy of his study, he would see what might be made of the king's subject and send it along if the result was satisfactory. Bach, the great republican of music history, added that he did not find the piano up to snuff; he still preferred his old clavichord, but the king was, after all, the king, and Bach would do his best. A few months later, Frederick received *"Die Musikalisches Opfer"* ("The Musical Offering"), a collection of fugues, canons, musical games, a trio sonata . . . and a magnificent six-voice ricercar, all on the king's subject. It is one of the great works of music, both in its expressive power and in the beauty of its vast learning. Piano music thus begins with what are arguably two of its greatest masterpieces, the three- and six-voice fugues, composed by a dour old fellow who didn't even like the piano.

As with Homer, there is some virtue in being first. Every modern writer who thinks he has made something extraordinary and new also ought to be troubled by the ghost of *The Iliad* rolling around in his head to remind him that whatever he thinks he has accomplished, he still stands on Homer's shoulders. So also has it been in the history of piano music; Haydn, Beethoven, Liszt, and Rachmaninoff gladdened the hearts of piano players, but the shoulders of Bach's first piano pieces still shadow them. It is contained in them but they were contained in it before they were ever an egg floating in their mother's womb.

The idea of "progress" except in the most narrow and shallow sense is more a marketing strategy than a description of the way the universe works. Things alter; circles grow larger, but they are contained within a greater circle, whose outlines we cannot see but which has always existed independent of human pretense.

When I stepped over two feet of open water to the island of music in the Golden Flower, I carried with me in my hands—in my very cellular organization—Pythagoras and Cristofori and Bach and Mao Tse-tung and the casting of the piano's iron frame in a Bessemer furnace and Red Guards with axes and a red book of harmony from Winnipeg. When my thumb passed under my palm to finger a scale, the primordial ooze of the Pleistocene still clung to the fingernails. My island of interior escape from the miseries of nerd-dom in high school was inhabited by a thousand generations who joined me on the piano bench. We only think we escape to islands; we forget the wind, which blows spores and ashes from all over the planet to keep us good company.

There is a paradox here that I cannot solve for you: it begins with the fact that the piano, though a public instrument, is, for those who love it, a private world. Peter Yates says: "Suppose I were on a desert island. And I had with me only my Steinway—or a Bechstein had washed up on the beach. Precisely the situation of a person who, after looking at his piano as ornamental furniture for a dozen years . . . suddenly sits down at it and exposes the keys to his fingers. . . . When I sit at the keyboard and start playing myself back into music, time ceases. The masters of the keyboard are my companions . . . though they must deplore my clumsiness. I am my own explorer, my own interpreter, my own false absolute." Sweet though this privacy, he goes on to argue that "music will not survive in the concert hall, if we do not keep it living in our homes." Music as a spectator sport dies if the spectators are not connected organically to what is made in public. If you think you have music when you buy a sound system, put on ear plugs, and turn up the volume, you are mistaken. Our millions of little islands of private homemade music make possible Carnegie Hall and the Vienna Philharmonic. This paradox is as true for literature or politics or mathematics as it is for music.

Pianos were still made entirely of wood till the beginning of the nineteenth century, but the desire for more sound and more notes as well as the technological advances in iron casting in the industrial revolution made possible the evolution of the heavy behemoths that have caused slipped disks and hernias for generations of piano owners foolish enough to carry them up and down stairs. Liszt was famous for demolishing the frail early pianos with his great power and ferocious technique. His scores, black with notes and thundering fortissimos, demanded iron strings held at enormous tension by iron pins in an iron frame. Inventors and engineers rose to the challenge. The piano, though still almost as hand assembled as an old harpsichord, is a true child of industrial technology. Mass production made possible cheap pianos, and by the end of the nineteenth century it was a rare middle-class house anywhere in the west that didn't boast a clunky upright in the parlor holding the generations of dead ancestors and prepubescent offspring in gilt frames. Somebody in every house could muddle

their way through a waltz, a polka, a hymn, a sentimental ballad—
or even a little Chopin and Beethoven and old Bach. By 1900 there
were seven thousand piano manufacturers in the United States
alone, and according to one probably reliable historian of the
piano, one of every six Americans was involved in some way in
the piano business—including producing the raw materials for
construction. My old black Raudenbush upright was made in
North Saint Paul, Minnesota, at a small family factory—in those
days a long trolley ride north from the Capitol. The Raudenbushes
made my piano sturdily enough to last since 1922 in decent play-
able condition. Many human beings manufactured in 1922 have
not survived so well.

A century later, those seven thousand piano makers have
shrunk to under a dozen, and the stragglers are mostly loss-
leader acquisitions by vast international conglomerates. Middle-
class houses chucked out most of the family uprights at garage
sales or dump grounds, filling their empty parlor space with
blinking screens that might play some artificial music for you if
you click the right mouse. No more hog bristles or interlocking
hammers. It's cheaper to buy a digital music program than to hire
a teacher and practice. Once, ordinary people investigated what
was new in the music world by buying four-hand versions of symphonies, operas, songs, dances. You found a brave friend—if you
were lucky, somebody you fancied and wanted to flirt with—
to bump hind ends on the same bench. Wagner, Grieg, Johann
Strauss came to life, wrong notes and all, under your twenty fingers and four flailing elbows. Now, summon music.com.org, punch
in your credit-card number, and you need never smell human
sweat from music making again.

There again—the paradox. The piano is on the one hand the
most public and sociable of instruments, a musical cement that

connects human beings, even whole communities to each other. G. B. Shaw said of it, "The pianoforte is the most important of all musical instruments; its invention was to music what the invention of the printing press was to poetry." The piano democratized an art. It gives ordinary people the history of music if they want it, just as cheap, easily reproducible books took Homer and Plato out of the monastery and the royal library to put them on the bookshelves of ordinary houses. But if the world is not to your taste, you can sail away to your private Encantadas where you can—in Herman Melville's description—turn yourself into an "isolato." I know. I've been doing it for years.

I sink into the music of a particular composer as if I were a sleepwalker. For six months, nothing but Brahms, for another six, nothing but fugues of Hindemith. Then six on "Carolina Shout" and others by James P. Johnson, then another six on the old-man music of Liszt. I never "perform" these composers. I play them only in a room alone. After a while some little stone from the unconscious rises to the surface of the brain. Whoever I've been playing delivers to me some insight about my interior life formerly a complete mystery to my consciousness. Brahms became the composer of mourning I had neglected to accomplish. Hindemith puts me in order when some exterior chaos threatens me. Haydn calms my fear of death. Beethoven gives me courage to stand up to foolishness. Johnson, Morton, and Joplin remind me I have a body. Liszt reminds me not to talk too much or to practice too much charm lest silence and loneliness extract their final revenge. Now I have been playing Gabriel Fauré for six months, the "Theme and Variations," the late nocturnes and barcaroles. His music writes me letters full of wisdom. A few words are already clear. Fauré is stingy with his musical materials, but profligate with surface beauty. The beauty hides (from all but

those who play him or who listen with the passionate attention of
a Daoist mystic) the precise, even steely, mathematical logic and
order inside the music. Those who do not like his music call it
gray. It eschews climax, and, when others might thunder or whisper, his pieces generally end in a calm moderate voice. I think
Fauré's letter to me says, "Be a little gray outside, it's all right. Pay
more attention to the currents running under the sea, less to the
noise of big surf pounding rocks." Bach, whom I play all the time,
brings me God, or the gods, or something I have no idea how to
describe. Neither did the poet Robert Bly.

LISTENING TO BACH

There is someone inside this music
who is not well described by the names
Of Jesus, or Jehovah, or the Lord of Hosts!

Bach may be what the universe has in mind next.

Glenn Gould, who played Bach (among other things) more
passionately than any musician of this century, embodies this
paradox of the public and the private. He was psychologically a
classic isolato, an island man in spades. He preferred phone talk
in the middle of the night to actual human contact. He swathed
his body (even in great heat) in layer after layer of cover—gloves,
sweaters, overshoes, overcoats, mufflers, wool caps—indoors, as
if he were afraid of the air itself. He preferred cold dead places—
the high Arctic was his notion of paradise. For years he ate only
steaks, then for more years only scrambled eggs. He disliked food
and thought it a bother to eat. He loathed playing for human beings and gave it up early in his career; afterward, he locked himself in recording studios in the middle of the night. He feared

germs so much he medicated himself to death. If ever a man was an isolate island, it was Glenn Gould. And yet. . . . Here's a prose poem I wrote about him in an attempt to get at the paradox of the piano.

GLENN GOULD, 1932–1982

A man who played the piano with as much genius as it is possible to contain in a human being said he trusted machines and electricity more than he trusted humans in a room. So hence, he would play only for steel wire and thin tape, genius forever saved from coughing, wheezing, and all possibility of disagreeable whispers and remarks.

He took his first machine, the piano, and chiseled, filed, and muffled it until it suited his music and was like no other such machine on earth—a name brand of one. He sat on his second machine, an old chair, which squeaked and rocked and comforted him.

He waited until the middle of the night to have perfect silence for his music, then moved his two peculiar machines into a sealed sound-locked room where not even the vibration of a human foot could ever be felt. There he played, safe at last from the rest of us, and even, he thought, from himself.

But when Bach or Haydn came on him, he started singing in a low and ugly hum, out of tune with everything his hands were doing. No machine could take this noise away or clear it out without losing the music too, so he was left with an awful choice. Give up principle or give up beauty.

He chose the music, hums and all, a glad hypocrite like us. Only failed ideals and wrong turnings will ever get you anywhere on earth or make anything with beauty or energy inside it. So now in the Bach F-sharp Minor Fugue or the slow C major tune in the Haydn sonata, the awful humming overwhelms the perfect technology, and everyone with ears tuned right is glad of it.

That hum is his ghost, still alive, but also it is the invisible audience sneezing and hacking; it is the ignorant applause after the wrong movement; it is pigeons in the rafters of the hall, cooing for bread; it is me blowing my nose and wiping my tears of joy in this music—in this odd, grand failure of a man.

Donne was right not only about men, but about pianos. They are all connected "to the promontory of Europe." Even two feet of open water in the Golden Flower will not protect us from history or our fellow humans. When the Red Guards fell on pianos with their axes, it was history and memory they were after. The old communists thought they could airbrush the consciousness clean, start history fresh. The Red Guards were only a deus ex machina that failed. Milan Kundera in *The Book of Laughter and Forgetting* describes the efforts of Gustav Husák's communist government to coax Karel Gott, Czechoslovakia's most famous rock singer back to Prague to help them. Kundera (no rock fan) says, "The history of music is mortal, but the idiocy of the guitar is eternal. Music in our time has returned to its primordial state, the state after the last issue has been raised and the last theme contemplated—a state that follows history." For Kundera, "Karel Gott represents music minus memory, the music in which the bones of Beethoven and Ellington, the dust of Palestrina and Schönberg, lie buried." This is the feel-good music of political manipulation. It wants us to forget. In our global capitalist world it wants us to buy things so it sings to us in elevators and Kmarts. Twelve bars of Bach played with attention and whatever skill you can muster will save you from these political and commercial demons.

The music that comes out of your piano is not an escapist pipe dream, an island floating in ether. It is reality itself. The sounds you make will travel farther than you ever imagined. Russell Sherman, a wise philosopher of the piano, says it well:

> To know the piano is to know the universe. To master the piano is to master the universe. The spectrum of piano sound acts as a prism through which all musical and non-musical sounds may be filtered. The grunts of sheep, the braying of mules, the popping of champagne corks, the sighs of unrequited love, not to mention the full lexicon of sounds available to all other instruments— including whistles, scrapes, bleatings, caresses, thuds, hoots, plus sweet and sour pluckings—fall within the sovereignty of this most bare and dissembling chameleon.

If, as a variation on the old game of choosing one book to take with you to a desert island, you choose instead one machine, forget your laptop or your cell phone. You want a piano (with tuning fork in case your island is humid). It will remind you what a pleasure it is to be a human being with a long history and the possibility of beauty still alive inside you.

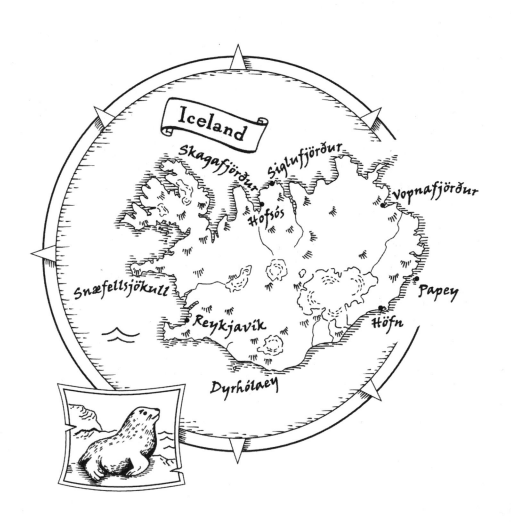

๛ Iceland 1979

THE BACKWARD IMMIGRANT, 1979

By sea, with a little bad weather in the Labrador Sea, gale-force winds, a twenty-foot swell, and a quick stop at a military base in Argentia, Newfoundland, to drop off a container of hamburger patties from Iowa, it takes eleven days to go from Portsmouth, Virginia, to Reykjavík, Iceland. You pass through the Grand Banks southeast of Newfoundland, where in 1912 a large cruise ship had trouble with an iceberg drifted south in the West Greenland Current. Radar, sonar, and prudent seamanship have shrunk the dangers considerably since then, but an iceberg is still an iceberg, and passengers have their imagination. If you leave on your trip just before Christmas, you will celebrate both Christmas and the New Year at sea. As you move north with the Gulf Stream, you sail from day into almost continual night. What little gray drizzly light keeps you company east of Boston shrivels to an hour or two south of Greenland. North Atlantic weather in late December doesn't offer much pleasure for sun cruisers. It seldom clears, but when it does your consolation is a view of northern lights beyond anything the land bound, much less the city dweller, have ever seen or can ever see. The sky turns into a circus of color and light. You are hundreds of miles from the nearest light source or human

being or building or even fireplace. Here is only black water and
sky and cascades of pink, gold, green, blue streamers shivering
across the darkness in front of you, behind you, overhead. Soon
the curtain closes and weather turns normal. Northeasters full
of sleet howl down the Denmark Strait or off the crest of the
two-mile-thick ice cap—the size of three of Texas—that buries
Greenland. The ship bucks like a crazed horse riding into the big
swells that crash over the hull; frozen spray glazes the world:
ropes, railing, decks, the brightly colored freezer containers of
military hamburger. Watch your footing. You don't want to slide
into that black almost frozen ocean.

What, asks Sensible Reader, is any sane person who doesn't
work as a seaman doing on board a freighter in the North Atlantic
in the middle of winter? That slightly touched person is Bill
Holm, on his way to teach American literature to Icelanders as a
Fulbright professor. He is thirty-five years old, a half-dropout
from academic life, and almost a full dropout from the American
economy. He applied to teach in Iceland for the shabbiest of
reasons—idle curiosity. As the grandson of four Icelandic immigrants to Minnesota, he grew up listening to old people speak
Icelandic, tell stories (always in English to him) of the stubborn
stoicism, quick intelligence, and fierce independence of the tribe
of his ancestors. In every Icelandic home he visited, he looked at
omnipresent shelves of books by ancient and modern Icelanders:
sagas, histories, *Independent People* by Halldór Laxness (the si-
multaneous pride and shame of the immigrants), and, more than
anything else, poetry, always poetry, endless leather-bound volumes of skinny lines in an impenetrable alphabet. That immigrant
community left him with—how else to say it?—a certain smug
arrogance at having been born an Icelander. To be an Icelander
meant to have poetry running in your veins and arteries, to never

back down before the rich and powerful because you were born
to what they could never buy or conquer. It was all incomparably
grand—this myth of the proud unbending farmer intellectual
hurling improvised sarcastic poems (in perfect rhyme and meter)
into the howling sea wind. A boy could do worse than have that
slightly fantastic and completely impractical mythic seed planted
in his brain. But what those old immigrants did not give him
was the language—without which, of course, it was impossible
to be an Icelander, or even a poet. Could poetry be written in
English? It wasn't only the Icelanders who lost their precious
language. North America is a vast continental graveyard of lost
languages from all over the planet. Sometimes language death
takes only a few years, sometimes a generation, or in extraordinarily stubborn tribes, two or three. After that, the deluge,
first only one language, glorious English, and then, arguably,
none at all, only inchoate muttering from ads and TV. English-
only fanatics and those who fret about bilingualism need not
worry. Time and American inertia will solve their problem. In
the case of the second-generation Icelandic immigrants (and the
rest of the north European midwest) the First World War jingo-
ism hurried this process of language death. By 1943, when Holm
surfaced, the extermination was complete. He grew up with rich
myths and nine Icelandic words, four of them profane, three of
them names of food, and two a greeting. So he wanted to go to
Iceland for a long enough time to satisfy his curiosity, maybe
even to learn a few more words of his parents' first language. By
1978 his parents were both dead in middle age, and he was left
(as they say in scholarly circles) with no primary sources to con-
sult except by medium. Was the real Iceland anything like the
romantic myths he'd grown up with? What peculiar atmosphere
above this harsh isolated island hatched these myths? When

you cut an ordinary Icelandic farmer, did he still bleed poetry and
eloquence?

When he got news that the Fulbright job had arrived, and
therefore someone else's money would get him to Iceland, he decided to take a ship to go slowly across the North Atlantic in winter, backward from his ancestors' journeys in the nineteenth
century. "You're crazy," said friends who did not know him well.
"You can be there in comfort in a few hours on an airplane." But
he was not fooled. He had flown in an airplane before—even to
Iceland—and he did not like it. The point of going far away from
where you are is, in fact, to be far away, to have inside your body
the physical sense that you are no longer where you were and have
gone to some trouble to get there, to move from one landscape,
one weather, to another. The airplane lies to you. It says you can
arrive at that charmless placeless invention, the airport, pay
some money, get squeezed uncomfortably into a sealed contraption, generally at night, belt yourself in next to strangers whom
you hope against hope are deaf-mutes, or monolingual speakers
of Armenian, try to booze your way into an uneasy doze, then
stumble out, enervated and stiff, a few hours later into an equally
charmless placeless airport half a planet away. These airports
probably play the same jolly bouncy traveler's muzak through dis-
creetly hidden speakers. And there you are—in Moscow or Hong
Kong or Nairobi or Lima, sleepy, grouchy, and far away from home.
The airplane has lied to your body. It wants to make you think the
universe comes easy. But Iceland is—and should be, like other
places—a long hard slow way from where the world looks normal
to you. If you arrive too quickly—anyplace—you will spend your
life never having actually seen anything at all except the No-
Smoking/Fasten Your Seat Belt sign and a still virgin vomit bag.

So Bill Holm asked the Fulbright commission to send him

slowly away by water. He bought a red used Ford Pinto, a car then drastically cheap because of a potentially exploding gas tank, packed it with books, a clavichord, two half gallons of Rebel Yell bourbon, a goose-feather coat, and his felt-lined arctic pac boots— good for saving your toes from amputation down to fifty below. He booked passage on the Bakkafoss (Bakka Falls—all Icelandic Steamship Company boats are named for the country's over-supply of scenic cataracts), leaving from Portsmouth, Virginia, a few days before Christmas. The Pinto disappeared into a sealed freight container, and Holm found himself in a two-room suite on the main deck, the only passenger (and the only true foreigner) on this mostly hamburger-patty, Wonder-bun, and smuggled-beer cargo ship. This was more luxurious than his grandparents' probably steerage tickets on a three-masted British schooner in 1878, but it was the best he could do to honor their journey west.

Western Minnesota is not oversupplied with saltwater harbors so this was Holm's first real experience on the sea. Bakkafoss was a working boat, all crew and all business. Even the Chinese cook was an Icelander by virtue of marriage. Most spoke a little English: move your ass, pass the potatoes, are you seasick?, big wind today. He soon found himself in a bridge game in a foreign language— *spaði, hjarta, tigull, lauf, grand* (spades, hearts, diamonds, clubs, no trump). His bidding provoked astonishment among the Icelanders. He used the Goren point-count system, they used the Italian. Few were anxious to be his partner after he had, for ex-ample, gone down six with a void trump suit. After a little lin-guistically awkward explaining, the game improved. The dummy frequently slid from one side of the table to the other as big swells whacked into the Bakkafoss's hull. His nine-word vocabulary grew to fifteen or twenty. He could now play cards in his grand-father's language.

Because he was a curiosity and a diversion, this strange
passenger—who looked like an Icelander, but played bridge like
an American, whose four words of Icelandic might frighten any
farm cow enough to kick over the milk pail—became a species
of six-and-a-half-foot tall, pink, ship's pet. He often made a pest
of himself in the control room at the top of the ship with its
panoramic picture window over the sea. He peered over the ship
pilot's shoulder, fascinated by this desk full of nautical maps, triangle, slide rule, compass. On a nautical chart the land is blank
except for a harbor or two but the sea is covered with language:
warnings, exotic names of shoals, currents, trenches, all unknown
to the land bound. The digital computer (even then in 1978) announced, in lurid red letters, the latest longitude and latitude.
The radar hums, the ship creaks, fifteen miles an hour, endlessly
chugging north to Newfoundland, then over the Greenland Banks
and the Denmark Strait to Reykjavík. The weather improves as
we go north, the sun comes out, the sea shines like blue-black
glass in the brief winter sun. The Canadian coast guard periodically barks out signals, mispronouncing Bakkafoss. Even the
squawking gulls that follow the ship seem more cheerful as we
head toward the Arctic. Gulls are great aficionados of garbage.
They follow the ship everywhere, our best, most loyal friends.
They know that human beings can always be trusted to leave a
trail of edible detritus in their wake. It all goes into the sea at last:
bread, fruit peels, coffee grounds, sheep bones, brandy bottles,
shit, piss, failed love letters, unread novels, and finally us. The
bright orange, red, brown cargo containers glitter in the slant
winter light, their refrigerator units purring steadily to keep the
hamburger patties cold for NATO. Why would any sane human
being ever set foot in an airport again if he could travel this way?

The great treasure of the control room, though, was the radio man, a wiry dark-haired fellow in his fifties named Sigurður Björgvinsson. Sigurður had learned decently fluent sailor's English and was clearly well read in many languages. He had one of those absolutely alive faces that seem always about to break into another idea that will settle a question once and for all or provide a piece of abstruse information from the *Journal of Bulgarian Geophysics* or a joke or a pun or a comic mistranslation of a word or, most often, a snatch of poetry—ancients, moderns, Icelanders, Englishmen, and often his own. His face would break into a grin, one eyebrow would lift, and his index finger would straighten to make the point.

Because he had the best English on the boat, or because he was a curious and friendly man by nature or perhaps because he had heard that Holm was a poet and an Icelander (at least by descent) and therefore in need of eleven days of mentoring before he landed in the motherland, Sigurður took him under his wing for the trip. He was the first real Icelander who befriended Holm and, in some ways, the most remarkable one he has met to this very day (though by now he's met several thousand other Icelanders).

Sigurður had been at sea for thirty years. He kept a globe by his radio station, where the sailors often came by to find out where they were. Somehow flat maps won't do for fixing the location of your own body on rolling water. It delighted Sigurður to twist his globe and show you where he had been. "To Brazil, to Singapore, to Africa—with stockfish for Nigerians, to Murmansk, so many times to Europe, and now to America, Canada, Portsmouth, Halifax, the Saint Lawrence, New Orleans. When you cross the equator, then you see the Southern Cross; the polar star disappears behind you." He traces with his index finger the Bakkafoss's route: "Here we enter the Gulf Stream, here we cross the Grand

Bank, where the Titanic went down" (stupid seamanship, he sputters), "here we pass the tip of Newfoundland where Þorfinnur Karlsefni settled Vinland—his son Snorri, the first Vinland baby, was the first American. Always an Icelander," chuckles Sigurður. "Here we swing wide south of Greenland because of drift ice, terrible gales in the Denmark Strait, then we round Reykjanes, where NATO buys hamburger, then we are home."

"Where do you live, Sigurður?"

"In Selfoss, the only flat place in Iceland and miles from the sea."

"Where is your favorite place?"

"Mývatn (Midge Lake) where I was born, of course. The most beautiful place in Iceland. Such fat sweet trout. And all the great poets are Þingeyingardl (the county of Mývatn). Every farmer there is a poet."

Maybe Holm's inherited myth had a small stone of truth in its gizzard . . .

"You know I am a communist. I have been here" (he points to Cuba) "twice, working on a brigade. I met Fidel. He is a remarkable man. And I have been here" (he points to the Soviet Union) "with a delegation of Icelanders."

By this point in their friendship, Holm had made clear his disgust for the Vietnam War, the stultifying greed and petty mindedness of American politics and business life. If this man so full of passion for ideas, generosity, humor, so in love with the planet and poetry is a communist, then God save us from Republicans.

Sigurður, an endless fount of poetry, decided to start Holm on his first lessons to make him into a proper poet. Having seen a half dozen of Holm's Minnesota poems—free verse all! even prose poems!—he politely demurred from judgment. "They have interesting ideas but it is so hard to judge the quality of a language not your own. Real poetry, Icelandic poetry, that is, is always written

strictly. Why, this poem, which has four rhymes and eight allit-
erations in four lines, can be spoken backward. The meaning is
opposite but the poetry is still correct and good." He recites it
both ways, then writes it down for me. He grabs my notebook to
scribble another four-line poem. "You must learn the rules of
poetry," he says, proceeding to explain them to me. "And you
must certainly learn Icelandic," he continues, and grabbing the
notebook again, declines a noun or two and writes down a little
vocabulary list. "Can you pronounce this properly?" he asks, and
proceeds to give Holm a lesson. Unfortunately, Holm, a lazy
student, never learned more than rudimentary ungrammatical
Icelandic, even continuing his unrepentant scribbling of free
verse—and prose poems. But a teacher succeeds if he touches the
heart of a student, to leave him alive and open eyed in a wider,
more complicated universe. Sigurður—son of farmers who had
never been to college—was a very great teacher.

Holm admired his enthusiasm most of all. Sigurður must then
have been fifty-six or fifty-seven, Holm's age now, twenty years
later, but hadn't yet collapsed into the middle-aged sour and
shriveled view of life that Holm saw (and sees) so often, even in
himself, in America. Sigurður showed off pictures of Magga
(Margrét), his wife, and their children. "They shall all have more
education than their father." Holm often went up in the middle
of the night to the control room where Sigurður tinkered with his
radio, getting marine weather reports, scratchy announcements
of passing ships. He kept trying to tune in Icelandic State Radio,
and one night east of Greenland it finally flickered in. "We are
getting close to home," he said. "Do you know what you are listening to?" The melodious voice of a middle-aged man talking,
a soft burr in which I thought I detected irony. I heard the word
Schweik. "Is someone reading *The Good Soldier Schweik*?"

"That is Gísli Halldórsson, Iceland's finest actor. He's a good friend of mine, a leftie like me. You must see him act and meet him when you are in Reykjavík. He speaks English well. He is a great man. Do you love this novel as I do?"

In this matter Holm could escape disappointing Sigurður. After Gísli was done reading, the teacher and student sat for half an hour recalling the pleasures of *Schweik,* the savage humor of its blasts at the stupidity of war.

The next day, word spread on the Bakkafoss that Iceland was in earshot and Gísli was reading *Schweik.* Half the crew huddled around the radios in various parts of the boat. Holm hoped the other half was at work making sure the boat didn't sink. "That's damned good! Very funny! I missed Gísli. You must learn Icelandic; it's better in Icelandic than Czech." Could this scene have taken place on an American freighter? Might the myth be true, or is the universe a quantum particle that organizes itself under the power of your watching?

Finally just after sunrise on the eleventh day (about noon at latitude 64 in January), a sailor spotted Eldey-Fire Island—a sheer volcanic rock whitewashed with seabird shit, which is the first land sighting of Iceland coming from the southwest. The island is inhabited only by colonies of skuas, gulls, guillemots, but it is Iceland. Home. Holm had never till that point, he thought, been in the presence of true patriotism—not love of ideas or politics or abstractions or money but a simple love of some rock that is physically part of your very soul, the rock of your being. Five warring political parties lived among those sailors; some would even march in a few months to protest the NATO base whose cheeseburgers they were about to deliver. But Eldey was Iceland in all its grand harshness. As we passed it in the half-light of January, the air was thick with thousands of flapping wings, a cathedral choir of squawks and croaks, the music of the Icelandic diving birds.

Holm gave Sigurður a Zep feed cap he had gotten from a cousin in Minnesota and photographed him on the front deck, grinning. Bakkafoss anchored outside Reykjavík harbor to await the customs man who would come next morning to inspect the boat for contraband beer (illegal in Iceland in those days). For our last dinner aboard, Ronnie, the Chinese cook, made ítalskt spaggettí (ketchup, ground sheep, and a little onion). It was served over mashed potatoes. "Noodles are too damned messy . . . ," said one sailor.

Holm had not quite duplicated in reverse his grandparents' exodus, but he had at least come slowly over a third of a planet of sloshing water to this isolate island. How else do you approach an island except by water? Are you a seabird or a seed blown by the wind?

The customs man appeared by motor launch next morning. He arrived at Holm's cabin with a look of grim determination. Not many foreigners arrived by freighter. Holm confessed to possessing somewhat over his one bottle allotment of duty-free whiskey. "You will be here a year?" inquired Vilhjálmur, the customs man. "It will not last long, and you will find good use for it." He thought Holm looked a bit Icelandic himself. A western Icelander, son of immigrants. Where were his people from? Mostly Vopnafjörður in the far northeast. "My people too," said customs man Vilhjálmur. "I think we are cousins. *Frændi* in Icelandic." *Frændi* is cognate for friend but means literally any male relative. "And your name in Icelandic is the same as mine, Vilhjálmur—William. *Nafni* (namesake) we call someone who has our name. Welcome to Iceland." Off he went in search of contraband twelve-packs of Budweiser hidden in the engine gears.

Just before Bakkafoss docked at Reykjavík harbor in the early winter dark, Sigurður came by with a book. "Here is the life of Jón Jónsson, a farmer from Mývatnssveit in the early nineteenth century. He taught himself English by trying to write his autobiography in it, though he had never met an Englishman and had no idea how the language was pronounced." When an English traveler arrived to visit Mývatn's volcanic wonders, he was told of a local farmer self-taught in English. He went to meet Jón, but couldn't understand a word—all Icelandic phonetics. They settled on conversing in Latin. "You will have a good time in Iceland," said Sigurður. They shook hands and parted. Holm didn't see him again for twenty years. He looked at the lights twinkling over Reykjavík, the shadow of the mountain covered with snow. He knew not a soul in Iceland—except Sigurður, who was soon off on another ship bound for Brazil or Nigeria. He thought of his own grandparents stepping down the gangplank in Quebec without a word of French or English, without a single face they'd ever seen waiting for them. It was four o'clock in the afternoon and pitch dark; a sharp wind off the Greenland ice cap rocked the boat. Holm shouldered his bag, walked down the gangplank, while some mad impulse flooded through his mind. He was tempted to start singing the few songs he knew out of Italian opera. He didn't, though who can be certain whether that fact is to his credit? Islands expect you to take impulses seriously, no matter how unlikely.

WHAT IS AN ICELANDER? 1999

Iceland, in Icelandic, is spelled *Ísland*. The *Ís* is pronounced "eese" as in geese or fleece. The old Norse had many uses for the prefix: *ísbjörn*—polar bear, *ísbrjótur*—ice breaker, *ísgljá*—a glittering sheet of ice, *ísgrár*—hoary (ice grey). Once a child looked over my shoulder while I put Icelandic stamps in an album. "Is there a country called 'island'?" Indeed there is, and it is a good name.

Iceland is my archetypal island, the island by which I judge all others. Whatever "islandness" is, Iceland is the incarnation of it. This is not a book of island biology. It is an inquiry into what wisdom or insight islandness might offer into the mystery of human character, its variety and eccentricity, and how that character either flowers or shrivels both in history and in landscape.

Human beings present a problem to writers of natural history in these peculiar last decades of our millenium. The rise of the "wilderness ethic" has led us to a form of demonizing human beings. We are the villains—the spoilers—of "nature." Our factories, our cities, our wars, our greed for electric comfort and amusement get stacked against the purity and beauty of such harsh places as, for example, the Great Dismal Swamp, the Himalayas, the antarctic glaciers, the Kalahari desert. We have met the enemy, as Walt Kelly used to say in *Pogo,* and it is us. Indeed there are too many of us; we breed grandly and without enough plagues, famines, and wars to trim our numbers; we stay alive and hungry too long. But remove us and our works from the definition and you have lowered the ante on nature too much. An angry essay on the industrial gobbling up of owl habitats should not remain unconscious of symphony orchestras, movable type, or the churches of Sir Christopher Wren—to name only a few of our better moments. Like the killer whale, who is simultaneously the most intelligent of our relatives and the most savage and brutal (though effective) hunter on the planet, nature is of a piece. It is a continuum and we are somewhere on it, a witch's brew of brains and bloody-mindedness, an inseparable emulsion, like the giant squid, the domestic poodle, the ripe blackberry, and the Ebola virus. Whatever nature is, we are it, in spades. We, ourselves, are the true wilderness. However ingenious the attempts of the human-mistrusting environmentalists to make Thoreau a member of their party, he knew very well that the wildness that preserves us is sunk into our interior bedrock. What happens to us happens to the universe. We contain multitudes, one at a time.

Icelanders make particularly good laboratory specimens to observe the peculiarity of human character because there are so few of them, so far away, so recently come (in geological or even historical terms) to so profoundly empty and new a place. When human beings arrived at Ultima Thule (as the Greeks, who had heard rumors but never seen it, called Iceland) about twelve hundred years ago, they came as close to finding a geographical and biological blank slate, a tabula rasa, as existed on the planet. The entire fauna consisted of the arctic fox—and he was probably a transplant, following the smell of carrion from the sea, drifting into a fjord on an ice floe discharged from east Greenland. In the long summer light, the air was loud with seabirds, seasonal migrants from half a planet away, but in the winter dark only the sarcastic raven hung around to fight the fox for the joy of picking at the blubber of dead seals and whales. No tweetie birds—because there were almost no insects and no rodents at all for them to eat. No reptiles or amphibians—Thank God! say modern Icelanders. The flora, though more numerous than the fauna, was not lush: mostly dwarf birch, grass, lichens, a few berries and tiny wild-flowers. *"Gjöri∂ svo vel,"* say Icelanders when they invite you into their parlors for coffee and cream cakes—be so kind as to come in and enjoy my humble hospitality. *"Gjöri∂ svo vel,"* said the island itself when the handfuls of Irish monks and Norse outlaws decided to sample its delights by living there a millenium ago. It is a skinny place, biologically. The table is not heaped high with succulent morsels. But *"gjöri∂ svo vel"* anyway.

David Quammen's wonderful book, *The Song of the Dodo,* is an encyclopedic compendium of the science of island biogeography and of metaphor. That's the job of good science writers: to fertilize the metaphors with doses of fact and speculation so the rest of us can imagine with more clarity and pleasure.

When we think about islands, Quammen says, we use three "crucial dichotomies": old versus young, small versus large, and continental versus oceanic. "These three dichotomies give pattern to a world of spectacular confusion." Thank God for spectacular confusion, says the poet to the scientist. May we all be liberated from certainty and its dark child: single vision. Let dichotomies flower everywhere and always.

Iceland is young, medium sized (40,000 square miles—about the size of Ohio or Kentucky), and vengefully oceanic. Continental islands: Britain, Vancouver, Newfoundland, Manhattan, were once connected to a mainland by a land bridge. They are generally close to continents, "surrounded by shallow water and therefore subject to reconnection to the mainland by a land bridge during episodes of lowered sea level." Their fauna and flora are most often continental.

Most oceanic islands erupted out of volcanic fissures deep in the sea, lava rising through saltwater, far from any continent. The sea, so smooth and flat on its surface is corrugated underneath with vast canyons and mountain chains, ragged seams where the tectonic plates that ride over the surface of the planet come together and pull apart, leaving great rifts open to the volcanic cauldrons seething in earth's heart. The mid-Atlantic ridge bifurcates Iceland, which owns the newest substantial real estate on the planet, Surtsey, an eruption out of the sea just off the south coast in 1963.

Continental islands start with a fauna and flora. Oceanic

islands start from scratch—as indeed the planet did itself—with nothing, except the wind and bird shit which eventually carry a little life onto the cooling lava. Iceland is so newly minted by nature, so far from anywhere, and so well protected by harsh weather and heavy seas that only the bravest life forms have any hope of setting up colonies there. They arrive by chance and survive by tenacity—like the human life forms, who also are recent immigrants.

Quammen, who has a great gift for the pithy expression of scientific ideas, says, "Island biogeography, I'm happy to report, is full of cheap thrills. Many of the world's gaudiest life forms, both plant and animal, occur on islands. There are giants, dwarfs, crossover artists, nonconformists of every sort. These improbable creatures inhabit the outlands, the detached and remote zones of landscape and imaginability; in fact, they give vivid biological definition to the very word 'outlandish.' . . . [Islands] are natural laboratories of extravagant evolutionary experimentation." I propose to extend Mr. Quammen's notion to human character and consciousness: to say that islandness also nourishes the evolution of outlandish and improbable human beings, that the brain and the imagination are fertilized in odd ways when seeds have to cross vast water to be planted in them. Size changes under the "peculiar conditions" provided by islands are almost linear: "toward gigantism, toward dwarfism." What do they hatch in Iceland, my motto island? Giants or dwarfs? Or some of both?

Here is what any walk down Laugavegur, the main shopping street of Reykjavík, will show you about species *Homo Islandicus:* they are tall—probably the tallest Caucasians in the world; they are fair skinned, though not so blond as the Swedes; they have tiny noses and, among males, almost absent buttocks and huge bushy oversized eyebrows; the same physiognomy occurs again and again, as if you were looking at a few vast extended families all settled together. Indeed you are looking at a concentration of cousins breeding with cousins for a thousand years—such are the effects of oceanic island isolation.

The Icelanders are a rigorously pruned population. Settlement began in 874. Prior to that, only a few scattered Irish monks prayed in their huts and oratories in isolated places on the coast or on nearly coastal islands. The population had reached 60,000 by the fourteenth century when the Black Plague thinned it by 40,000. The population recovered to 45,000 by 1707, when smallpox slimmed it down to 30,000. It had barely begun to rise again when, in 1783, the largest volcanic eruption in the history of the country (which had already endured hundreds of sizable and satisfactorily destructive eruptions in the previous nine hundred years) covered vast sections of the country with poisonous ash, killed a few people initially, but wiped out almost the whole population of horses and sheep. The Red Cross was not delivering surplus cheese in 1783, and the massive famine in the next decades almost finished off the Icelanders. The Danes, then the colonial overlords of Iceland, offered to settle the surviving bedraggled remnants of the Icelanders in Denmark. But if you've lived on your own island, how can you bear to forsake it for a mere continent? The Icelanders stayed, surely now among the poorest specimens ever to occupy any part of the planet. When another venomous volcano, Askja, erupted in northeast Iceland in 1875, killing the sheep and burying the hayfields again, my great-grandfathers gave up and moved to Minnesota, where settlers were offered 160 acres of free land and a promise of no volcanoes. Minnesota, while well aquainted with other natural miseries, is unafflicted with active volcanoes.

The shriveled breeding stock in 1800 gave birth to all of us who are genetic Icelanders. Only 800,000 Icelanders have ever lived, hardly an afternoon's work for the Chinese. With so few of them, they have made a hobby—some might call it an obsession—of keeping track of everyone's name and statistics. Any Icelander who knows his grandparents' names (or even their farm name, and all Icelanders do) can, with a little research, find thousands of relatives going back a thousand years. Modern geneology software can shorten the process to a half hour—with a few hours extra if you intend to print out the four or five hundred pages of your ancestors.

Icelanders are enthusiastic quarrelers. Their history and sagas are chock-full of bloody fights over money, sex, politics, wounded pride, horse races, breeding rams, insulting poems. Any provocation seemed to satisfy the medieval Icelander's desire to pick up his ax to lop off a few of his neighbors' limbs. The violence in this now pacific, almost crimeless tribe seems today safely sublimated to political (or even literary) quarrels. Icelanders these days hurl sentences instead of spears.

But they hurl them vigorously. They still like a good fight. The liveliest recent brouhaha is inspired by the work of a neurologist, Kári Stefánsson, who founded Iceland's first biotech company, deCode Genetics. Stefánsson means to file in his computers the DNA of every living Icelander, and the DNA codes of dead Icelanders back to 1915. What he has found (no surprise, given the population pruning and the meticulous geneological records) is that Icelanders form very few family groups and that their DNA can be used to trace the hereditary propensity to diseases or even (as he has found) to longevity. The centenarians tend to be related to each other, as do the schizophrenics, the asthmatics, the epileptics, the hypertensive, the cancer prone. Iceland provides a limited stock, a perfect control group, that is large enough to

include most human miseries we try to understand—and ultimately to eradicate. The possibilities for medical research are immense. Somewhere in Icelandic heredity, in some mysteriously
malformed DNA, may lie the cure for cancer or the secret of living
a hundred good years. Of course, the possibilities for pharmaceutical exploitation—and profit—are also immense. At the moment, Stefánsson's company owns the DNA intelligence. Rumors
abound of financing from mysterious pharmaceutical conglomerates. Meanwhile, the Icelanders quarrel grandly over these
substantial questions: who ought to own the DNA coding for an
entire country—and even for me, a good old American boy whose
DNA is pure Icelandic? Who profits? Who ought to?

Darwin thought the key to his evolutionary theory lay in thorough investigations of the development of island life forms. The
Galápagos, like Iceland, isolated oceanic islands born of volcan-
ism, provided Darwin with the first evidence for his ideas for *The
Origin of Species*. Alfred Russel Wallace, who actually beat Darwin
to the punch with the idea of natural selection, did his research in
the islands of the Indonesian archipelago and authored in 1881
what is still an extraordinarily useful and comprehensive compendium called *Island Life.*

Stefánsson, like any good biological investigator, was able to
imagine this forlorn northern island as science's most valuable
control group, while modern computer technology enabled him
to figure out a way to make the information useful. Still, the
question stands: To whom do we write our checks for the mystery
of life itself?

Meanwhile we are left with the less scientific question of
how island isolation affects human character and history. Is
an Icelander different in kind from say—a North Dakotan or
a German or a Ukranian, to take only three continental places?

Could Sigurður Björgvinsson have been hatched in Nebraska or
Beijing and not at Mývatn? Does anything of island peculiarity
still roll around inside Bill Holm with his suddenly lucrative DNA
code? Does being named "island" give you a leg up into the ether
of giants and dwarfs? I'll give you three little metaphors for
island peculiarity, a historical place, a bird, and a very great book.
Make of them what you will.

If Icelanders were Muslims, Þingvellir would be Mecca. The old
Parliament Plain, thirty miles east and inland from Reykjavík, is
Iceland's holy place. The original land takers, who settled Iceland
after 874, had become numerous enough in the early tenth century to need a government, but having left medieval Scandinavia
mostly because of royal quarrels, their thinking was clear on the
subject of kings. They wanted no part of them. What's the alternative? Let us have law. We shall make a legal code, appoint a law
speaker (a sort of chief justice), gather at an appointed place, and
settle our own disputes among ourselves. "With laws shall the
land be built up but with lawlessness laid waste," says the hero of
Iceland's greatest medieval book, *Njal's Saga*. Old Njal was himself
a crafty lawyer, the greatest in Iceland, according to the anonymous saga writer. Where then shall this assembly of quarreling
free citizens meet? Ninety percent of Iceland, including the whole
interior of the country, consists of bare lava, rough volcanic
desert, a half-dozen sizable glaciers, quicksand, tundra, high
mountains of black stone covered with snow, boiling fumaroles
of sulfurous mud that would melt the fat off your bones in a matter of seconds, and vast stretches of gravel that turn into brown
cutting blizzards in the omnipresent gale-force winds off the

polar ice. It was not, to put it mildly, a gentle or easy place that the UR-DNA chose to settle into to make a civilization.

But Þingvellir in the southwest quarter of the country is an obvious oasis, a fifty-square-mile lake stuffed with an overpopulation of succulent pink trout, a large flat valley of fertile farm land, enough underground hot water to take a bath (and heat the house), and, running through it all, a curiously symmetrical ridge making what came to be called the Almannagjá, the canyon or rift rock of the people. Perched on the canyon rim is the law speaker's rock, a natural amphitheater and sounding board from which the chief justice could recite the legal code yearly and hear the disputes brought to him by the citizens gathered below him. Also it provided the speaker with a head start or a quick getaway should the disputants not like his verdict and try to kill him. There was plenty of law in Iceland, but no official enforcement. The idea of police had not yet been born.

At Þingvellir, the Icelanders found hay for horses, trout and lamb chops for dinner, dwarf birch and rift walls for shelter, so they assembled yearly, building their "booths" of sod covered with colored wool, gossiping, trading, drinking, debating, flirting, and always quarreling. Here, in the year 1000, the saintly warrior King Olaf of Norway delivered an ultimatum to the Icelanders: become Christian at once, give up Thor and Odin and horse eating and infant exposure, or be invaded by a large army which would put to death with axes any pagan Icelanders they happened upon. By such gentle means does our Lord make his way into the hearts and souls of the heathen. The Icelanders pulled at their beards, picked at their lice, sucked on their trout bones, and said *yow-yow* with an in-sucking breath many times. Then a farmer from the north named Þórgeir (whose ancestors, the sagas tell us, included Þórir Snipper, Grím Hairy-Cheek, Ketil Trout and Hallbjörn Half-Troll) proposed the following solution: "The first principle of our laws . . . is that all men in this land shall be Christian and believe in the one God—Father, Son, and Holy Ghost—and renounce all worship of idols. They shall not expose children at birth nor eat horseflesh. The penalty for carrying on these practices openly shall be outlawry, but they shall not be punishable if they are done in private." And then, the saga writer tells us, "People went home from the Alþing." Last summer, the tastiest sausage I found in an Icelandic meat shop was labeled *folaldakjöt*, horse veal. The Icelanders, though superstitious (as if trolls and elves and Thor and Odin still stalked the gullies behind your house), may be the least pious people on the planet. Is that an island solution for the armed might of the single truth? Do what's necessary. Survive. Mind your own business. Go home from the Alþing and feed your sheep.

Þingvellir is Iceland's first national park, one of the "Golden Triangle" of tourist attractions for the Iceland stopover on the way to Europe. The other two legs of the triangle are Gullfoss (Golden Falls, one fine cataract among many) and Geysir, the original volcanic waterspout that gave its name to the English language. Geysir is now worn out and quiescent, but Strokkur spouts dependably every few minutes to give damp tourists a thrill. Despite the always intelligent and informative commentary of the Icelandic tour guides, I suspect most tourists have little idea of what they are looking at when they stand at the third leg of the tour, the Almannagjá overlook. They see a green plain with a river running through it, distant volcanoes of greater size, a large pea green lake, the sharply peaked gables of an old fashioned Icelandic farmstead (now summer retreat for both the prime minister and the bishop), a charming and astonishingly expensive little country hotel, an old white church and graveyard, and the weirdly symmetrical rift that runs for miles below them. If they stroll into the people's gorge, tourists find themselves standing on one of the great metaphors on the planet: the mid-Atlantic ridge that bifurcates Iceland. Stroll west and you touch North America, stroll east and you are back in Europe. The two sides are gradually pulling apart at the rate of four-tenths of an inch a year. At the first assembly in 930, the mountains to the east were thirty-nine feet closer to your feet. Iceland has not broken in two because upwelling lava has created new real estate. You stand on the border between two worlds, constantly moving away from each other. This hypotenuse through mid-Iceland continues north past Jan Mayen, an island with a mammoth volcano east of Greenland, then veers over to Spitsbergen before it disappears under the polar ice cap. It moves south through the mid-Atlantic past the Azores, the Canaries, Saint Helena, Tristan da Cunha till it meets the antarctic plate south and east of Tierra del Fuego. Iceland is either the eastern-most island in North America, or the western-most island in Europe. Take your pick. I like the idea of both, the Icelanders standing with spread legs, braced sturdily as if riding on a hayrack pulled behind a baler, one foot planted in each hemisphere and the continents rolling apart under them.

The earth quakes continually in Reykjavík as Europe and North America slide away from each other with occasional jolts and hiccups, but I never felt one when I first lived there. Unlike California quakes where one chunk of continent tries to bulldoze its way under another, Icelandic quakes generally enlarge the country. I finally felt one in the summer of 1998 while I was having coffee and cake and rúllupylsa on flatbread in the apartment of an old friend in Reykjavík. For a few seconds, the cup rattled in the saucer, the coffee table trembled, the collection of family porcelain displayed on a shelf rattled and pinged. The sound of the earthquake itself resembled a muffled thunderclap deep underground. In that tiny moment, when the earth is no longer solid under your feet, you realize that the whole planet, like the whole solar system, the whole universe, all the cells and blood and muscles in your own body, are in a state of continual motion. There is no nirvana, no stasis, no calm, no still point in a turning world. Even dead, you continue moving. Everything is energy, endless nervous energy. By God, both Einstein and William Blake were dead-on right. "Energy is Eternal Delight." "$E=mc^2$." An occasional earthquake brings this truth back home inside your own body. The mountains east of Almannagjá must have moved a fraction of an inch farther away from Minneota while we drank ten more drops of coffee and buttered one more piece of rye bread to hold a slice of salmon. Even the rye bread had a little adventure on the coffee table and tasted so sourly sweet it must have enjoyed the trip. I heard later on the evening news that the epicenter of the quake was at Hveragerði, thirty miles east of Reykjavík and just south of Þingvellir. It's a town full of hot-spring greenhouses where the Icelanders grow their own bananas in the long arctic winter. The bananas—and cucumbers and tomatoes—all survived the five-point-something quake without incident. The only casualty was a television set which rattled off its shelf, shattering into hopelessly unreassemble-able fragments.

Þingvellir makes a good metaphor to think both about Icelanders and about islands. It is itself an island of fertility and gentle beauty in an ocean of harsh lava. It is heavy with history and memory—even for non-Icelanders. The roots of modern democracy—the first kingless assembly of free and equal citizens—met here to govern themselves. Athens, its only possible predecessor, was closer to oligarchy—and in Iceland women were always the equals of men in prosecuting lawsuits and doing real-estate business. Aud the Deep-Minded was one of the powerful chieftains of medieval Iceland. Finally, while California is in danger of falling into the ocean, Iceland grows steadily by a few square yards a year. It shows us creation in process, the DNA of the planet itself. And finally it asks the same questions Icelanders ask of DNA: Who owns real estate from inside the planet? Maybe Ralph Waldo Emerson can help propose an answer in his poem "Hamatreya": "'Tis mine, my children's, and my name's" say the land-proud Concord farmers, but "Earth laughs in flowers, to see her boastful boys / Earth-proud, proud of the earth which is not theirs; / Who steer the plough, but cannot steer their feet / Clear of the grave." So laughs the DNA and the mid-Atlantic ridge. So laugh the ghosts of the proud old chieftains who fought it out in the people's gorge. And the earth itself sings, "'How am I theirs, / If they cannot hold me, / But I hold them.'" That advice from Emerson ought to cool your avarice "like lust in the chill of the grave."

I am not a bird watcher, though I count many of that fraternity among my best friends. I listen to them comparing "life lists," sighing at the mention of pileated woodpeckers, recalling the pursuit of sandhill cranes, checking their *Peterson's Guides* and spiral notebooks. When asked about a bird I respond whimsically that I can identify crows and owls, but that I imagine most birds, when I see them, not named and noted, but browned in butter and roasting in a pan.

I first came to consciousness that something wonderful existed in the sky above my own head in Iceland. The birds themselves gave me no choice.

Iceland, so poor in mammals, reptiles, insects, is home to

some of the richest marine life on the planet. As if to compensate
for the frugality of earth, water is profligate with edible creatures: whales, sharks, shrimp, herring, lobster, cod. Where dinner is available, seabirds gather and prosper. Iceland is feeding
and breeding grounds and migratory destination for enough
birds to make it a desirable tour for curious ornithologists.

Both tourists and Icelanders often chat about favorite bird
species. Birders, like oenophiles, are connoisseurs: Oh, the puffin!
What a splendidly designed bird; how awkward in air, but how
graceful in water! The cabernet is exquisite, so much fruitiness,
so much more body and authority than this thin pinot! When humans practice such rituals of discrimination, they say nothing
about nature since neither bird nor grape can be superior one to
the other. Nature is various, not hierarchical. What you hear is
a metaphor for the character of the speaker; we imagine that the
bird or the wine that pleases us describes our inner lives. Preference offers insight only into the preferer, not into the thing itself.

Icelanders do not go to bed much in the summertime. From
early May till mid August night disappears. The sun feints setting
for an hour or two, but even on cloudy days leaves the world lit
by soft gray light. After the long winter dark, why sleep through
this? A few years ago I came back to Reykjavík after a long absence
to visit old friends and to see that light again. Human beings go
slightly mad in it; they begin behaving strangely, like characters
in Knut Hamsun's books. *Pan, Victoria,* and *Mysteries* are closer
to plain realism than any southerner is likely to understand. At
midnight I announced to my friend Wincie that I wanted to see
a lighthouse and hear the sea. "I know the place, if the *kría* allow
us permission to go." "I am not about to ask a bird's permission,"
I huffed. "We'll see," she said, and off we went. Seltjarnarnes, a
skinny peninsula, juts west into the sea at the end of Reykjavík.

It is a fashionable place to live, even though your windows are often caked with salt and in winter storms the unruly sea sometimes tries to break down your doors to barge into your living room. In places, the peninsula is only two streets wide and from the top of any house you can survey the sea in all directions— except backward to the modest skyline of Reykjavík. We drove past suburban villas of poured concrete, a gaily painted modern school, a church, a garage, a marine repair shop.

The peninsula finally peters out to bare grass, ending at the lighthouse on a tiny island connected to the mainland by a causeway. We parked in a gravel lot, got out, and began strolling toward the lighthouse in the gray quarter dark. "Stay on the path," said Wincie. The air soon erupted with harsh shrieks, the whirring of wings overhead, not friendly noises. The arctic tern in Icelandic is called *kría*. To pronounce it, trill the *r* violently, bring the long *e* (*í*) up through your nose and accent the first syllable as if with a sledgehammer. Repeat. Again. Shout it with vigor but no order or unison. Louder now. Clever Reader! You have just discovered onomatopoeia—the naming of a thing by vocal imitation of it. *Kría! Kría! Kría!* In English, the arctic tern, in Latin, *Sterna paradisaea*. I stepped a few feet off the path to pick a wildflower when another squadron of crying terns dive-bombed my head. They looked like they were heading for the eyes but might settle for drawing blood from the scalp or tearing hair out by its roots. Was this a flashback into Alfred Hitchcock's imagination? I covered my face and head with my arms in full retreat. "They're breeding now in June," said Wincie with a smug face. "Very protective and absolutely fearless. Such a small bird! I love them best." So do many Icelanders love them, though that love is shaded with a healthy respect.

The arctic tern is, indeed, a small bird—at least compared to its closest cousins, the gulls and skuas. A bit over a foot in length, it weighs less than two pounds. It is a sleek, compact bird, mostly white with a black head (looking a little like a Hasid wearing a yarmulke) with a bright orange beak, shapely forked tail feathers, and powerful looking wings that seem too long for its compact body. The *kría* needs powerful wings; it is the champion migrator among birds. It summers and breeds in the high Arctic (all the way to the edge of the polar ice), laying its eggs and hatching them in large colonies, sometimes thousands of pairs, in whatever grassy meadows it finds next to the sea. *Kría* is a fish eater, diving from thirty feet up to scoop up small fish, shrimp, krill, and if the sea larder is empty, insects. Two of their many peculiar charms: they hover in midair—like oversized hummingbirds; unlike their gull cousins they lack webbed feet and are poor swimmers—odd for a seabird. At the end of the brief arctic summer, when the hatchlings have learned to feed themselves and fly efficiently, the tern colony packs up and flies far south. It winters in Antarctica after flying (not in a straight line and never over land) twelve to fifteen thousand miles. The yearly mileage on a tern's odometer reads somewhere in the vicinity of twenty-five thousand miles—over the mid-Atlantic from one harsh end of the planet to the other. For compensation, they spend most of their lives in light, flying from one endless day to another.

Their name is their song—in Iceland; they sing it over and over in their harsh raspy voices as they are trying to jam their orange beaks straight into your eyeballs: *Kría! Kría! Kría!* I am me, and I don't care how big you are. Get your ass away from my future.

Wincie is not the only Icelander who admires the fierce pugnacity of the *kría*. The Icelandic newspapers annually announce the first arrival of *kría* at the pond in Reykjavík, usually in early May. Winter is over; light is back; our friends, the *kría* have traveled twelve thousand miles to bring us spring greetings. Last year, the *kría* closed down a suburban golf course outside Reykjavík by deciding to nest somewhere on the fairways. Even your five iron is not an adequate defense against those aggressive beaks. The golfers played elsewhere till the *kría* finished their business and moved on.

But the *kría* too has enemies besides us. Skuas, the giants of the gull family, are heavy-bodied, hook-beaked, claw-taloned, predatory bullies. They live at the top of the food chain, monopoly capitalists of the gull tribe. They steal what they please and ravage what they will. They are fearless, even of humans, and much more than arctic terns, look capable of doing us serious damage if we cross them. Katharine Scherman describes the skua's visit to a tern colony:

> With their sharp talons and hooked beaks the skuas will play havoc in the nesting area when the terns begin to lay their eggs. They will pluck the eggs from the open nests in sand or gravel; assail the parents bringing food to their young; chase them at sea to force them to drop their fish catch; will even seize a bird by the tail, drag it down to the water and hold it there until it gives up its food. Entire colonies of arctic terns are sometimes harassed beyond endurance by the activities of one pair of skuas, and disperse without laying a single egg. At other times, of eggs successfully laid and chicks hatched, not one will reach maturity.

This reminds one of descriptions of Indian massacres in the old West—the Wounded Knee of the *kría*. If Mussolini or Slobodan Milosevic or Rockefeller or J. P. Morgan had known the skuas, they may have loved them. Remember our preferences mirror our inner life. Icelanders respect the skua, but take the side of the brave-hearted though undersized *kría,* who comes so far to keep them company for a little while.

Snæfellsjökull, according to Jules Verne's novel, opens into the center of the earth. That's unlikely, but it is nevertheless one of earth's most mysterious and beautiful mountains, a mile-high extinct volcano topped with a glacier that rises as if straight from the sea at the end of a long peninsula seventy miles northwest of Reykjavík. On a bright day Snæfellsjökull seems, from Reykjavík, to float up on the horizon as if connected neither to earth nor water but instead had gathered up light in its pink tinted ice cone to hover a few feet above the north Atlantic.

New Age mystics call it a "power center," a convergence of invisible harmonic forces that circle the globe and connect this Icelandic volcano to Stonehenge and the Pyramids. That's not likely, but W. B. Yeats thought stranger things. I have spent, I suppose, a couple of years of my life in Iceland, but have seen Snæfellsjökull only for a few hours, and only at long intervals. I joked to Icelanders that I was waiting to see Snæfellsjökull for twenty-four consecutive hours before I went home. You will be here a long time, they said.

In the summer of 1998, the sky cleared. Old friends from England were visiting Reykjavík, so we drove north to visit the magic mountain. We stayed at a New Age camp of an affable and curious Icelander named Gulli Bergman. An imitation Stonehenge with a crystal at the center stood outside our hotel window, framing the nearby glacier that glowed all night. Old lava flows made a little shelf of land around the massive mountain. Here lava cooled into cliffs of columnar basalt that seabirds colonized by the millions, leaving the cliffs, of course white with centuries of guano. Gulli took us on a tour around the mountain in his jeep. He was a great fount of stories from Icelandic history and folklore—hauntings, murders, witchcraft, and sorcery in the local farmsteads. Every stone was remarkable, heavy with supernatural lore, as Gulli described it. After rounding the north side of the mountain we stopped at a little village, Hellissandur, to go to the community shop, the center of every Icelandic hamlet. Dodging a tern or two we made our way in the door. Terns occupied the whole village, thousands of them circling every patch of grass. It was impossible to walk outdoors. Parents equipped children with helmets. Most life retreated indoors till the *kría* had finished their business and flown back to Antarctica. Did anyone suggest driving them out, moving them to an uninhabited stretch of coastal meadow? No. After all, the terns have to nest too. It's just their nature. The Icelanders lived calmly in yet another Alfred Hitchcock village. Maybe harmonic lines do converge on Snæfellsjökull.

At dinner at Búðir, an old and famous restaurant south of the mountain, I ordered puffin and *svartfugl* (guillemot). They were delicious. After dinner, at about eleven o'clock, we drove two-thirds of the way up the mountain to explore a murderer's lava-cave hideout and set foot on the bottom of the glacier. Standing on that ancient ice three thousand feet above the Atlantic, I would have believed anything you told me—the terns are bodhisattvas in new incarnation, the gates of paradise can be entered from the top of the glacier, the brilliant cook at Búðir was two thousand years old, the moon is made of black diamonds. The *kría* seemed good protectors of that magic landscape.

Halldór Laxness, Iceland's epic novelist and Nobel Prize winner, wrote a fragrant and wonderful novel about the peculiar atmosphere of Snæfellsnes, *Christianity at Glacier*. The bishop of Iceland is disturbed by strange news he hears from Snæfellsnes church and its priest, Jón Prímus. Jón has let the church fall into disrepair, stopped holding services, and spends his time shoeing horses and repairing primus stoves—thus his nickname. Rumors circulate of secret burials on the glacier, a giant salmon waiting to be reincarnated as Séra Jón's long absent wife, Úa. The bishop's young emissary travels north to investigate. He finds the world there even weirder than he imagined. He interrogates Pastor Jón one day on the nature of God.

> *Pastor Jón:* . . . God has the virtue that one can locate Him anywhere at all; in anything at all.
> *Embi:* In a nail, for instance?
> *Pastor Jón, verbatim:* In school debates the question was sometimes put whether God was not incapable of creating a stone so heavy that He couldn't lift it. Often I think the Almighty is like a snow-bunting abandoned in all weathers. Such a bird is about the weight of a postage-stamp. Yet he does not blow away when he stands in the open in a tempest. Have you ever seen the skull of a snow-bunting? He wields this fragile head against the gale, with his beak to the ground, wings folded close to his sides and his tail pointing upwards; and the wind can get no hold on him, and cleaves. Even in the fiercest squalls the bird does not budge. He is becalmed. Not a single feather stirs.
> *Embi:* How do you know that the bird is the Almighty, and not the wind?
> *Pastor Jón:* Because the winter storm is the most powerful force in Iceland, and the snow-bunting is the feeblest of all God's ideas.

The preference for the snow bunting reveals the character of Pastor Jón as a man and the heart of his theology. What is he? Buddhist? Pagan? Pantheist? Or like many Icelanders, merely a man who has come to regard fixing stoves for his neighbors as the highest religious duty?

What does the tern tell us about the Icelandic inner life, about what it means to be a tiny tribe living on an isolated island that keeps threatening to swallow them whole? Like the terns the Icelanders have always been great travelers and seamen. After all, they discovered Greenland and North America, traveled far into Russia, to Constantinople, to Rome. But they always came back to Iceland, not because it was an easy place, but because it was their place, home. When armies of Norwegians, Danes, Germans, British cod fishermen, threaten them, they raise their voices and sharpen their beaks to protect their eggs. When volcanoes, earthquakes, avalanches, flying icebergs threaten to bury them, they step aside till the natural fury is spent, then continue nesting. Maybe even my sporadic reappearances in this odd island are the voices of my interior biological homing pigeon. Maybe none of these fanciful notions are true, but only that some humans admire small feisty creatures who stand up for themselves, who refuse to be bamboozled by size and power. Carry a steel umbrella if you decide to go birding in a tern hatchery. They will be singing to you: *Kría! Kría! Kría!*

℮

Credit-card mania has arrived in modern Iceland, everything now chargeable on your VISA card: groceries, traffic tickets, false teeth, real estate, Big Macs. "Look," says my friend, the half-Icelandic, half-American Wincie, daughter of Jóhann and Winston, the Janus who points one eye at each of the sliding plates of Europe and North America. "See how beautiful my new Landsbankinn VISA card is!" as she tries to beat me to the punch paying for a round of drinks (three for twenty-five dollars) at a Laugavegur bistro. She beats me so I get to admire her VISA card only briefly on its way to the house credit computer. It shows a squished globe, a flat two-dimensional earth in shades of pale blue and grey. At the bull's-eye sits the crown jewel: Iceland, surrounded by vast water with a little chunk of Greenland just to the west, the Americas on the remote left, Eurasia and Africa on the far right, the southern hemisphere receding into the distance under the raised card number, all paying court to Iceland in the center.

Why should that seem odd to you, Sensible Reader? The solipsist's view is that wherever you are is the center from which all points are equidistant. We are all solipsists of one kind or another. Americans should understand that best of all, since most of us, resident in the richest behemoth empire on earth, are often only partly conscious that other places actually exist, or that languages other than English might be spoken in daily life. The Chinese print all their maps with China at the center, and their very language confirms the fact for them: Zhong-Guo means middle earth—the center. I once saw an Australian map with the hemispheres reversed top to bottom, Australia in lordly eminence at the center, looking down on Italy, Mexico, and the far distant United States and Britain.

If the round world has to have a center, why not Iceland? All islands, to some degree, fall into this island solipsism. They have no borders but water, the only true unconquered power on the globe. Come to the edge of the earth in any direction and you fall into the salty kingdom whose only lords are whales, sharks, squids the size of apartment buildings, who pay taxes neither to you nor to anybody else.

Icelanders, who take literary matters seriously and whose chief products of the last thousand years are all made of language, recently elected Halldór Laxness's epic novel *Independent People* as their "book of the century." I am not the only reader and admirer

of this grand book who might up the ante a little more to crown
it one of the human race's books of the century. It is the story of
Bjartur of Summerhouses, an impoverished, uneducated, gruff,
unruly sheep farmer in the northeast, who in his desire to be "independent," to make his own way in the world, accepts no gifts or
help that might obligate him to others, thus managing to destroy
two wives, several children—and any sympathy or fellow feeling
the reader might have for him. He is simply an impossible bas-
tard. He is obsessed with sheep; their tapeworms and diseases
are more serious to him than any that destroy the human beings
around him. He starves his family to feed his livestock. He allows
nothing, neither ghost nor human to interfere with his stubborn
honor—his imagined independence. Many of the novel's early
Icelandic readers saw Bjartur as a libel on the Icelandic character.
Some still do. Yet most readers wind up loving this stubborn
wretch, and finish the novel soaked in tears. It is a very great and
strange book. Laxness calls it, not without reason, an epic, though
it is a sardonic one. It contains as much of the pity and grandeur
of human nature that readers expect in Homer or Virgil. Who
could imagine so much life confined within the covers of any
single volume? It was published in Iceland in 1934/1935, translated brilliantly into English by J. A. Thompson, became a Book
of the Month Club selection in 1946, and finally was the primary
impetus for Laxness winning the Nobel Prize in literature in
1955, a great honor for this tiny population of 250,000 readers of
Icelandic, but perhaps even more for the noble old language itself.
Something new and grand could still be made from the ancient
word hoard of the sagas and *Eddas.*

For almost fifty years *Independent People* disappeared from
print in English. Because Book of the Month Club members had
(and still have) to remember to put a stamp on a postcard, make a

black X, and then (hardest of all!) put the card in the mail before the due date, a few hundred thousand hardbound copies arrived, probably unwelcome, onto the bookshelves of middle America. The gaggle of names like Gunnvör or Kolumkilli or Bjartur on the first few pages defeated the attention span of most readers. This same principle works for the books of Dostoyevsky, Tanizaki, or García Márquez adorning the bookshelves of readers who prefer characters named Bob, Sean, Lisa, and Jennifer garnished with a plot that moves right along, thank you very much.

For lovers of the book, this meant a great chance to acquire a library full of copies in mint condition, dust jacket and all, at ridiculous prices. Hardly a garage sale, estate sale, thrift shop, or used bookstore was without a forlorn copy or two that the owners surrendered with pleasure for a nickel or a dime; sometimes those with more business savvy asked a quarter or a half dollar. A cousin of mine who loved the book as much as I—he had, in fact, introduced me to it when I was thirteen or fourteen—started a contest to see who could corral the most copies. Eventually we pooled our resources and between us maintained a steady stack of about a hundred. Even with 1980s inflation we held to our rule— no copy could be bought for over three dollars. This was not, however, a library to be hoarded as an investment. Like Gideon New Testament pushers, we evangelized for Laxness. If some new visitor arrived in Minneota, we baited them by reading a few pages aloud, telling an anecdote, quoting some poetic gem from Bjartur, or, if they were Icelandic by descent, shaming them into reading the book as their ancestral duty. Only one rule: this copy is yours if you promise to read it. Should you reappear in Minneota you will be given a verbal quiz. Should you disappear forever, the integrity of your word is a matter between you and your higher power. Go in peace. Take and read. Bjartur and Ásta await you.

Independent People finally came back into print in January 1997, through the good offices of Brad Leithauser, a novelist and poet (not an Icelander!) who fell in love with the book as a young man, and then—a not unusual consequence—with Iceland itself. In a fine essay on Laxness that serves as introduction, Leithauser shrewdly observes that *"Independent People's* first chapter summons up the days when the world was first settled, in 874 A.D.—for that is the year when the Norsemen arrived in Iceland, and one of the book's wry conceits is that no other world but Iceland exists."

Well, does it? Isn't this the essence of islandness, this sense that your world is self-contained, as in the old epics, where beginning, middle, and end circumscribe the knowable world, and beyond that only sea and sky exist?

Bjartur takes his daughter Ásta Sóllilja (beloved sun lily) to the little village at the end of the fjord when she is thirteen. Prior to this she has seen nothing but the farm, the meadow, the river, the enclosing mountains. They live perhaps twenty miles from the coast, three or four valleys, three or four small mountains to climb—on foot. They walk all day, when they finally arrive at the top of the last pass, Ásta has this experience:

> "Father," she said in a perplexed and hesitating voice, "where are we?"
>
> "We've crossed the heath," he replied. "That's the ocean."
>
> "The ocean," she repeated in an awe-stricken whisper. She went on staring out to the east, and a cold shiver of joy passed through her at the thought of being fortunate enough to stand on the eastern margin of the moors and see where the land ends and the ocean begins, the sea of the world.
>
> "Isn't there anything on the other side, then?" she asked finally.

"The foreign countries are on the other side," replied her father, proud of being able to explain such a vista. "The countries
that they talk about in books," he went on, "the kingdoms."

"Yes," she breathed in an enchanted whisper.

Ásta had lived at the center of the VISA card; now she sees what
stretches out around her—everything else.

The First World War brings a little welcome money to the
Icelandic sheep farmers. When Europe explodes into insanity, far
away Iceland always prospers—briefly. Bjartur and the neighborhood farmers discuss European politics over snuff and a nip of
home-brew schnapps. Bjartur, no sensitive New Age male, says:
"Oh, let them squabble, damn them. . . . I only hope they go on
blasting one another's brains out as long as other folk can get
some good out of it. There ought to be plenty of people abroad.
And no one misses them." That's island solipsism bloated into
xenophobia, though Bjartur has an understandable point. The
same European economic and political system that imploded on
itself in 1914 had ensured Bjartur's life-long poverty.

The Fell King, Bjartur's neighbor who is prone to lengthy ex
cathedra orations, delivers a strange one to express his view of
the war. A sheep doctor had brought the Fell King a foreign book,
in which he examined the pictures of France and Germany "as
closely as circumstances allowed. And I came to the conclusion,
after minute scrutiny and conscientious comparison of the pictures, that there is no fundamental difference between France
and Germany at all, and that they are actually both the same
country, with not even a strait between them, much less a fjord."
They both share mountains, woods, cornfields. The inhabitants
look exactly like each other except for differing hairstyles—
shades of Lilliput's big-endians and little-endians, low heels and

high heels. Judging from the sheep vet's pictures, one breed looks not a whit less stupid or wise than the other. Therefore, the Fell King concludes that "in strict reality France and Germany are exactly the same country, and no one in full possession of his faculties can possibly see any difference between them." That's the center of the VISA card, the island mind, talking again, except this time, unlike Bjartur's venom, the Fell King's pompous rhetoric gives the lie to any reason ordinary humans trot out to justify blowing each other to smithereens because they believe there is some difference between them. Observed from the isolation of a remote island, it all looks like complete bloodthirsty irrational madness. And it is. The Fell King is exactly, dead-on right, a jack-leg moral philosopher capable of putting the human race to rights on the question of war. If you live at the center of the VISA card, it may be easier to see that big picture clearly.

Laxness, who seemed eternal as the mid-Atlantic ridge, died at ninety-five in 1998. With the exception of a few rabid anti-communists who never forgave the old man his flirtation with the Soviets, the whole country mourned their great writer. Americans do not mourn their novelists with quite so much intensity. Laxness, as a last ironic gesture, chose to be buried from Iceland's only Catholic church, a grey neo-Gothic cement cathedral that crowns a hill in the middle of Reykjavík. He left Iceland as a teenager to join a Benedictine monastery in Luxembourg, but like most Icelanders found chastity, poverty, and obedience unsuited to his character. He became an enthusiastic atheist and communist, then a democratic socialist, then a conservative, finally—probably always—a skeptic, with a few other ideological flirtations in between. He changed dance partners often; I suspect this came from his basic Icelandic mistrust of absolute truth. He argued even with himself, vigorously assaulting his own opinions at any given time. At bottom he was an ironist, whose only faith was in narrative itself, the power and truth of stories. Since stories are made from experience and imagination, they can't be pigeonholed into absolute truth. A good story is a slippery matter.

To honor Laxness after his death, Icelandic State Radio broadcast a tape of *Independent People* read by a famous actor, Arnar Jonsson. Gísli Halldórsson, the first Icelandic radio voice I'd heard, reading *The Good Soldier Schweik* twenty years before, had also recently died, so in a way, the Icelanders simultaneously honored two of their great literary traditions: writing stories and listening to them. The whole country stopped to hear their peculiar epic read to them. The radio played in shops, taxis, offices, fish plants, cow barns, kitchens. Commuters sat in their driveways listening, the engines idling until the chapter ended. I was in Reykjavík when Bjartur killed Búkolla, the cow. Bjartur, no cow man, gives in to the pleading of his wife and children for milk and butter. A cow costs money, eats hay, takes barn space. He is a sheep man, a real Icelander. Only decadent foreigners expect to drink fresh milk or slather butter all over perfectly good hardtack. He needed no butter or milk to be capable of doing a day's work. An independent man doesn't waste his money and risk debt on a useless old bag of bones of a damned cow. Cows are for women. Now a sheep is a man's animal. He goes on—and on—but finally gives in to the massed weight of his family, though he continues sputtering behind a cloud of snuff. But hard times and bad weather come again. Sheep die of mysterious ailments. Hay rots. The new hay freezes under unseasonable blizzards. The price of mutton collapses. There is nothing to eat for either animal or human. Búkolla grows ever bonier, her teats almost dried up. Yet the reader, like the author, and like Bjartur's wife and children, has come to love the old cow with irrational intensity. I propose that no cow in literature (or probably life) was ever created or described with such tenderness. The reader feels the growing gloom as the food supplies dwindle, the weather moving from disaster to catastrophe. Finally Bjartur (who very likely has no choice) kills old Búkolla. You think to yourself: my heart is being rent by the death of a damned cow? This is not possible! It is possible. Your heart is rent—soundly. You are lost in the spider web of a master storyteller.

I walked into Wincie's parlor just as Búkolla expired and the radio faded away. She was blubbering, sobbing, "The old son of a bitch murdered Búkolla. I can't listen anymore. It's too sad." Tears falling, soaked handkerchiefs, a clutch in the chest, all over Reykjavík, all over the fjords and villages and fish factories and farmhouses of the whole forty thousand square miles of Iceland, all over every radio room of every Icelandic ship at sea—tears, tears, tears. The cow is dead. Oh, what any writer in history would have given to have written that book for those people. By this point in this masterly epic, you, too, have come to love Bjartur with as much intensity as you loathe him, you love the cow, you love Asta, you even love Bjartur's damned sheep and his rotting hay. The world that emanates out from the center of the VISA card has become an ever so much more complicated place. There will, in fact, never be any simple answers to anything again, nor any simple feeling in your own body. Congratulations, Sensible Reader! You have discovered literature—the mystery of a story made from language. You are likely to be a more interesting person from now on, though you will never be happy again in quite the same way.

When you go to a cocktail party or any kind of get-together in America these days, you are besieged with opinions and preferences: "I feel that a woman's right to choose is central to the campaign." "Pistachios are really the most exquisite of nuts." "Since I found these French running shoes, I can do five miles much more quickly. They cost plenty, of course, but. . . ." None of these fascinating remarks are ever followed by what might be their only redemption: "I once met an old man in Morocco high in the mountains. He was carrying an enormous burlap bag of pistachio nuts, and had the ugliest face I have ever seen, one eye out, two or three blackened stumps of teeth like vampire fangs. He stopped me on the road, spoke a little English, and asked whether. . . ." Who finally gives a damn whether you like pistachio nuts, or can run fifty miles in ten minutes in your $250 sneakers? What bores we have become to each other in America! Somebody often tries to perk up these evenings with jokes: "Did you hear the one about the priest and the minister and the rabbi who were up in a plane with two parachutes?" These jokes are made like little tin coffins, closing in on their dead mechanical contents with a metallic twang.

Real stories grow from paying attention to experience, to cultivating your eye for detail, and to real feeling, for without genuine emotion, you can never have genuine humor in your talk or in your life. I am not the only occasional visitor to Iceland to have noticed that here, at the center of the VISA card, straddling the bucking tectonic plates, with the *kría* hovering overhead like a fishy-smelling hummingbird on steroids, narrative not only survives, it prospers both in life and in bookstores. The old instinct that crafted the sagas seems coded into the traditional DNA.

At any gathering of Icelanders you hear stories or silence. Sometimes, particularly at cold sober or official gatherings, long silences settle into rooms, punctuated only by an occasional sigh or a *yow-yow*. If you are tempted to express a preference for pistachio nuts or give a commercial for your running shoes on these occasions, you should certainly keep your mouth rigorously shut. After particularly lengthy silences some Icelander might, with a

sigh, repeat the old cliché, "An angel is flying through the room,"
to which a famous wit of the last generation once responded, "I
wish the damn fool would quit flapping his wings so loudly." But
a few Brennivíns always loosen up the Icelandic shyness and reserve till stories start pouring out: from daily life, from history,
from reading, first-rate gossipy tales about bishops and cabinet
ministers and bankers, ghost stories from your grandfather's
home district, adventures of eccentric relatives and of travel. The
atmosphere is competitive, one story rolling off another, one
Icelander trying to best another with a fantastic tale that will
leave the group dazzled. In the long summer light, these chains
of stories go on till early morning. In the long winter dark, they
pass the time waiting for light.

I remember one evening in Wincie's parlor a gathering of
young Icelandic writers, filmmakers, translators, Einar Már
Guðmundsson and Einar Kárason together told the tale of hearing the news of Elvis's death while they were shoveling fish in a
fish pit in the Faroe Islands. Friðrik Þór Friðriksson, Iceland's genius filmmaker, who has filmed stories and scripts by both Einars,
his old schoolmates, topped them with a tale of being tracked
down in the middle of the night at gunpoint, in a hotel room in
Brazil by Interpol. His passport had been stolen in Italy by a famous terrorist who had been planting bombs all over Europe dis-
guised as Friðrik Þór. The police tracked him to Sao Paulo. He
was drunk and asleep in his bed when he found himself staring
down a gun barrel. Top that! If, at this moment, you are tempted
to express a preference for pistachio nuts or to ask the assembled
yarn spinners to extinguish their cigars because of the dangers
of second-hand smoke, you should under no circumstances do so.
It is good to be in a room that trusts narrative.

Einar Már Guðmundsson is poet as well as a novelist. What

Icelander isn't if you scratch him? He imagines Homer, the singer
of tales in Reykjavík on a rainy afternoon:

> One rainy afternoon,
> on a ship from a much travelled dream,
> Homer the singer of tales arrived in Reykjavik.
> He walked from the quayside
> and took a cab that drove him
> along rain-grey streets
> where sorry houses passed by.
>
> At the crossroads Homer the singer of tales turned
> to the driver and said:
> "How can it be imagined
> that here in this rain-grey
> monotony lives a nation of story-tellers?"
> "That's exactly why," answered the cab driver,
> "you never want to hear
> a good tale as much as when the drops
> beat on the windows."

That's what you do on islands on rainy afternoons. Tell stories.
Sing. Let the songs travel out from the center of the VISA card
over the sea to moisten the opinionated continents.

REYKJAVÍK AND THE FARM, 1979

The gang plank that stretched from Bakkafoss to the solid ground
of Reykjavík turned out to be a border between worlds in more
ways than Holm imagined on that dark January afternoon in 1979.
No one prepared Holm for the pitching and rolling that went on
inside his body for a week after eleven days in the Atlantic. Why

won't the ground stay still under my feet? he thought. Is the
whole island cut adrift from its bedrock, sloshing with majestic
slowness around in the sea looking for a new anchorage with better weather? He sat at a table laden with cream cakes and open-
faced sandwiches of salmon, smoked mutton, vinegary rullapylsa,
waiting for the plates to begin their sliding. He clutched his coffee cup tight to keep it steady. When the ghost of the sea began
dying inside his bloodstream, he grew sad and restless. Iceland
dropped anchor in its old mooring and stood still. How boring
steady land must be to a working seaman. Holm heard stories
about seamen who would come joyfully home to their families—
for a week or two—and then like Melville's Ishmael begin rest-
lessly haunting the harbor, hoping for the next sailing before the
bedrock settled back inside.

To travel from 1979 America, still reeling from its Vietnam hang-
over but gearing up to elect Reagan, the god of shopping and forgetfulness, to Iceland was like entering a time capsule for 1949,
or 1939, or 1929, . . . or 1200. The paved road extended only from
the northern city limits of Reykjavík to thirty-five miles east just
outside Sigurður's home in Selfoss. The national highway that
circled the island was a rough gravel track full of stones, potholes,
washouts, wild 16-percent grades going straight up steep mountains, tracks bulldozed out of scree on cliffs hundreds of feet above
the Atlantic. The last section of road, over the treacherous black
glacial outwash sands under Vatnajökull in the southeast, had
been completed only recently and still washed out often. Call
ahead if you're going there, said the locals. The bridges over the
gritty glacial rivers were frail one-lane wooden contraptions
that didn't look as if they could hold up a respectable semi with
a half load.

Beer was illegal—except that every Icelandic basement was
equipped with a hydrometer, a capper, and ten bubbling gallons
of homemade lager. The grocers offered rutabagas, waxy yellow
potatoes, cabbages, rutabagas, yellow onions, rutabagas, cabbages, potatoes, and rutabagas. Brown lettuce (when available)
was $3.00 a head. I once saw a rock-hard avocado for $5.00, and a
green pepper for $3.50. These prices were, keep in mind, in 1979
currency. Multiply them four or five times for 1999. The butcher
counter offered whale, old horse, horse veal, mutton, fish-flavored
skinny chickens (raised on fish scraps), tough beef, and, if you
were wealthy, a little smidgen of pork. Ordinary people ate boiled
fish with boiled potatoes and as much sugar, butter, and whipped
cream as could be compacted on a plate.

Reykjavík traffic was full of two-cycle East German Trabants
that sounded like berserk lawn mowers belching great clouds of
petroleum fumes—plus Wartburgs, Ladas, Moskvas, old Buicks
and Mercuries and Dodges (even a tail fin or two)—and for those
who had business on the national highway: vintage Land Rovers.
Gas, $4.00 a gallon; whiskey, $50.00 a bottle (at perhaps a dozen
almost unmarked state liquor stores scattered at difficult places
around the country); import taxes 100 percent on almost every
import good.

The five daily newspapers (one for each political party) raged
away at each other, full of high-voltage invective, until Saturday
when they all published a special fat section of *minningargreinar*,
lengthy and flowery obituary essays on the geneology, character,
and accomplishments of every dead Icelander for the previous
week. Iceland is likely the only place on earth where the obituary
is a literary form—which sometimes gives surprising birth to
great gems of prose. State television operated from four o'clock
in the afternoon till about ten thirty at night, six days a week,

eleven months a year. No TV on Thursday (we need a day off) and none in July (who in their right mind would watch television when it's light all night?). The Christmas commercials (done in a lump) featured singing jingles puffing new books of poetry. State radio (the *only* station, like TV) offered novel readings (like *Schweik*), melancholy Icelandic folk songs sung by the Siglufjörður Men's Choir (mostly herring fishermen), café ballads by Sigfús Halldórsson (Iceland's Hoagy Carmichael), a recipe hour (which featured the *actual* ingredients of italskt spaggettí—ground mutton, a little onion, salt and pepper, and ketchup), and the live broadcast of funeral ceremonies, particularly of old ladies who had hatched vast families.

Inflation gobbled away at 100 percent a year. Banks offered 60-percent interest on savings but got no takers. The whole country was overdrawn by mid-month. Either spend your salary fast or lose it. Holm's first Fulbright salary—prorated, thank God, to American dollars—was 350,000 krónur a month. By the time he left it was 750,000 krónur. Holm was briefly a millionaire for the first and only time in his life. Icelanders went shopping with fat wads of 5,000-krónur notes—the largest denomination. The note bore the grand face of Einar Benediktsson, one of Iceland's great twentieth-century modernist poets, a sort of Norse Wallace Stevens. Benediktsson was equally famous in Icelandic political folklore for the legend that he almost sold the harnessable power of the northern lights to the English. It's probably an apocryphal story, but it certainly demonstrates the possible usefulness of a large poetic imagination to the national economy. Hard-currency accounts were illegal, so Icelanders hoarded marks, pounds, Swiss francs, dollars. A lively local black market flourished for dollars, turkeys, Parmesan cheese, and Budweiser. The marriage of the fish economy and the modern welfare state had almost turned Iceland into the world's north-ernmost banana republic. The irony, of course, was that Iceland actually grew its own bananas within a cat's whisker of the Arctic Circle in the volcanic steam greenhouses of Hveragerði, a little town just east of Reykjavík. One of Holm's favorite Icelandic post-cards pictured a pink-cheeked white-blond girl with a toothy smile caressing a stalk of ripe Icelandic bananas. Holm sent many of these cards to folks at home to announce his watery arrival in the old country.

His other favorite postcard was a photo of whale cutters with their flensing knives, hip boots, and rubber aprons, trimming enormous slabs of white blubber off a bright red whale roast the size of a pickup truck. The card announced "Greetings from Hvalfjörður" (whale fjord), the lovely fjord just north of Reykjavík where the country's only whale fishery processed and sold fifty whales a year mostly to the insatiable Japanese market. His American friends must have thought, arctic bananas and whale burgers . . . what a strange place!

They were right, of course—Iceland *is* a strange place: half Europe, half the wild west of North America (the pop hit of the year was "I'm an Icelandic cowboy on my Icelandic pony / Just coming from Snæfellsnes"). The mid-Atlantic ridge is a good metaphor for the place, in some ways the first outrigger of American imagination, with its egalitarian ethos, its rough fron-tier landscape, its island isolation from European shenanigans and wars, but in other ways very ancient European, the last cus-todian of the ghosts of Viking civilization. Because it was so far off normal trade routes and because Icelanders are linguistic re-actionaries of extraordinary stubbornness, the language remains almost unaltered since settlement; modern schoolchildren can read the thousand years of sagas, histories, and poems with relative ease in their own modern language. Try reading *Beowulf* and the *New York Times* together and you will see what linguistic isolation and stubbornness mean.

The sea is the real road around Iceland, however many airplanes fill the air. If you fly like the tern, you are still grappled to the sea, your only fuel depot. Holm, born so far from the sea, in a dry, flat, snowy place, began to understand that fact in Iceland, the power of saltwater. If it is possible to make so silly a claim that one is born in the wrong place, he might still make it. Maybe the job of writing island news begins with a plunge into interior water to see what wisdom lives far from the roads that meander over the plains of a continent.

After the sea settled down inside him and quit rocking his bed all night, Holm found a basement flat in a suburb of Reykjavík in a house full of magnificent paintings, fresh salmon, and hospitable hosts. He moved in his clavichord, which he had carried with him on Bakkafoss, tuned it, and began his daily morning regimen of an hour of Bach fugues. Upstairs he found a Danish spinet. Páll and Erna seemed to enjoy hearing him practice, so he started learning Schubert's big A Major Sonata, a soulful piece that suited the gray sea and serrated ridge of mountains visible through any window. He tried a few words of urban Icelandic pilfered from the *Teach Yourself* series, but discovered two impediments to language learning: almost all the urban Icelanders spoke English with ease, and it pained their ears to hear their beloved language butchered.

He started teaching in the English department at the University of Iceland, housed in a concrete villa formerly owned by a prime minister. Almost all his colleagues were British; he was the lone gunner for American literature. The students, a brilliant and completely multilingual lot, seemed a bit put off by the wildness of real American voices: Henry Miller, James Agee, Edward Abbey, Walt Whitman, William Carlos Williams, Carl Sandburg. Education in Iceland tilted east toward Europe. Still, he had a good time haranguing and evangelizing for Walt and the native genius. The students were shyer and more reserved in class than he would have expected from his experience of American Icelanders, but when he got roaring drunk with them at the frequent student parties, some hitherto silent student, floating in a sea of vodka and home brew, would lean lopsidedly onto his chest and say: "Bill Holm, you don't know your ass from a hole in the ground about T. S. Eliot. You are dead wrong. I translated *The Waste Land* into Icelandic. . . ." News to me. And when sobriety resumed, so did shyness. I enjoyed every minute of it.

Two peculiarities of Icelandic entertaining surprised Holm. When Icelanders are invited for dinner or when they have parties, they love dressing to the nines: tuxedos even, patent-leather shoes, elegant dresses for women. Páll, Holm's landlord, gave a party for his pals in a blizzard one night—mostly high government officials and successful businessmen, a stag party. "Surely they won't come," Holm consoled him, as the sea a few hundred yards across the road disappeared under sheets of horizontal snow. "They will be on time," Páll said, burying a couple of bottles of Brennivín (Iceland's schnapps, affectionately nicknamed "the black death") inside the growing snowdrift outside the front door. At seven thirty, a four-wheel drive bus slid into the driveway and out poured thirty penguins, all in formal black, slipping through the drifts on their leather soles. They each downed a shot of freshly chilled Brennivín (a traditional Icelandic gesture of welcome) before coming in to warm up to serious partying. The blizzard continued, unabated. The four-wheel drive bus showed up promptly at one o'clock in the morning, and the thirty now wobbly guests waved their farewells as they disappeared into the snow. Icelanders resembled Minnesotans (at least of the last generation) in this regard: if nature has condemned you to life in a continuously foul climate, you have no choice but to ignore it and proceed with your plans. If you wait for the weather to improve before doing anything, your bones will have crumbled to fine dust.

The second peculiarity is a lovely one. Icelanders seldom appear for any occasion—a party, dinner, even a "visit" over coffee—without fresh flowers. Liquor stores, grocers, gas stations may close, but the omnipresent flower shop is always open. Maybe this habit, too, is a function of living with an excess of dismal weather.

Holm loved Reykjavík, a moderately small town full of chamber music, theater, bookstores, eccentric citizens. No taverns in those days, but he was in cahoots with his next-door neighbor, a witty marine biologist, brewing a barrel of bitter. Holm liked the ordinary daily diet of salt mutton and peas, rye bread and herring, boiled haddock and waxy potatoes, and plenty of good chocolate. He joined one of the many splendid choruses in town to lend a tenor to Beethoven's Ninth—in Icelandic! Icelanders, like all Scandinavians, are addicted to choral singing—mixed, women's, men's, children's, whatever the combination—and they do it well. Whatever northern reserve frosts the surface of daily life disappears in the heartfelt, even sentimental, singing of a chorus. He made friends that he has kept for twenty years after, the marine biologist who took him on mussel-gathering expeditions in tidal pools, the wry lexicographer who regaled him with bilingual limericks, the half-American schoolteacher who was his bridge partner and his greatest source of insight into the Icelandic soul. Plenty of beautiful women. Plenty of fine cooks. Plenty of well-read conversational jousting partners. Plenty of musicians to play with him—flute or violin sonatas. Why go home? he often thought. Why did my great-grandfather ever leave?

But there remained one clinker. To be an Icelander, or even to live there, you must have Icelandic. The kindly Icelandic priest, Séra Bragi Friðriksson, who met Holm at the boat and helped him settle into daily life, kept gently trying to teach him a few words, to goad him to say something—anything—in Icelandic. One of Séra Bragi's parishes was at Bessastaðir, the president's house on a little peninsula a few miles outside Reykjavík. Americans always express astonishment that Bessastaðir, a handsome but unpretentious old manor house from the eighteenth century should be unguarded, unlocked, almost unattended to by any authority. If you knock at the president's door, the president answers. If you go to the little church next door to his house for the regular services, he or she (both are possible in Iceland) might invite you next door for coffee and a little something. International terrorists seem, thank God, not to have discovered Iceland, so it still behaves like a civilized country. Holm often found himself recruited to contribute a loud tenor addition to the music at Bessastaðir. Iceland's president at the time, Kristján Eldjárn, sometimes appeared for services and invited Séra Bragi and the big American (almost Séra Bragi's size!) for coffee and chat. Kristján disingenuously referred to himself as a simple Icelandic farmer from Svarfaðardalur in Eyjafjörður in the north of Iceland but he was, in fact, a distinguished (though self-taught) archaeologist and historian, a fine writer and a great wit and raconteur. In other words, an ordinary Icelandic farmer. Over sherry, cakes, and coffee, he found out that Holm was from Minneota, a town well known to old Icelanders for being full of nineteenth-century immigrants. "So you are Icelandic, but have no Icelandic? That will not do. You must go north to a farm and learn something." On being told that I was a poet, he asked, "Are you a proper poet or an *atóm skáld* (free verse modern poet)?" *"Atóm skáld,* I'm afraid." "My son is one too. But you should at least learn the proper rules." First Sigurður, then Bragi the priest, then Kristján the president. Holm had now been given orders, almost, it seems, by both nature and culture.

One of Holm's students at the university, Július, had returned for a degree in literature in his late forties. In his other life he worked for the ministry of agriculture. Holm told Július about the advice he'd gotten to go out to a farm. Július knew a good one, right in the middle of the area of northeast Iceland that sent most of the immigrants to Minneota a century before. "It's the right farm for you," Július said. "No one speaks English. You will have to speak Icelandic or keep silent." Holm, afflicted with garrulity from birth, couldn't quite imagine not talking. Desperation might even drive him to learn a little Icelandic.

His old friend Howard Mohr, the writer from western Minnesota, stopped to visit Holm in Iceland on his way to Europe. Those were the days of cheap jolly boozy Icelandair flights to Luxembourg—the counterculture express. Howard loved Iceland, drank home brew, and exchanged sallies of wit with Holm's next-door neighbor Jón, the marine biologist, ate the only pizza then extant in Iceland: ground mutton, farmer cheese, and canned tomato sauce on flatbread, watched whales being winched out of the sea to be flensed of their blubber. To cap his adventure, he decided to ride with Holm in his potentially exploding red Pinto halfway around Iceland to the farm, then fly back to Reykjavík to make his connection to Europe.

They started their trip on a bright June day driving east from Reykjavík, past the end of the pavement in Selfoss, thirty miles out. Now 350 miles of rough gravel greeted them. They passed the saga farmsteads from *Njal's Saga*, Iceland's *Iliad;* first Njal's farm where he was burned alive inside his house with his wife and sons; then Gunnar's farm at Hlíðarendi, which he loved so much that rather than save his life by going into exile, he looks backward after his horse has stumbled and says the most famous sentence in Icelandic literature, "How lovely the slopes are, more lovely than they have ever seemed to me before, golden cornfields and new-mown hay. I am going back home and I will not go away." He dies, of course, because of it, ambushed and murdered inside his own house. That sentence must describe something of what the sailors on Bakkafoss felt when they saw Eldey after eleven days at sea. Americans have always misused and misunderstood the word "patriotism." They use it as a blunt instrument with their opinions attached to the club head. The love of your own countryside has nothing to do with foreign policy, burnt flags, taxation or a Maginot Line against immigrants at the border. It has to do with light on a hillside, the fat belly of a local trout, and the smell of new-mown hay.

After Gunnar's farm, the glaciers began, Eyjafjallajökull and Mýrdalsjökull, both old volcanoes capped with gleaming ice. At the first roadside waterfall, Skógafoss (Forest Falls), Holm and Mohr stopped for the night at a boarding school doubling as a summer hotel. Not a tree in sight at Skógafoss, but a garland of fine mist and a properly resonant boom as the water thundered over the cliff on its anxious run for the sea a few miles south. In 1979 Icelandic summer hotels offered spartan simplicity—a sleeping bag on a classroom floor, the school showers, and everyday school lunch food. That night Holm and Mohr dined on boiled fat mutton, mashed rutabagas, and something with whipped cream, washed down with near beer (the real stuff being still illegal).

When they came to spread out their sleeping bags after dinner, Mohr experienced one of his Icelandic shocks. Among their room- mates was an Icelandic family, dining on a homemade picnic sup- per's main course: svið, blackened singed sheep's head. Mohr had a sort of mystical culinary experience at the sight of the blond, rosy-cheeked, eight-year-old daughter cutting out the eyeballs and the cheek meat with a pocketknife and downing them with lip- smacking pleasure. Three groups shared the room, the Icelanders, a handful of German tourists, and the wandering Minnesota boys. Though light still flooded into the classroom windows, everyone bedded down around midnight. It is a curious thing to try to sleep on a hard floor in a roomful of strangers who not only do not share your language but have just been munching away on the eyeballs out of a black sheep head. Holm took a stiff nip out of his traveling flask and soon fell asleep, but Mohr was restless. The mutton and rutabagas and whipped cream soon went mightily to work in Holm's now sleeping digestive tract, and the night was evidently full of impressive explosions—answered by a softer chorus from the Germans. Mohr took note of the night and has been telling Holm the story of it for twenty years. Isn't that the reason to have adventures and to tell stories—so that humans can give each other affectionate gifts of wisdom and humor over and over for a whole life? Everyone needs their own comically noisy and fragrant night in their own Iceland next to their own treeless Forest Falls.

From Skógar, they drove east to Vík to see puffin cliffs on Dyrhólaey (Door Hole Island), the southernmost point in Iceland. The sea cut the door hole in a black basalt slab that juts south and rises above a black sand beach. Here crashes the biggest surf in Iceland. When the wind blows right, the rollers hit the beach with nothing to interrupt their progress north from the Antarctic coast. Look at the globe: that's a long stretch of water without the petty interference of land to slow it down. Holm and Mohr spent an hour skipping flat black stones into the surf.

East of Vík you pass over the two vast glacial outwash sands below the glaciers of Mýrdalsjökull and Vatnajökull. Volcanoes periodically explode under those glaciers, hurling icebergs in the air, causing huge floods of meltwater, obliterating everything in a few minutes that stands in their path to the sea. These are eerie places, black quicksand and waste stretching for miles, behind them the pale glaciers with fire in their bellies. The black gravel road seems too frail even to hold a red car from falling under its squishy skin. Mohr is famous for his fanatical safety consciousness, taping corners in his kitchen, driving fifty-two miles per hour, warning family and friends against risky behavior. For years he has pestered Holm about his habits: reading novels while driving eighty miles per hour on county roads, smoking Camels, and poaching eggs in bacon fat. Mohr reads out of the *Icelandic Road Guide* that Mýrdalsjökull has erupted with Swiss-clock dependability at regular intervals since settlement in the ninth century. It is forty years overdue for an eruption. Mohr glances out the window nervously at the shining glacier. The horizon has disappeared out the windshield, no end in sight of the endless black sands. "Drive faster," says Mohr to Holm for the first and only time in their lives.

They stayed that night in the upstairs bedroom of an old farmhouse at Skaftafell, once the most isolated and arguably the most beautiful farm in Iceland, set on a steep slope, entirely in the shadow of and surrounded by Vatnajökull, the highest and largest glacier in Europe—the size of Connecticut. Somehow the glacier protects this farm from wind and weather and warms it. The grass and wildflowers are lush, the sheep fat, the cloudberries and rhubarb sweet. The old farmer and his wife spoke little English. Their parlor was lined with leather-bound books—geneology, poetry, history, treatises on sheep disease. The old lady fed us thin pancakes and *vínarterta* and strong coffee. The old man walked us to Svartifoss (Black Falls), a glacial waterfall entirely made of perfect symmetrical columns of columnar basalt as if carved of black marble by giants. We went to bed at midnight in sunshine again but slept more peacefully than at Skógar.

Look at a map of Iceland. The south coast is smooth and round as a baby's bottom, no place to land a boat or hide from heavy seas and gale winds. When you round the bend to the east, you pass the first harbor town, Höfn, which mysteriously enough means harbor. Try pronouncing it. The ö sounds like a German umlaut, the *f* somewhere between a *p* and a *b*. Take a deep breath. Say it fast and loud. Höfn! Höfn! Agglutinate the consonants! It is, of course, a hiccup in English, a grandly comical noise to the foreign ear. Accompany your tries at Höfn! with a lurching of the shoulders. Why not have fun with your mouth? And with your language? The Icelanders certainly do. Höfn is lovely, a lobster fishing town and until the last year or two, a NATO radar surveillance station watching for Russian submarines. Höfn is ringed by sawtooth mountains and chilly lagoons full of ice chunks broken off the glacier waiting to slim down for their last trip into the sea.

Follow the map north on the east coast. It looks a saw blade, endless deep narrow indentations, the east fjords, narrow water walled by steep mountains, a little fishing town at the bottom of each of them. Holm and Mohr rounded Höfn and drove around each and every one of these fjords, one grander and lovelier—and emptier—than the next. The greatest advantage for travelers to being born in the flat grass of the Midwest is that the smallest relief in the landscape gives pleasure and joy. When, as in the

east fjords of Iceland, you arrive at a landscape that might even
deserve the encomium of sublimity, you enter a state of almost
childish wonder. Can this much beauty be good for you?

Finally Holm and Mohr reached Egilsstaðir, the market center
for northeast Iceland and, after a few wrong turnings, found the
local road going north to the farm where Holm was to live for
the summer. Mohr looked at him with a wry face. Mohr was leaving for Reykjavík the next morning, then on to Luxembourg,
London, Paris, Berlin—the centers of European civilization. The
ready-to-explode Pinto bounced north over rocks and potholes,
past grazing sheep and horses, old well-used-looking farmsteads,
a ridge of snowcapped crags to the east, a milky blue glacial lake
(Lagarfljót) with its own resident monster to the west. This was
not Reykjavík. They hadn't heard English for three hundred miles.
East Greenland was the nearest landmass. Sixty miles north,
the sea was already pocked with drift ice. Cold rain pelted the red
Pinto's windshield. "Holm, you are crazy," said Mohr. "You are
thirty-seven years old, too old for this sort of thing. I wouldn't
dream of doing it." Holm smiled (I think . . . he must have smiled),
"And I have dreamed of this for years, and wouldn't dream of
doing anything else." They pulled into the long driveway of
Gilsárteigur, seven hundred kilometers from Reykjavík, farther
from Minneota, farthest of all from the United States in every
sense. If you are going to try an island on for size to see if it suits
you, then you had best get to the farthest end of it, to make damn
sure that it is not a mere continent in disguise.

Though Iceland was settled by sea-going Vikings and the
whole economy to this day comes from the sea, the land takers
soon after settlement laid down their oars to raise sheep and hay.
Icelandic farming, however, never resembled the crop farming
of Iowa or the Ukraine. With a growing season too short and soil

too thin to nourish anything much beyond native grass—the
Icelanders raised hay. When Gunnar looked back to his "cornfield,"
he probably saw a tiny patch of barley or some other hardy small
grain, and his farm was hundreds of miles south of Gilsárteigur.
In the northeast farming meant sheep—unlike any sheep you
have ever seen, unless you have watched them in Iceland. The
breed arrived here a thousand years ago, and remains unaltered
by the genetic experiments and crossbreeding that have transformed most domestic livestock in the rest of the world. The same
is true of the Icelandic horse, probably even dog and cow. Here,
at the last edge of Europe (or the first edge of North America),
Icelandic domestic animals were preserved in splendid isolation.
What is true of the grammar and structure of the language is
equally true of the sheep. The gamey—and delicious—lamb chop
whose bones you gnaw tastes as it would have a thousand years
ago. That lamb dined on the same flavor of grass that grew in
1,000, growing the same wool. It is against Icelandic law to import foreign sheep (or horses or any other animal). The great
threat to Icelandic survival has not come from volcanoes, earthquakes, or glacial floods, but from microscopic foreign bacteria
that periodically try to wipe out their whole animal or human
stocks. An Icelandic sheep has grown no more resistance to foreign
visitors than the Hawaiians had to Captain Cook's bacterial calling
cards. The Icelanders have grown fond of their sheep in the last
thousand years—fond may be an understatement, obsessed is
better. They intend to protect them.

Remember David Quammen's description of the peculiarity of
island biodiversity: giants, dwarfs, mutants, sports. All Icelandic
domestic breeds qualify for those mantles. You have never seen
anything quite like them before, and, unless you stuff them to
take them home to admire on your mantelpiece, you will have to

go *there* to see them now. They live in a biological time warp.
You can come visit if your hands are clean and your pockets are
empty, but they will not come calling on you in your modern foreign parlor.

Like the sheep, Icelandic farm architecture hadn't changed
much for a thousand years. Building materials changed but only
in the last century. The immigrants in the 1870s and 1880s left
low, cramped, damp turf farmsteads, a series of sharply gabled,
grass-roofed sheds arranged in a connected row. Frequently the
only wood in them was the door and roof frames. Poorer farms
had floors of packed dirt; the more prosperous manor farms
splurged on rough plank floors. A central living space (baðstofa)
had the only fire or warmth, cramped beds built into the walls
(everyone slept in the same room for centuries), a rough table, a
few stools, a stinking chamber pot, one door open to the animal
barns, another to the storage rooms for tools, grain, butter churns.
Rain leaked through the sod roofs; the turf walls exhaled damp
manure-rich fumes; the single fire blackened the ceiling and
clouded the room with acrid smoke, probably whale oil or peat
lumps. And always, of course, the bookshelf stood there in odd
majesty.

The few surviving old-fashioned turf farms are now museums,
national relics to remind the Icelanders of their own history,
sometimes surprising foreigners who cannot imagine literature
being made in these crowded, disease-ridden, clammy little hovels. The Icelanders might respond to that puzzlement by saying:
Where else do you imagine that literature is made? In drawing
rooms? In formal gardens? At beach resorts? The *baðstofa* of a
turf farm makes a perfectly good setting for W. B. Yeats's "rag and
bone shop of the heart."

After about 1920, farms began to be built of concrete, but the general principle of architecture remained the same. Animals, humans, hay, tools, all together in a row, one door opening to the other, the smells and warmth of the one keeping the other company. Gilsárteigur was such a farm: the horse barn connected to the house, the old sheep barn underneath (the house was built on a small slope). Two grown children of Snæþór (the old farmer) farmed the land, living in separate wings of the big rambling farmstead: sister Gunna and her husband, Jón; brother Bjössi and his wife, Salla. The thirteen-year-old sister, Kidda, lived there too, along with two little boys working for the summer: Siggi and Guðmundur, both twelve or thirteen. The farm boasted several hundred sheep, all named and recorded in a book of sheep geneology, a fine herd of Icelandic ponies with shaggy manes and no-nonsense faces, a few wandering chickens, and a dependable old brown cow who furnished the family's milk and cream to whip for pancakes.

Into this melange of Icelandic speakers arrived the thirty-seven-year-old Holm, erstwhile poet, professor of American literature, and piano thumper, who had spent his first decades trying to escape manure and hay on a farm in western Minnesota and who possessed a twelve- to fifteen-word workable vocabulary of Icelandic, a pocket dictionary, good intentions, and, suddenly, a sense of deep terror and loneliness at the prospect of what he had gotten himself into. The family welcomed him with fine un-sentimental warmth, fed him coffee and a pancake or two, and showed him to his room: a small bed built onto the wall of a steeply gabled room. The bed, about five and a half feet long and narrow, had an Icelandic eiderdown *dúnsæng* (quilt) folded at one end. Holm was (and is) a heavy, broad-beamed fellow six-feet five-inches long. Gunna looked him over quizzically and said (in Icelandic, of course), "We didn't know you were so damn big."

Holm, trying to be polite in his pidgin Icelandic, butchered a sentence or two in an awkward attempt to set her at ease and reassure her of his gratitude. Mohr sipped a little coffee, ate a pancake or two, watched Holm fumble for words, and soon left for the airport, Reykjavík, and Europe. On the way to town he told Holm once more that he was crazy, but added, "This might be one hell of an experience." So it was.

Holm had done his best since childhood to forget the rhythm of farm life—alike anywhere on earth: Iceland, Minnesota, China, Madagascar. Fix the machinery, wait for the weather, vaccinate the sheep, shovel the shit, cut the hay, fix the machinery, wait for the weather, shovel more shit, castrate the lambs, turn the hay, fix the machinery, breed the ewes, milk the cow, wait for the weather, rake the hay into bundles, fix the machinery, find the wandering sheep, gather in the hay, wait for the weather. All this punctuated with coffee, fried sheep heart, coffee and cake, mull over the weather, boiled fish, contemplate the sheep, more coffee, TV news, a Swedish documentary on cod breeding grounds, a Czech soap opera, one more cup of coffee, maybe a card game, bed, check the weather, fix the machinery.

All rhythms have a few hiccups. In Iceland, farm days were divided not into light and dark, but rather wet and dry. Icelandic ground, untended, exists in a state of perennial saturation. Most grass grows not in flat meadows but in something resembling a heavy sea—rolling lumpy clumps and hummocks punctuated by squishy bog. It must be drained and flattened before grass can be mown and gathered. Every farm has a home hay field where nature has been altered and improved—the *tún*. During hay season the *tún* is the subject of worry, fear, veneration. Out there grows the hay that keeps the horses and sheep alive for the long winter. On the size and quality of the hay crop depends the future of

Icelandic civilization, as any farmer might modestly tell you. On Gilsárteigur, the summer's chief job, other than worrying about the hay, was to construct a new silo, a proper storehouse for the hay—now transformed into silage. Holm, whose idea of a building project involved piling cheese and roast beef and tomatoes on rye bread, often found himself loading a wheelbarrow full of cement, pushing it up a ramp to be dumped into a concrete mold. When the hay finally dried enough to be gathered, the whole farm shifted into high gear. The idea of working till dark, then rising at dawn doesn't make sense on the Arctic Circle. Keep pitching bundles till the hay is finally safe from the demon rain. After twenty years of using his shoulder muscles mostly for strenuous octave passages in Liszt études, Holm found himself, after a few days in the hay, sore enough to be in need of liniment, chiropractors, and pity, though he got none from the Icelanders—shoulders were meant for pitchforks, pitchforks were meant for hay in dry weather, and hay was meant to preserve the civilization of Iceland and to provide whatever dinner might appear on your plate. Holm's residence in Iceland entitled him, like any third-world guest from the United States, to the use of Iceland's national health service. Still sore, he visited a doctor in Vopnafjörður who heard his story and inquired, "Aren't you too old for that sort of thing? Take an aspirin and rest it," adding, of course, this being Iceland, "What farm did your grandparents come from? Perhaps we are cousins. . . ."

One morning over coffee when it was too wet for hay or cement, Jón asked Holm a question in a genial voice. Holm missed the drift of the question, but not wanting to be impolite so early in the morning nodded affably and answered *yow-yow* (yes). After coffee he followed Jón to the old shit pit in the nether barn where he was handed a fork and shown a honey wagon. *"Gjörðu svo vel."* Like most slow language learners, Holm answered yes to all

questions he didn't understand—most of them. If the consequence of ignorance and laziness is an afternoon in a shit pit,
language students might grow smarter faster.

Even on farms that grew their own meat, Icelanders ate fish
more than anything else—except whipped cream and coffee, of
course. Fish was not only cheaper, it was soul food. Icelanders
deprived too long of a boiled haddock with fat, either butter or
mutton cracklings, poured over it get jittery. They lose their edge.
Since Holm was the owner of a functional, not yet exploded red
Pinto, he was given the happy responsibility a few times of driving to Borgarfjörður, the next fjord east, to pick up fresh fish from
a local fisherman—probably a cousin.

It was always an interesting trip to Borgarfjörður. From
Gilsárteigur and anywhere north you could see the grandest
mountain in a long ridge: Dyrfjöll (door mountain), a fine square
crag with a jagged door in the middle as if a pass for heroes either
up into Valhalla or down to the netherworld. Even in the July sun
the snow never disappeared from its high slopes. From Gilsárteigur
the road north passed farms with names familiar to Minneotans.
Half of Holm's American neighbors had roots on these farms. The
last farm before rounding the bend east and over the pass to the
fjord was called Kóreksstaðir, an odd Irish name. The west slope of
Dyrfjöll rose just behind it. This was the farm from which Holm's
grandfather Sveinn Jóhannesson Holm and great grandparents
Jóhannes Sveinsson and Soffía Vilhjálmsdóttir had emigrated in
1885. This was the mountain he had missed seeing every day of
his life by happening to be born in Swede Prairie township in the
middle of North America.

After Kóreksstaðir the road bends east and up. To the west and
north you look back over an immense tidal marsh, the Héradsflói,
where Lagarfljót, the long lake with the resident monster, and

Jökullsá á Brú (Glacial River with the Bridge), a nasty gray gritty river, all empty north into the Arctic Sea. The stony path climbs steeply up a mammoth sliding scree pile. The road is only a bulldozed path through the scree. About five or six hundred feet above the sea stands a cross anchored in cement. The inscription, in Icelandic, tells you that this scree mountain is inhabited by the troll Naddi, whose great pleasure it has been since the middle ages to kick up avalanches of scree to slide travelers abruptly downward into the churning surf a long way below. Your only hope for making it over this mountain alive is to offer a prayer to pacify Naddi, thus making sure the good angels are on your side. The prayer is cut there—in Latin. As Holm stood mumbling his verbal bribe to the resident troll, a few slabs of scree dislodged themselves and slid down a long way. Click click click as the scree tumbled over itself. Holm looked at the Pinto's gas tank, then down, then up, then drove briskly to the other side of the scree slope into Borgarfjörður. Holm, though neither devout nor superstitious, offered Naddi a kind word every time he went over that pass. Too bad his safety-conscious friend Mohr went home, he thought. He'd have enjoyed Njarðvíkurskriður—the Njarðvík Scree.

The first farm on the way to the small harbor in Borgarfjörður is named Geitavík (Goat Bay). This lovely farm on a cliff was the home of Pauline Bardal's mother. Pauline was an old Minneota Icelander, a friend of Holm's parents, his first music teacher, and the heroine of his old essay, "The Music of Failure." Geitavík is famous to Icelanders because Jóhannes Kjarval, their greatest painter, lived there, and many of his most surreal landscapes have the color, shape, and texture of this countryside. The liparite mountains in Borgarfjörður look blood red, as if Utah had moved to the Arctic. Dyrfjöll seemed even grander and craggier here on the east slope. A few horses grazed in a field, sheep ambled over the dirt paths in search of grass, a dog barked, a cow stood at attention to be milked, a few flies buzzed in the chilly air. The road ends in Borgarfjörður. The way in is the way out—over the scree. Perhaps a few hundred people live in this isolated sublimely beautiful place: farming, fishing, shooting reindeer, poaching seabird eggs, drinking coffee, staring out to the sea north of them, reading old poems, taking snuff, drying fish on long racks exposed to the wind, admiring reproductions of the famous paintings of their backyard. In a place like this, silence is comprehensive. What century is this? Where are the others on the planet? Here is only the sea and its continual breathing, and the blood-red mountains and the ice not far to the north. Holm strolled around in the meadows and along the beaches for an hour before driving down to the boat to fetch his dripping plastic bags of fish—cod, haddock, halibut, steinbítur (ocean catfish), skate, red belly. He always thought long thoughts, as Longfellow's old poem says, before driving back over the scree with a quick prayer and a respectful nod to Naddi.

Scratch an Icelander and you will find a theory on the proper preparation of boiled fish, as you will with a Russian about borscht, a Texan about chili, a Chinese about dumplings. A fish is a weighty matter, to be considered before it is eaten. Farmers preferred not fresh fish but a peculiar Icelandic variant called *síginn fiskur*, where the fish is hung outdoors over a line to be dried a bit and aged till it develops flavor—perhaps fifteen minutes before it might qualify as cat food. Fresh fish is not preferred. Holm always returned with some sadness from these trips with his damp white bag a few hours out of the sea knowing that he would have to wait a few weeks before tasting that succulent halibut, by then grown hoary and fragrant, bathed in a sauce of mutton fat. Though he came to sympathize with the taste for *síginn fiskur* after a while, he continued to prefer fresh fish.

Icelanders are not early risers, particularly not thirteen-year-old Icelanders. As in every peasant culture on the planet, it is the job of young girls to milk cows. It was Kidda's job. At thirteen she was a dreamy girl still stepping delicately onto the cliff edge of whether to become a woman or not. For the summer she put off deciding, instead electing to become better acquainted with her dreams. This required not rising early. The old brown family cow, whose name was probably Búkolla, sauntered up to the fence next to the house, hung her melancholy head into the yard, and gave expression to her swollen teats with long imploring moans. She was usually attended by a menagerie consisting of the sheep dog, the cats (waiting for spilt milk), a few chickens, and a mentally challenged runt brown sheep that had been exiled from the flock. Holm remembered watching this wonderful tableau every morning, then hearing the voice of Gunna, *"Farðu á fœtur*, Kidda!" (Get to your feet! Get out of bed!). Then, after a painful interval, Kidda appeared pulling a sweater over her still drowsy head, grabbing the three-legged stool and pail to relieve old Búkolla's misery where she stood. The cats snapped to attention at the ping of the squirting milk into the bottom of the tin pail. The squeahunkie sheep rolled his crossed eyes as if he had no idea what was going on but might be enjoying it. Lord, lord, lord, thought Holm as he took a mental photograph of this scene, in what century do I live? Do I like this one or the other one? Is this some great old novel I have wandered into? Or maybe an old Icelandic poem with the full panoply of rhyme and alliteration, about a young girl milking a brown cow on a summer morning a few miles south of the Arctic Circle?

Jón and Gunna then had one daughter, Svandís, two years old. She was a white-blond, pale-skinned little wisp of a creature with an eternal smile full of baby teeth. She had just discovered

language, babbling to herself happily in something resembling
ancient Sumarian from which a few Icelandic words would emerge
now and then like seabirds coming out of a fog bank. It amazed
Holm that Icelandic, so difficult for foreigners to pronounce decently with its consonantal clots, trilled *rs*, and long soulful diph-
thongs, danced effortlessly past Svandís's trainer molars. She
spoke better and more Icelandic than a thirty-seven-year-old
intellectual who was working at it, and, though her observations
frequently had a quality of French surrealism about them, her
grammar and enunciation were perfect. She chanted phrases over
and over to herself, presumably because she enjoyed the sound of
them, and no one had demanded of her the boring regularity of
reason. Sometime in mid-summer she discovered *"áttatíu og sjö."*
Eighty-seven. Over and over. Good morning, Svandís. Eighty-
seven. Time to go potty. Eighty-seven. Eat your peas. Eighty-seven.
Do you love your daddy? Eighty-seven. Once the men came in for
lunch from haying, and Svandís (whose name means swan—a
good one for her) leaped into the big dumb foreigner's lap, smiled
wickedly at him, and said with great good cheer: eighty-seven.
Holm looked at her as seriously as he could and said, eighty-eight
(áttatíu og átta). She scurried off his lap as if he had showed her
a cobra. Never fool around with women of any age when they put
their mind to charming you. Cold reason is not useful on such
occasions. By the next week, she had discovered questions: *"Hvað
er þetta?* (What is this?)," and it soon became the next building
block of her budding communication skills. "Where are you,
Svandís?" "What is this?" "Time for bed." "What is this?" "What
is your name?" "What is this?" When she asked Holm her question, he answered, "eighty-seven." He was not asked again. He
hopes that since she is now presumably a grown woman, she has
forgiven him for his impertinence, but if he were to meet her

again, he might lift one eyebrow and ask her what came after
eighty-six and whether it could be identified.

Holm's best Icelandic teachers were children, particularly the
young boys Siggi and Guðmundur, who worked with him in the
hay and cement operations. They could hardly imagine that someone so big and old could be so clumsy and incompetent, could
butcher the simplest phrase—just as he sometimes tipped over
the wheelbarrow or fell off a horse. But they were kindly boys,
filling in a word he needed, correcting some completely unthink-
able grammar, as if he were an oversized but retarded adolescent
in need of help to survive. But like most Icelandic boys their age
in 1979, they were swept up in the cowboy craze, loved tales of
the wild west and stories of shoot-'em-ups at the Snæfellsnes
corral. They had seen his Minnesota license plates and imagined
a land of pointy boots, heavy sidearms, and swinging doored sa-
loons. He tried to explain to them in his primitive Icelandic what
Minneota was really like, a land of five-buckle overshoes, stoical
snoose-chewing farmers, and millions of pigs—which were hardly
in need of a roundup or in danger from rustlers.

What is your house like?, they asked, imagining a slightly win-
terized covered wagon. Holm's attempt at describing his house in
Minneota led to his best disaster. Thinking slowly in bad Icelandic,
he described an old white square frame house built in 1895 next
to railroad tracks, close to a water tower and a Norwegian church.
A few years earlier Holm had bought an old stuffed moose head
at an auction sale and hung it on his front porch. He thought it
a good enough detail to mention to the boys and thought he had
enough words to do it. But the moose head stumped him. What
the hell was moose in Icelandic? Too late to call for a dictionary.
He charged ahead, throwing in the English word, hoping for the
best. Siggi's eyes grew wide. "How big was the moose when he was

alive?" "Oh a thousand pounds, maybe. His antlers are four feet wide." "Are moose always so big in North America?" "Sometimes bigger." Their faces showed clearly that something had gone terribly wrong. A little while later he discovered that moose was an exact cognate for the Icelandic "mouse." The ungainly name for moose (who don't exist in Iceland) is *stórt Bandarískt elgdýr* (big North American elk-like animal). Siggi and Gudmundur looked at him a little strangely after that unconscious out-Texaning of the Texans' renowned boasting skills. A thousand pound mouse indeed . . . sometimes bigger. In retrospect, it sounds like a good evolutionary idea, something Quammen might expect to happen on an isolated island.

As Mohr suspected, the farm was one hell of an experience. It felt to Holm not just like moving four hundred miles from Reykjavík or three thousand miles from Minnesota, but back fifty or a hundred years in the century, an island suspended in time as much as in water and that these lovely people existed as characters in an interior ballet, the intricate dance of another life, another world, moving to music of a solemn delicacy, a melancholy beauty that threatened sometimes to break his heart. On the other hand, they were lively young farmers probably wondering what the hell they were doing harboring this big eater who could neither talk intelligently nor do a good day's work. Holm found out later that they were all in fact his cousins, their great-grandmother the sister of his great-grandfather. They were much too civilized to be Gíslasons, but they were nevertheless.

Only sporadically did the outside world break into this island pastoral idyll. To call Reykjavík meant turning the crank on the wooden phone box and announcing to a live Icelandic "Central"—in Icelandic—what number you wanted and who you were calling. Central probably also wanted to know if you had any business wasting your money to call these people whoever the hell they might be, but she said all this in rapid enough Icelandic that he missed it. Holm once had to call Minneota and it took several hours and much complicated negotiation to even make a connection. There will be a special room in a special hell worse than any Dante imagined for the inventor of the satellite phone, the car phone, the cell phone, the beeper, the caller ID, the call waiting, the answering machine, voice mail, and any other contraption that will be invented by the time the scribbler Holm finishes this sentence and rests his ball-point pen to end it with a period—not a dot. In this torture room a thousand phones will ring continually and loudly in a cacophonous disorder and every one will be a telemarketer selling you yet another phone. This will happen for the rest of eternity. You asked for it. You got it. Meanwhile, in 1979, a phone call from the outside world signified something and required some trouble and effort. Otherwise, the wind blew, the seabirds cried, the horses whinnied, but sometimes for hours nothing happened at all but silence and the planet turning slowly around on its interior axis.

Holm did miss one machine—the piano. He tried cold turkey for a few days, but finally asked Gunna if there were an unoccupied piano anywhere in the neighborhood. At the school across the road, of course, at Eiðar. Just ask the headmaster for a key or ask my sister Þórhalla. Off Holm went on foot, down the long driveway, across the gravel road with *The Well Tempered Clavier* and a few Beethoven and Schubert sonatas clutched under his arm. He looked up the words for key, permission, piano. The headmaster spoke English; Þórhalla did not, but she invited him for dinner anyway. She was a professional cook. He accepted with delight, spent the afternoon thumping Bach and Schubert and a little ragtime, finishing the day with salmon garnished with mussels and a dill sauce, a starter of curried shrimps and a finisher of cream cake in sufficient layers to make a strong impression. Fjóla (Violet), her daughter, was eight, a perfect age for expressing the fact that adults are usually mistaken and incorrect. "You do *not* say it that way. You say it *this* way," she said to the slow-witted foreigner. "That is silly. No one says that. *This* is correct." The blond Violet was a fine instructor. Would she had had a cleverer student. Describing the shoulder of a road (*öxl* in Icelandic) caused great peals of laughter from Þórhalla, Fjóla, and even small Snæþór at two. *Öxl* connects your arm to your torso. Roads have edges. When Holm was telling a story about the liturgy in the American church and said "Heilagur Draugur" (Holy Ghost), all three of them fell off their chairs. Ghost in Icelandic is reserved for the malevolent undead. The white dove on the other hand is only an *andi,* a breath, a spirit. It was a fine night and Holm lingered late. He would spend many lovely nights in that flat, and they all became fast friends—even Fjóla, who was often stern with him.

Holm remembers walking slowly home from Eiðar that night. It had rained all day, gloomy fog hanging like a gray shroud over the mountains. Bach and salmon and laughter and the company of lovely women had made him unconscious of weather, but now, at maybe two thirty or three in the morning, the sky cleared. The snowy tops of the mountains gleamed in soft light. Terns cried and circled their nests in the distance. He was too far away to be a threat. The Gilsá (the Gil river) that gave the farm its name burbled along a few feet from him coming down fast from the mountains to join the milky Lagarfljót on its last miles before the sea. A pair of still-awake white horses watched him with great solemnity. The light thickened. He did, by God, start singing Italian songs and skipping like a tango dancer as he shuffled along the gravel driveway to his narrow bed with its eiderdown quilt. Something inside his body rolled over and sang to him: now is the time for praise. It is good to be a human being. It is good to be alive on earth. No matter what misery or stupidity track you through the rest of your life, you have lived this night. You have seen the sun beat back the fog in the middle of the night. He looked at the grass. It seemed to him now the beautiful uncut hair of graves. He looked at the lupine and the angelica and the Iceland poppies. They seemed to him proof that the whole creation was a kelson of love. No wonder this damned island had hatched legions of poets from the time human beings first set foot here. It unhinged you from the world of getting and spending, though that world continued spinning too, minding its own business tonight.

The summer was coming to an end, and he would have to go back to Reykjavík to teach American books and resume his other life. Now he had two hundred and fifty—maybe five hundred—words of Icelandic all glotted together without the grammar that enabled them to make sense. But it was, to quote Mohr, a hell of an experience. On one of his last weekends in the country, everybody stopped work early to go to a *sveitaball,* a country dance in Reyðarfjörður, the fjord just south of Egilsstaðir. They all piled into the Gilsárteigur Land Rover: Jón and Gunna, Bjössi and Salla, Þórhalla and Vilhjálmur for the trip south. They were armed with 7-Up bottles of landi, the Icelandic white lightning, and Holm may have added a flask of Scotch smuggled from Reykjavík. Þórhalla volunteered to be the designated sober driver, a necessity in Iceland even in those days, while the rest of us enjoyed the fruits of farm chemistry to loosen up the soul a little.

Icelandic country dances are remarkable; they begin late and go till the last dancer drops, often at an hour when puritans rise from bed. The invariably skilled bands play every conceivable sort of music: old time waltzes, polkas, fox-trots, sambas, bossa novas, cha-chas, tangos, rock and roll, country western, square dances, funky chickens—and probably if you asked them: pavanes, galliards, minuets, and gavottes. Everyone dances with everyone, children with grandpas, mothers with sons, old with young, choose your sex but choose somebody. They dance hard, and they dance steady. They are not shy about moving their feet and often old farmers are astonishingly graceful ballroom dancers. When they have worked themselves into a sweat, they go to the parking lot with flasks and swig grandly on white lightning. Sometimes they get drunk and fight—but it feels more like ritual than passion or hatred. Sometimes they get randy and kiss everyone in sight and make outrageous propositions for dalliances. The actors at an Icelandic country dance are not small hearted or timid, and they don't like it very much if you insist on being a purse-lipped disapprover or a constipated puritan. A dance is a serious matter, and you had damned well better enjoy it.

And so we all did. Holm can no more dance than he can speak Icelandic or play hockey, but that night, by God, he danced. He flirted. He made a fool of myself. He kissed several women he had never met. He did not fight but he laughed, and then he danced some more, probably destroyed thirty or forty perfectly respectable Icelandic toes. He may have been the tango king. He doesn't remember. What he does remember is Þórhalla's laughter as she loaded them all back into the Land Rover to drive an hour north from the sloshing Atlantic at the bottom of the long fjord, back home, home on the island where he first shouted out to all the interior angels: The hell with continents. Let me die here where I can be thrown into the sea to circle the planet forever as a pink whale, spouting the foam of poetry up into the chilly air.

⌇ The Island of Pain

WE'VE DONE A GOOD JOB at the end of the twentieth century of mushing up our sweet language. Poor English! We have politically corrected it, castrated it, euphemized it, bureaucratized it. All nouns can now be verbed. We parent the brat, workshop the poor defenseless poem, journal in our journals, dialogue together. Lord have mercy on us for our insults to language, but who is snooty Holm to imagine himself superior to the fashion of his age? Therefore, I propose to newly verb a perfectly respectable noun.

It is possible to island a man, to sever him from whatever promontory, Europe or otherwise, that connects him to other men. Pain is the instrumentality of islanding. Pain assumes many disguises when it comes. The simplest disguise is intense physical pain, the body at the outer limit of its possibilities for survival. Interior pain is more complicated, the black melancholy that sings to you of suicide, that sees every passing train or deep gorge as the only ally. Sometimes, if the black music is not quite loud enough or if your inner gyroscope rights itself, you simply amputate lumps of time from your memory. These lumps disappear leaving only mysterious holes in your life.

In fifty-six years I have been islanded three times by the body, and once by the soul. I have been, and am, a lucky man, a reasonably sturdy piece of work, and the universe has let me off lightly, only delicately grazed with the death bird's wings. I cannot imagine many readers who have lived so long who could not match or even best me grandly. I tip my hat to them. They will know what I am talking about.

Make a mental picture of yourself—your body, your clothes, your habits, your loves, your work, the people around you, your memories, your pleasure at the odd flickerings in your own brain. This accumulation adds up to a human being with your name, whom your mother, your lover, your neighbor recognizes as you. Now island this mental picture. Cut away the memory of the you that makes you you. Let it drift to open water, no boundaries left for others to cross, no bridges for them to come on shore. No past. No history. No future. No expectations. Only now. The island of now. You are not a human being. You are not you. You are pain. You have been islanded.

By the age of forty, I had survived the deaths of parents, the failure of a marriage, financial ruin, a collapsed career, a few disastrous love affairs, the usual stuff, nothing special. While certainly not trifles, these events had not managed to island me. I was still Bill Holm, an intact though eccentric sensibility, with a reasonably sure footing in the universe.

My Aunt Clarice, Uncle Abo's widow, lived a few houses away from me in Minneota. She was a kind and dignified lady, who kept her plump nephew supplied with homemade brown bread and Icelandic *vínarterta*. Her son and daughter-in-law were coming to Sioux Falls for a college-class reunion in early June. Clarice asked me if I wanted to drive her to Sioux Falls and have a chance to visit my cousins. Of course I would. Early on a sunny Sunday morning we set off driving ninety miles southwest, Clarice telling family stories, I watching weeds and wildflowers in the ditches next to the county roads. Clarice had brought a fresh caramel roll

or two. I had a thermos of coffee. A sweet pleasant morning in
the Midwest, nephew and seventy-year-old aunt happily chatting
in the front seat of a Chevy. Eight miles from Sioux Falls the small
county road merges into Interstate 90, roaring trucks, diesel
fumes, no wildflowers. I remember feeling an eerie discomfort in
the middle of my body as we turned onto the big highway. I fell
silent, I suppose, as Clarice continued talking, wondering aloud
which exit we should take to find the Holiday Inn. After a while,
she looked at me and asked if I was feeling all right. She was a calm
woman who had endured much disaster, a good companion for
this morning. I felt as if someone had jammed a red-hot serrated
knife into the top of my thorax. I said something foolish, "A little
pain, must have been something I ate, would you mind driving
the last few miles, should be gone in a minute," and then no
speech. I opened the car door, tried to get out to move to the passenger side, and the knife in the gut literally knocked me over
onto the pavement at the shoulder of the road. Thank God Clarice
could drive a car. Most farm women of her generation couldn't.
We drove on to the Holiday Inn, every seam in the concrete road
a turning of the interior knife blade. We found the Holiday Inn.
I tumbled onto the grass trying to find some bodily contortion
that would stop the turning blade. My cousins came out to have
a look, the desk clerk from the motel arrived, someone said, "Get
him to an emergency room." I had never been to an emergency
room, never been to a hospital except to visit. I didn't want to go.
I didn't want to be seen, observed, commented on, pitied. I wanted
them all to disappear and leave me alone with my interior knife.
I wanted to crawl under some porch in the darkness like a dog to
bury myself in wet dirt. I wanted them all away—far away, dead
or silent or gone. I didn't care. I was islanded, properly islanded.
I wasn't Bill Holm. Not a human being. I had no relatives, no

friends, no Aunt Clarice, no history, no future. Only me and my knife alone on our island. No, that's wrong. Not even me, only the knife, all open sea in every direction circling out from that knife. There is no more profound loneliness in this universe than the islanding of pain. No one is now allowed to love you, help you, or even best of all, kill you fast to end the turning of the knife. A cheery psychologist might suggest that you make friends with your pain. At a certain level of intensity, that is impossible. The pain doesn't want friends, nor does it want tolerance, forbearance, stoicism. It wants you. It is you.

The Sioux Falls emergency room was a sleepy place on Sunday afternoon. I offered only minimal excitement. The nurse asked me where I hurt. I pointed. She asked if I had a family history of heart disease. "Madam," I said, "unless my interior anatomy differs greatly from other humans, that is not the heart, it is the gut." Maybe Icelanders have misplaced hearts, but I doubted it. Maybe an ulcer. Maybe. She handed me Maalox. I drank it. I gagged. When the milky remnant hit my esophagus, the knife turned grandly and knocked me down again. Here's a prescription for Demerol. Go see a doctor in Minnesota and get a thorough workup. I took enough Demerol to endure the ninety miles back to Minneota. Clarice drove.

I had no health insurance, of course, having taken leave from a college replacement job, so I spent two or three grand I didn't have to get a diagnosis. I was islanded by a gallstone. I was allergic to milk, poisoned by ice cream. Several surgeons were anxious to help me out, quoting cash figures of eight to ten thousand. They promised to relieve my misery with more misery (a big cut in those days) and large debt. The pain went on for days. I Demeroled myself into a semiconscious state now and then, but mostly I was awake—or the interior knife was awake. I tried to barricade the house against human beings, to keep from them the pleasure of seeing me writhing and groaning. I wanted no food, no love, no kindness. I wanted the knife out or death. Actually I was incapable of desire—of wanting anything. Nothing went through the head—a flat line. That knife was Napoleon's Saint Helena. Only the little bile tube clogged with its gritty white stones was alive. Bill Holm was in exile, causing no trouble.

When the knife surrendered (or sailed away in temporary retreat) after about a week, I felt my humanity come back as if from the dead. I could move, wash, breathe, speak language. I had still not eaten, the terror of food too great. Food brought the knife. I called an old friend in Seattle, a doctor, and asked for his wisdom about gallbladders and surgery. He advised reluctance. "Surgeons love gallbladders," he said. "It's a big cut, but an easy one, and a good fat fee. They're knife happy, the surgeons." (At the mention of knife, I winced, the memory of islanding still powerful in my body.) "You're too damn fat anyway," my sensitive nurturing doctor friend continued. "Here's a list of what you shouldn't eat. [It included almost every imaginable pleasure in the four basic food groups.] If you're not careful, it'll hurt you. You might even lose some weight, and the stones will very likely break up and pass. If the gallbladder ruptures, you'll die horribly of peritonitis, but what the hell? Save your ten grand."

I did. I had a few more smaller meetings with the knife. I ate with great care like a barefoot dancer on broken glass. I lost thirty pounds. I asked my doctor friend if whiskey and coffee were permitted. "Certainly. No fat in whiskey. That'll do in your liver." I counted on my liver's forgiveness and poured a stiff drink to toast the return of Bill Holm from his lonesome island, his regrappling onto the promontory of humanity.

⁊

The second islanding traveled almost to the top of the body. While only a fraction of mankind ever becomes conscious of the interior presence of the gallbladder—like the appendix an anatomical anomaly soon to be evolved out of existence, only a very few lucky humans ever travel from cradle to grave without having adventures with their teeth. Teeth occupy the island of universal human misery; they are the cement that binds us together in fellow feeling. Mention teeth in any gathering past first youth, and you will hear story tumbling over story, one misery topping another, one complaint competing in eloquence with the next. We tell those stories with more ease to each other than cancer or stroke or Alzheimer's tales because we are confident that whatever suffering our teeth may inflict on us, they will not finally kill us. Few die of toothache. But the teeth can island us as efficiently as any organ of the body.

I once went on a poetry tour of small towns in Minnesota, three then-young writers traveling from hamlet to hamlet giving readings in churches, nursing homes, libraries, town parks. Since most of the audiences had no idea what a poetry reading was, nor had ever been to one, we kept the readings cheerful and light hearted, full of singing and humor. In the middle of one tour, my mouth called attention to itself, and I found it impossible to maintain the cheerfulness quotient. I snarled at gatherings of the innocent elderly, snapped at my fellow poets. Finally I islanded down to surly silence with occasional moans and whimpers. I had never had a toothache quite like this one; my jaw ached and felt swollen as if I had a baseball crammed in it, my head throbbed, my shoulders and arms felt as if they were bruised and beaten, even my sciatic nerve quivered from hip to ankle. Water was a torture to the mouth, as was air blowing into it. I was not in good humor; I was not, in fact, in any humor at all. I had disappeared again, islanded by whatever the tooth had decided to do to me.

My old friend John, who knows me well, said it was time to quit fooling and find a dentist. "I'll finish the tour," I growled. "It'll pass." Ignoring me, he called his own dentist in a town twenty miles away. The dentist himself was too busy to see me, but since it seemed an emergency, his old father, a retired dentist, would have a look on his way to play golf. I was to arrive very early in the morning so the old man could still make his tee time. It will not surprise you that some of the most skilled and enthusiastic golfers in America are dentists.

I (or something that had the vague outline of my body, but was in fact only a confused jumble of pain receptors) arrived at seven o'clock in the morning. A jolly-looking man in his seventies, wearing a loud plaid sport coat (and probably golf shoes), came in. "So we're having a little toothache, are we?" How hateful to be referred to in the plural when you have ceased being even an individual of the species. "The toothache is doing very well today, thank you, but I think Bill Holm has disappeared." He pried open my mouth. "My, my, what a beauty! You'll feel better without that. It's a good size. Probably need a saw and pliers." He brandished a novocaine needle. "A good what?" I mumbled. "You have a crooked wisdom tooth, grew cockeyed right into the jaw." A wisdom tooth indeed. . . . What wisdom lived in yet another useless evolutionary appendage that didn't know enough in its pin-prick DNA brain to grow straight? The old man hummed as he worked, a country western tune, I supposed. He yanked and pried and grunted for what seemed several days, but in fact was only a minute or two. "It's a beauty," he said, holding a bloody fang in his pincers for me to admire. The moment the malevolent tooth left the mouth, Bill Holm came down the birth canal into himself again, a human being for better or worse. Instantaneously the arms and shoulders stopped aching, the head ceased throbbing, the sciatic nerve quieted from thigh to toe, the baseball was gone, traveling over the plate, up toward the Milky Way for all I gave a damn. I was filled for just a moment with true wonder at the infinite complexity of the wiring in the human nervous system. What a piece of work is man that a tooth should do this to his whole body and then—just—stop. I thanked the old dentist. "Have to rush. Almost late for the first hole. Have a nice day. Toodle-oo." I took home the chunk of bony wisdom in a plastic bottle to remind me.

I taught at a Chinese university for the 1986–87 year in Xi'an, the old Tang dynasty capital. The experience of living in China proved half terrible, half joyful: a loathsome political bureaucracy hell-bent on terrorizing, humiliating, and chiseling its own citizens, but a year grappled to a lovely bunch of students and ordinary people—funny, smart, generous, and stoical to a fault in the presence of daily chaos. I wrote a book about my experiences that year; more than one reader noted that the only place the author traveled that seemed detestable without redemption was Wuhan. The Chinese themselves refer sardonically to Wuhan as their nine-headed carnivorous bird and as an oven. The town, a sort of Chinese Chicago where goods pass from north to south over the Yangtze River, has a gritty, bad-tempered feel about it. The beauties and antiquities that grace countless other Chinese cities have disappeared from Wuhan under the bludgeonings of incessant floods, invaders, revolutionary uprisings. Not a swell place.

So, lonesome for China and my old friends and students, I violated my own advice to steer clear of the nine-headed bird. I took a job teaching literature in Wuhan in the spring of 1992. In retrospect, I ought to have trusted intuition better, but retrospect is the cheapest view of any human action. On islands, the hell with "retrospect." When you find yourself islanded, "retrospect" is the cruelest non sequitor of all. Avoid it.

I left from Seattle, where I had just finished sitting at the long dying of my old friend, the doctor, in December of 1991, then returning in early February for a memorial dinner he had requested in lieu of a funeral. The doctor had warned me, all through his last illness, against going to Wuhan. I wrote most of the China book in his house in Seattle, so the doctor had heard all the stories. "Don't go," the doctor said. "It won't come out well." The dinner was melancholy, a cloud of artificial gaiety drooping over the evening, a sad crab Louis followed by broken-hearted filets finished by weepy Napoleons and nostalgic cognac. Half the guests were themselves dying and would be dead in six months. Someone played Brahms intermezzos, all minor, all full of grief. A few sad speeches. Some attempts at humorous anecdotes. Plop. Good night, friends, see you all soon—though of course no one would, or could, or did. The next day Marcy and I flew first to Shanghai, then on to Wuhan to begin our second teaching adventure in the middle of the Middle Kingdom.

Though Wuhan looks on a map like a continental belly button, it is in fact a city almost islandized by the merging of two huge rivers, the Han flowing south into the now mammoth Yangtze. Thus it is a city of vast bridges connecting the three physically separate cities that make Wuhan: Hankow, Hanyang, Wuchang. I had read Su Dongpo, China's great poet of the Song dynasty, for whom Wuhan was a city of political exile, misery, and heat. I thought I had braced myself for it. We arrived at the airport on a sunny cold February morning, loaded books into a ramshackle van from the school, to cross the long Yangtze bridge, scene of

bloody battles in the '30s, the '40s, the Cultural Revolution of the
'60s and '70s, and only a few years earlier, the student rebellion
of 1989 when the bridge was occupied, marched over, and fought
for by students and police. Below, the murky Yangtze looked like
an enormous brown drainage ditch. In its gut, tons of Tibetan
and Szechuan dirt moved like a watery belt across China's belly
toward Shanghai and the sea. The river fell fast from four miles up
in the mountains, then rushed through the soon-to-be-dammed
three gorges, finally reaching its sea-level floodplain just east of
Wuhan. It divided north from south China: above it—wheat
fields, desert, grassland, forest, then Siberia; below it—rice paddies, swamps, half a billion farmers, Hong Kong, the South China
Sea. Blow up the bridge over that big brown river—by now an
emulsion of factory goop, human shit, and Himalayan gravel—
and you cut China in two. The bridge, naturally, is well fortified
by green-suited soldiers.

South of the Yangtze sat the school, a technology college with
a foreign-language department. Three of my old students—
friends, bridge partners, comrades in adventure—taught there.
My lonesomeness for their company, and for the bizarre juxta-
positions of Chinese daily life, had tempted me to violate my instinctive mistrust of Wuhan. The van pulled up at our home for
the semester, a grey cement ruin, half the windows cracked and
loosely boarded, the roof sagging. The eternally smiling foreign-
office woman (or waiban—barbarian manager) apologized.
"We're redoing the building but haven't finished." They hadn't in
fact begun. "The downstairs apartments are closed." They had
flooded, over and over. We slogged up the dark stairs, mud caked
into the gray cement, smell of mildew and rotted wood, rooms
closed and airless too long, mouse turds, a net of interlocking
spider webs. "You have lived in China before, so you are used to

the inconvenience of daily life," said Smiley the *Waiban*. "It is a very large apartment." Large indeed. It boasted a broken mildewed bed in one bedroom, a black propane tank with a hose to a single burner in the kitchen, a couple of three-legged chairs, a crooked stool, a couch with visible springs, a theoretical orange plastic rotary phone (it was never connected), a toilet that leaked water when you sat on it, a grimy bathtub with a primitive water heater that boiled water for thirty seconds on the days when it worked. "It's a bit dangerous," said Smiley, "so we'll replace it"—which they didn't. One large closed room was entirely filled with construction garbage: broken window frames, a rotted mattress, wet two-by-fours. Nothing in this flat had been washed or dusted for months. Balancing on the three-legged chair left you with a muddy ass—decorated with a garland of crushed spiders. "See you in my office to officially welcome you," said Smiley as she disappeared. As we discovered shortly, all the water was turned off at eight o'clock every evening, connected again at six o'clock in the morning; the electricity disappeared dependably two or three days every week; raw sewage sometimes bubbled up out of the bathtub drain. From the balcony we looked down on a colony of rats that scurried about hell-bent on errands. The rotted wood in the windows and door frames housed a family of poisonous tropical centipedes, half a foot long, who enjoyed sharing your bed occasionally. But worst of all was the absence of color: bare wood, bare cement, bare floors, plastic wall paper so long unwashed that it was now uncleanable glum beige maybe once a faded yellow, a filth-caked colorless gray world. We later discovered that the foreigners' guest house, as it was called, was a remnant of the Japanese occupation of Wuhan in the '30s, officers' quarters for the most hated and feared brutalizers of the Wuhanese. We inhabited an evil ghost of their bloody history. If it flooded and collapsed over our heads, any normal Chinese would cheer. Invaders gone at last, and good riddance to them.

At the official welcome, we were greeted stiffly by Smiley and the assembly of big potato university officials, lukewarm green tea in covered blue porcelain cups, all the overstuffed chairs pushed against the walls so that we all stared out into the cloud of dust motes drifting toward the empty center of the room. Speeches vowing eternal friendship between nations, the solidarity of peoples, the progress of the "Four Modernizations" for feudal China, much smiling and awkward translation, more tea— hot water poured out of a tin kettle to rejuvenate the soggy leaves at the bottom of the cup by pretty serving girls with bored sullen faces. Then came the warnings—what not to mention, the thing that did not happen on June 4, 1989—still unhappened three years afterward. I took notes that day and afterward made a little found poem from the mouths of Chinese cadres. A psychologist would call these remarks "denial," but a human being would call them lies. That's where the lizard in the poem comes from, the old lizard of public lies.

OFFICIAL TALK IN WUHAN: 1992

When nothing has happened there is no need
to mention it, it would only prove
embarrassing if certain policies
were brought up, though of course
everything, as you see, is fully
ordinary, moving forward, though without
any backward to move forward
from, and everyone smiles and is
happy, doing their part, though of what
they are not too sure, only little

months or years have disappeared,
nothing much and nothing serious if
a little time goes quietly away
here and there, and isn't mentioned because
there's no need really, besides what
good would it do anyone, it might
cause painful thoughts and you can
see for yourself clearly the shops
are full, there's plenty to eat, the future's
just around the corner, and the past
is looking better every day. Meanwhile
an old lizard the size of a bulldozer
perches on the flat cement roof.
All the sleepers in their cold flats
listen to his raspy breathing all night,
watch his scaly tail hang just over
the edge, wave back and forth past their window,
thud into the wall now and then
like a hanged body blown
against the gallows by the east wind.

Thus fortified I began teaching. The first shock was the discovery that, having spent considerable money and taken considerable trouble to ship American literature texts to China where
they were (in any recognizable form) unavailable, I was scheduled
to teach only British literature. My only immediate examples
were poems of Wordsworth or Yeats or sentences of Dr. Johnson
that I carried around in my head. "A slight misunderstanding,"
said Smiley. Indeed.

The next shock was section B. I always began teaching simply,
speaking slowly, keeping to an elementary vocabulary, reading
an easy poem or story. In every other Chinese class I'd taught, I
found myself quickly surprised by the intellectual alertness and

language skills of the students. Then I would raise the discourse level toward thunder and humor. But not in section B. The simplest English defeated them, blank bored faces, utter incomprehension, a cement wall. After a few manic weeks of trying to assault them, I asked one of my old students what the hell was going on. "Section B is . . . special. They failed their entrance exams but they paid money—good money—for degrees. They are children of high cadres who are—can you say?—not so quick. But degrees are necessary in the new China." "Why am I teaching them?" "They paid for you."

More shocks followed as the weeks passed. Cold rain fell incessantly, temperatures hovered barely above freezing, no heat at all—only a primitive electric iron stand that first smoked ominously and then blew out all the fuses in the building whenever it was plugged in, the roof leaking in twelve places (I counted over and over), stories of official corruption, swindling on contracts, skimming state money allocated for foreign salaries, sad stories of political abuse, thought examinations, self-criticisms written from threats and fear, a magnificent artist in porcelain now teaching toilet design, more rain, a cold damp bed, a chair collapsed into smithereens under my now bruised butt, pilfered mail, Smiley visits again, more sheets of sleet sweeping down the Yangtze, more section B. Still, as always in China, there were pleasures, a magnificent cheap hun-dun restaurant a few blocks away, lively political discussions and storytelling, dinners at the modest flats of our three old pals and former students, a duplicate bridge tournament, some smart new students in section A and section C, even a half-dry though gray chilly day now and then.

But one thing completed the breaking of Holm's heart already recently half broken from watching the long awful dying of his old friend, the Seattle doctor. From 1987, when I had left, till the

spring of 1992, China had declined; I saw the mean-spirited bullying of any Chinese intellectual foolish enough to cling to idealism
by the lowest human pond-scum officials who would lie, cheat,
sell out their friends, connive, and plot at the expense of the innocent as easily as they smiled when you entered a room. One
day I taught Yeats—for I needed no textbook for this poem with
its drowned innocense, its tale of blood:

> The best lack all conviction, while the worst
> Are full of passionate intensity.

I announced to sections A and C and probably even to the un-
comprehending B, who said, "This poem is only about Ireland in
1920. It has no relevance whatever to China and its current inner
state, and it makes no allusion whatever to anything that certainly did not happen recently. You may safely disregard both the
language and content of this poem."

But I could not weep for my anger. What I saw wound me into
a knot of fury, grief, frustration at my inability to do anything at
all, coupled to the certainty that any action I might take or scenes I
might make could only harm those I loved and respected in China.
I would wake abruptly in the middle of the night to sit bolt upright
with clenched fists, cursing, demanding, like Job, some answer to
"why?" On these nights I often terrified the sane woman sleeping
next to me on the damp broken bed with the cold rain dripping
onto the musty quilt. She saw everything I saw and more.

The brilliant sculptor who designed toilets invited Marcy
and me and a couple of Chinese friends to see his private studio,
a ramshackle room in a Hankow slum that turned out to be a
gallery crammed with delicate and lovely art. We rose early on
Saturday, took the long jammed bus ride from the college to the

big river, where we joined another mob to board the ferry to the
northern shore. I remember half-starved children, women in rags,
gnarled old men with flat, dead faces, the beaten-down urban
poor of China, then, now, forever. I remember a dwarf who came
to stare at the six-and-a-half-foot, pink-faced, now almost white-
headed barbarian. The dwarf stared up, up, up, then touched the
foreign leg as if it might be a talisman to add a foot or two to his
height. The sun was out for the first time in weeks and did its
best to inject syringes of light into the murky Yangtze. We spent
hours admiring the toilet maker's art, then it was dinner time.
We ate Wuchang perch, rice pancakes, fish flavored pork, and hot
chili bean curd, washed down with many bottles of good local
beer. The food, as so often in China, was splendid even in the
most unpretentious hovel of a restaurant, and there was laughter
with it, but somehow a melancholy sleepiness settled over me. I
supposed I was feeling Virgil's tears in things. As we crossed back
over the river in half dark, rain started to fall again. Then the long
slow bus down to the college street. The rain had turned the street
to greasy mud for the last half-mile walk to the college gate. We
all walked slowly, me slowest of all.

A block or two from the gate, a great invisible boulder fell from
the damp sky and landed on my chest. I did not cry out, did not
make a noise, did not call the woman or the sculptor or my friend
the Fish a hundred yards ahead. I did not lose consciousness. I did
not lose my wits. My heart had cracked; I was islanded again, marooned alone with nothing but the black sea for a thousand miles
in any direction. When they missed me, they all came back to find
me leaning against a tree, face ash gray. I snapped at them, "Get
the hell away. I just need a little time to get home to bed. Leave.
Go. Damn you, don't look at me." The invisible boulder pressed
into the chest, as if a celestial boot heel pushed against it, trying

to smother me. The gallbladder was a sharper island, the tooth larger, but this . . . this was the heaviest island. It anchored on top of me. This was the weight of a million years of oceans rising and falling, mountains washed away, bones sucked into swampy muck, a glacier growing almost audibly, crunching rock as it swelled to begin sliding downhill.

None of these metaphors occurred to me as I leaned against the sycamore tree on the grimy street while the passing Chinese stopped to stare, wondering when the pink, now turned gray, barbarian would fall forward into the mud. I thought of nothing but to drive them all away, friends, strangers, the ghost of the by-now dead Auntie Clarice. I would not be seen on this island. Death or life. One or the other. Now. The hell with you all. Go!

I walked the last block or two to the college, each step weighing fifty tons. Someone called Smiley. A masked nurse arrived with a cotton oxygen bag that looked like a feeble bagpipe bellows. I waved it away. Fish tried to calm me. Marcy tried. I snarled. Children gathered to stare. Everything in China is public: murder, love, sex, death. I snarled again, a caged island. An old Shanghai sedan arrived, piloted by the school driver summoned from his bed. We drove to a military hospital. When we arrived, someone summoned a gurney. I snarled again and walked in. I laid down on a dirty blood-stained sheet. A flurry of Chinese. Stethoscope. Blood-pressure cuff. Questions: Are you diuretic? What? Sugar sick? No. Get me my pants. Myocardial infarction. On the next blood-stained gurney, a bleeding young woman, a terrified man by her side. Smell of urine and Lysol. Get me my pants: I'm leaving. A hypodermic. Put this under your tongue. Don't chew. Good night, sweet prince.

The next days are shrouded in sedative fog. A dirty room with blue peeling walls. A piss cup. Faces. The weight gone. Now only a mental fog and a tube or two or three going out. One sentence only obsessed me: get me my pants, get me out of here. Smiley appeared. Another flurry of Chinese. I am the subject. I want only to be absent. Inedible food. Gray fishy broth. Mealy rice. Get me my pants. I've got to go. Get the hell out of here. Leave me alone. Take these goddamn tubes away.

I lay there two weeks, though they lasted centuries. Students came, old friends, Smiley, Marcy always, an old doctor, a young doctor, a pretty nurse to cut toenails—I called her Cat for her gravelly voice and tall lithe body, an old ugly nurse who, missing the vein, jammed a tube into my leg till it swelled to the size of a tree stump saturated with glucose and Chinese herbs.

Through a mist of language, I became gradually aware that I was the subject of a bureaucratic money quarrel, the military hospital wanting to charge Smiley a fortune for keeping the foreigner, Smiley wanting to end the drain on her skimmed budget. I harangued for my pants and escape, but was cautioned to practice forbearance—till the money wars were settled. I still had the vague suspicion that the reaper was not quite ready to gather me in, but they all kept assuring me of my frailty. If you want to become frail, lie still in a bed for two weeks; frailty will lie down to join you. One night I violated everyone's orders to stay prone and walked around the room. My feet stung and I was dizzy. The next night, weary of piss cups and bedpans, I walked down the long hall in the middle of the night to the filthy communal squatter which served as the hospital toilet. The lovely Cat came to check my toenails again, and this cheered me up a little. I wanted my pants.

That army hospital was the most profoundly lonely island I ever occupied. Half terrified of dying, half full of rage and claustrophobia, I wanted simply to disappear from anyone who had ever seen or known me. Let this catastrophe run its course in darkness.

After two weeks I was retrieved back to the filthy flat. Well-wishers arrived. I wanted to scourge them from the temple but practiced patience. I sneaked a few smokes, had a few bowls of fragrant hun-dun from my favorite food stand, began to anchor my island back into the world.

One night, the next-door neighbor, a Maryknoll nun, came over to chat with Marcy. I grabbed *Letters from the Earth* and laid down on the mildewed bed to enjoy a few pages of Mark Twain. Past the edge of the book I noted an enormous red-pronged centipede crawling toward me fast from the next pillow. I hurled Twain at the monster and shouted. Marcy and Sister Mary, thinking I'd died at last, scurried into the bedroom. What the hell is that? Marcy chased it to the door then crushed the half-foot long demon. It did not die easily. "Why it's a poisonous centipede. Quite nasty. We had them in Korea. They always come in families," said Mary. We did not sleep well that night under the damp quilt. The next morning Marcy found the tail of another centipede under the bedroom door. She trapped it into a tea jar, then clamped the lid tight. That afternoon, Smiley the *Waiban* appeared for a financial chat. We showed her the jar. She winced. "How ugly! I don't know what they're called." She lied, of course. They are called in Chinese: *wugong,* a homonym for her employer. The next day we left for Hong Kong. When a poisonous centipede with a red pincer crawls out to your island, leave. Fast.

In Hong Kong I saw a Chinese cardiologist who sent me to a Seventh Day Adventist hospital for an angiogram—cash on the barrelhead: $3,500, we take American Express. One more time I had neglected to have health insurance, and medicine waited with open palms and itchy fingers to punish my negligence. Naked in a room full of lead suits, I had the pleasure of watching on a TV monitor a ten-foot pig wire shoved up into the arteries.

The Chinese cardiologist said I was in grave danger, but a quick bypass—a great bargain for fifteen or twenty thousand in Hong Kong—would save me. The next day I went to the airport to buy a ticket from Hong Kong to Minnesota. There, a more prudent doctor advised me to take an aspirin daily and try to practice better habits. The *wu gong* crawled through my dreams for a long time. I often heard in my inner ear the voice of my dead doctor friend imploring me: Don't go. Don't Go. I'd gone—and discovered an island farther from the mainland than any I ever imagined on earth.

In this little Chinese adventure I heard the louder flapping of the death bird's wings. This, probably, was the penultimate islanding that will ever happen. One more and out. That is that. Yet, oddly, as the heart cracked on that muddy Chinese street, the fear of my own disappearance was not the primary surging inside. I feared most the disappearance of my membership in the human race, of being islanded once and for all. I wanted not help but flight, to crawl inside the sycamore tree I leaned against as the stone pressed down on me, where I could be neither seen nor touched nor addressed in any language. As a boy on my father's farm, animals disappeared when they were wounded or ready to die. All of them—dog, cat, pig, cow—shared this deeply coded mammalian instinct to disappear. Islanding seemed not strictly a human phenomenon, but was echoed everywhere in nature, everywhere except in sentimental novels whose readers apparently took a prurient interest in the private miseries of islanded characters. I shared no such interest; I preferred characters clearly alive or clearly dead, including my own.

I wonder, to this day, if the Wuhan islanding didn't represent an old cliché that grew a concrete body, a leached-out metaphor come back to life. The heart literally broke—not from cholesterol but from grief, suppressed anger, a collapse of faith and trust in human decency. Random events coagulated into a stone and sank inside, but at the bottom of pain the life force itself decided it would not be finally islanded and swam for shore with all its power. Maybe in this event lay the wisdom of the old liturgical prayer: "The sacrifices of God are a broken spirit: a broken and contrite heart. O God, thou wilt not despise." Who the hell wants a broken heart? Maybe we all need one now and then in order to see the world with any clarity.

When the body islands you, the details stay clear inside you forever like some ancient Russian icon whose colors glow with greater intensity as the centuries pass. But when the soul islands you, it carves great chunks out of your life. You are the amputee who looks down at his absent hand to imagine the ghost thumb twitching or the disappeared index finger pointing directions. Your nervous system invents a phantom out of air, but the real thing is gone forever.

I've lost six months of my life, and its disappearance was so complete that for years I never realized it was gone. At fifty-six, a man has quite enough half years to keep track of anyway. The hell with six months. If a recovered-memory shyster tried to get it back inside me, I'd drive him out of the house—with a gun if necessary. No matter though. Memory disappears for good reasons, and it not only ought to stay gone, it will. You resuscitate only phantoms.

I lost half of 1961, from the night of my high-school graduation until my second semester as a student at a college in western Minnesota. I spent the first eighteen years of my life loathing the farm, the high school, all sports, the constipated timid-hearted small-town culture, American business mania, hypocritical religiosity coupled with smug ignorance of the rest of the world. Is that an extensive enough list for a young fellow to spend his energy loathing? I longed for college—my only escape, where, presumably, civilized people read books, drank wine, played chamber music, said sophisticated and ironic sentences to each other, and made love grandly. Don't judge this foolish young fellow too harshly, Sensible Reader. It is the job of the young to be passionately discontented with the world, filled with high-minded contempt for any interference with the grandeur of their own yearning, their plans to reinvent civilization right. We age toward ironic resignation fast enough. Anyone so young who thinks that present reality is just ducky has already died at puberty and will certainly begin smelling quite terrible inside before he is finally embalmed. Staying entirely alive until you achieve your death requires you to start at the top of the hill with the brakes off so that you can pick up a little speed on the way downhill toward senescence.

I had planned my escape: graduate and go. My father had given up on me as a future farmer, and my mother already had my bags packed to do what she herself had dreamed of doing thirty years before but couldn't. A week after graduation, on a warm day in early June, my father, Big Bill Holm, had a massive stroke while chasing cattle with a neighbor. I know this fact, but I do not remember it. He was shuffled from podunk hospital to podunk hospital, badly treated by ignorant and inattentive doctors who abandoned him as a hopeless hemiplegic, his voice still intact but his body ruined. I know these facts too, and I was certainly present through every hour and day of his misery, but I do not remember it. His farm machinery along with his pack-ratted farm

junk and all his livestock—cattle, pigs, chickens, geese—were
sold at auction at the hilltop farm homesteaded by his father and
grandfather. The Allis-Chalmers combine went, the Farmall M,
the old 1020, the swather, the binder, the plow, the drag, all the
drills and chisels and grease guns and socket wrenches that keep
a farm running. All for sale. Come and get it. I was certainly
present at that sale but I do not remember it. My mother rented
a cold-water flat in a house owned by one of her brothers and
moved my father, now islanded in his crank-up invalid's bed, to
town. She packed up thirty years' accumulation of family furniture and goods and crammed them into the bottom half of a
square, white, frame house, a drafty semi-ruined relic from the
late nineteenth century. I must have helped. I must have been at
least present. I do not remember. Relatives came to her to try to
make her talk sense to her fat, lazy, shameless son, to make him
give up the foolishness of college—no money for it, no health
insurance, a ruined father—to stay home and farm his grandfather's land like a proper son. My mother would hear nothing
of it. I was surely present at and involved in these quarrels. I remember not a thing. I must have packed my precious books and
scribbled poems, some clothes and soap and towels, and begged
a ride 120 miles away to college. My mother never drove a car,
and I was forbidden by scholarship rules to have one on campus.
How did I get there? I have since been told, but I do not remember either packing up or arriving. I started college, signed up for
classes, did poorly in some and well in others, made friends, met
people. I do not remember. None of it. All gone. A mental alien
abduction minus the aliens. I was islanded by memory, disappeared from the human race for a little while.

Around Christmas my mind began coming back into itself. I had
survived a semester, even pleased a teacher or two with my strange

wits, made friends who have lasted for almost forty years, fallen in love at a great distance with several women, and written two or three lines of passable poetry. The details of life cleared, as when the wind dies down after a blizzard so you can finally see across the street that others are still alive too. But not a minute of those last six months ever came back to me then, nor have they since.

Why did they go? Why this islanded absence from consciousness? Your guess is probably as good as mine, but I'll give you mine for whatever wisdom there might be in it. For eighteen years I had been carefully fabricating the mental picture of my escape. I imagined myself gone—daily. Elgar's pompous march bleating out of trumpet bells sang to me the song of final liberation. I was a classic spoiled boy, the creation of my mother's thwarted ambition to escape her farm life. My relation to my father—any eighteen-year-old boy's relation to his father—was, to make an understatement, awkward. Bill Holm was a farmer— complete and whole, unimaginable as anything else. I think that he never in his adult life worked for anyone: he had never cashed a paycheck. His own mother, widowed when he was three, had moved her family to Minneota to raise them in 1909, but my father left school to return to the farm as soon as he was a teenager. The farm had by this time been lost in a 1920s land speculation debacle, so he simply returned there to spend twenty years buying it back. He emerged finally from debt in 1943, the year his first and only son was born. He was a scrupulously honest and foolishly generous man; he loathed tightwads, sneaks, those eaten by greed and ambition. He wanted only to be clear of debt, so that he could be his own man on his own land. Once he stopped work on a sunny dry day to go to town ostensibly to fix a tractor part, but actually to drink beer and play cards with his buddies, to have a good time. He ordered his hired man to stop work and come to town with him. Ralph said there was plenty of work to get done on

the farm with the good weather, and that's what my father paid
him to do. "Goddamn it, Ralph," said my father. "It's my goddamn
farm, and if I want to pay you for coming to town to keep me
company, I can goddamn well do it. Work can wait till tomorrow."
Ralph, it goes without saying, has loved and admired my father
and his memory for fifty or sixty years. My father was a large-
hearted man. He loved humans more than money.

But more than anything else, he was a large-bodied man. He
did not live in an intellectual world though he read novels every
night before bed; his was the physical world of sweat, muscle,
hard dirty work. His exterior was rough, his voice loud and profane, his skin leathery from wind and sun, his hands mammoth
and gnarly. He swore grandly—though unconsciously—but even
the ministers (whose church he attended once a year from duty)
forgave him for it. His sentences ended with a bellered "eh?"
though he was not Canadian. Salesmen and strangers were sometimes frightened of his bluster and physical size and power, but
they quickly discovered his interior mildness—even a desire to
please others. I never saw him strike a live creature—human or
animal—but he would beat his combine or tractor mercilessly
with his cast-iron fists when they had broken down at an incon-
venient time. He could, of course, have killed any sentient creature with those extraordinarily powerful hands, but no one who
had met him for five minutes worried about it. I wrote a prose
poem about his hands long after he died.

BIG BILL HOLM

This strong, nervous, profane man loved whiskey, stories, and
laughter. He had a velvety spirit but the alligator hide of a blond
man who sat on a tractor in wind and sun too long. I got dragged
along with him into the Powerhouse when I was a boy, while he

and Uncle Avy Snidal, with his clawed thumb—the only remains
of his hand, and Einar the Mayor Hallgrimsson and farmers from
north of town sat around drinking, waiting for the combine to get
fixed. He goddamned this, and goddamned that, and goddamned
a politician as "an asshole too dumb to piss with his pants full."
Finally one of the farmers snuck down the street to the hardware
store, came back with 60-penny spikes, and Bill Holm with grunts
and "ehs" got coerced into his trick. He took out of his striped
overalls pocket an old red handkerchief, full of oats dust and
sweat, and wrapped it around the spike. He bent the handkerchief, turning the big nail into a perfect V. Some farmer always
picked up the bent spikes that clunked to the bar and hung them
together like fence links. Those souvenirs from his strong hands
went home from the Minneota liquor store while I sat in amazed
silence wondering at my father's power. After a while, a couple of
farmers gone one whiskey over the top of the dam started argu-
ing about the right time to sell cattle, the best soybean fertilizer,
the cleanest barn. Voices rose; closed fists began circling the beer
bottles. My father, who liked loud talk but hated fights, came up
behind, locking a vise-grip hand affectionately on each neck:
"Hell, boys, let's have a drink over here, I'll buy." The fight ended
before it started, throttled by that spike-bending thumb pressed
into a neck. What good is strength if you have to use it? That's
what my father taught me without meaning to.

Despite inheriting his size, I was, in fact, a delicate moody
boy—a mama's boy—lost in books and music, lazy, willful, bored
by the farm. My father loved me, though he must often have
looked at me with a bleary eye and thought, "What creature have
I hatched?" And I would look at him, his shit-caked overalls, his
red face, his callouses, his string of goddamn son of a bitches, and
I would envy the prissy soft-spoken white-shirted fathers of the
town boys. But I could escape! I was going to college! The whole

universe beckoned, and I would never have to see the damned farm again except in passing! Excelsior!

And then the stroke. And then the end of it all, the collapse of the intricately imagined life I had fashioned for myself in the private recesses of my consciousness. The island of blessed escape sank and the black island of entrapment rose under my feet. It was unbearable to see this powerful man languishing crippled in a bed, longing to die, but unable to do it. For my father was now islanded by pain—both psychic and physical—that I still cannot get my mind around. For five years he lay waiting for some happy circumstance to carry him off once and for all into oblivion. My mother waited on him day and night for those five years, slept on a pallet at the foot of his bed. She hated it. He hated it. I was simply a vapor drifting in and out from some interior Kathmandu or Addis Ababa. I was working hard to remember nothing at all. My mother was a fiercely passionate woman, one of whose passions was loyalty. For all of their noisy quarrels, the two were bound to each other with unsentimental love, and she would have kept him alive for a century if she could have managed it.

Meanwhile, those six months of my life got into a canoe and paddled off out to open water. Presumably they found an undiscovered island—some bleak and stormy outcrop washed by icy tides—where they unpacked their bags to make camp until I summon them back. I will not now summon them. I exile them to the island of forgetfulness for eternity. I remember quite enough.

That is what it is like to be islanded by body and by soul. It has happened to you too, Sensible Reader, and it will happen again—to both of us. Maybe, in spite of all my linguistic fulminations, English really does need one more peculiar verb, if the universe keeps taking it into its head to island a man every now and then. Mostly, we live through it.

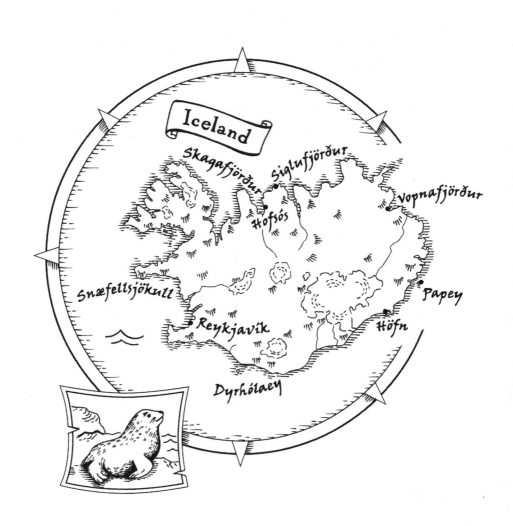

Iceland

Skagafjörður
Siglufjörður
Vopnafjörður
Hofsós
Snæfellsjökull
Papey
Reykjavik
Höfn
Dyrhólaey

⁀ Iceland 1999

THE OUTLAW'S ISLAND, THE POPE'S ISLAND, AND WHAT WE MUST DO TO BE CIVILIZED

After that summer on the farm in 1979 I thought hard of becoming an Icelander, of saying toodle-oo to the United States once and for all. What would I miss? Television? Kmart? The Pentagon? Cheap gas and whiskey? Winter baseball tomatoes? Richard Nixon? Fundamentalists? Big Macs? Whitman, Ives, Emerson I carried with me wherever I went, whoever cashed my tax check. My parents were dead, my marriage ended, no children waited to greet my homecoming with joy. My friends had credit cards and could damn well use them if they wanted to see me. I had no job waiting. And what job would I find? Another go at academic pettiness? (what I called "politics for midgets"), teaching students so bored with literature—even language itself—that they stared blankly at you as if you were a television set tuned to the wrong channel? Why not, in Confucian fashion, light a candle to ceremonially ask atonement from all my emigrated ancestors, then come home to the island where my DNA belonged?

But—always a but—I missed not the United States but the English language as it is spoken by ordinary people, even by phlegmatic Minnesota farmers. Not the English spoken in the academy, the government, the church, the striving suburbs, but the true music of everyday speech in tavern, coffee shop, hog yard, old folk's home. Here I heard metaphor, feeling, humor as I would never hear them in Icelandic or any other language. They exist there, of course; no language anywhere has ever been or can ever be without them, but I was too old, my ear too fixed, to hear them. If I wanted to write books, I had to go home and sink into language like this: "Didn't you used to be somebody?" a woman was asked by an old farmer at a blood bank. Or the old lady staring out the laundromat window at the funeral procession: "You know, I never seen a hearse pull no U-Haul." Or the two old Norwegian farmers meeting at the post office on a snowy morning in Wendell, Minnesota: "Sorry to hear about your wife how are the roads?" Then a long pause, as if deep in thought: "There's a big drift out by Larson's woods but she went fast." The United States, such a graceless, bumbling idiot of a country, so in love with guns, shopping, television, and primitive religiosity, goaded me into language. Somebody had to be around to try to improve it—to kick the dead language and worn-out ideas in the hind end. So I went home.

I wrote books. I taught school. I traveled to every place I could afford, or had an offer. I fell in love again. The United States, astonishingly, even began to seem normal to me one more time. As Bertolt Brecht said, "I wear / A derby on my head as others do." While Iceland crept sideways into my prose or poetry as a metaphor, I didn't go back for almost twenty years. Was I afraid that if I went I would stay forever—the hell with English? Was my romantic view of either culture or landscape merely a phantasm, some interior projection unconnected to reality? Or was it merely the fact that I had other places to go and no large extra doses of money—so necessary to even stay alive in this expensive island?

I know answers to none of these questions. Some intuition told me to stay away for a while, so I did. Never insult or ignore your intuition.

Finally, in 1997, intuition changed its mind and, like Eliot's pub keeper announced, "HURRY UP PLEASE IT'S TIME." I left, this time by air. Bakkafoss took passengers no more.

Was this the Reykjavík I left in 1980? Or, like Rip Van Winkle, had I slept through a generation or two? Four-lane motorways with spaghetti junctions circled the town, there were miles of new concrete office buildings and blocks of flats in the favorite no-nonsense modern rectangle style, and Kringlan—the enclosed mall of Iceland—adorned muzak, health food, and computer shops, a yuppie market with kiwi fruit, mangos, and whole-grain pasta. Downtown Reykjavík now had both vegetarian smoke-free cafés and little bars on every corner with draft beer, cognac, and tattooed purple-spiked-haired metallic body-ornamented citizens reposing behind black mirror glasses. TV had arrived from Europe and the United States seven days a week and all of July—CNN, soaps, rock videos, shopper channel. Every driver in Iceland (now stocked with cars sufficient to enjoy real traffic jams) chattered away over cell phones, laptops on the seat next to them waiting to be pulverized when the air bag explodes. Where were the sheep? The crank phones? The gravel roads? The basement vats of illegal home brew? The old farmers who knew ten thousand lines of ancient poetry and could improvise a passable imitation of them instantly? My God, the Icelanders had even taken up golf—ringing the city with putting greens decorating the lava. All the toys and habits of high-tech industrial capitalism had arrived in less than two decades at Ultima Thule, this island of books and ghosts once the outer margin of the habitable world.

It had, of course, happened before. Everything has happened

before, so many times. A quarter of the way into the century, just after World War I, Iceland skipped over the Renaissance, the Industrial Revolution, and the Enlightenment to proceed directly from the middle ages to the modern world, like some mad Monopoly player not stopping at Go. Tractors, cars, electricity, radio, airplanes, a fully mechanized fishing fleet arrived in an eye blink at a country still living in the twelfth century, as if some medieval serf had stepped out of vespers in a Gothic cathedral to find a new Plymouth waiting for him, all eight cylinders purring. World War II finished the modernizing so that Reykjavík, when I arrived in 1979, felt like the America of my childhood in the '40s and '50s. At the end of the century, it seemed a science-fiction novel come to life. Maybe they'd even thought of doming the country to tame the undependable arctic weather once and for all with climate control.

But the old Iceland survived too, under all the high-tech glitter and market-economy glitz. I am not the first traveler to have been worried about the arrival of modern life in this magical backwater of an island. Literary travelers (with the exception of Richard Burton, who preferred Mecca and Salt Lake City) have for the last two hundred years all fallen prey to the seductive myth of Iceland: the land of farmer intellectuals guarding their precious language like a dragon squatting on a gold hoard, hurling intricate poems by the thousands into the teeth of blizzards arrived from the Greenland ice cap.

In 1936 W. H. Auden and Louis MacNeice arrived in Reykjavík, both twenty-nine years old, the two leading young poets of their generation. MacNeice knew he was an Irishman, but Auden—all his life—fancied himself an Icelander by descent. He thought Auden an Anglicization of Odin, the old Norse god. It's a good ancestry for a compulsive scribbler of poems to claim, and while

Auden may or may not have been right in the physical sense, he was certainly right about his spiritual descent. *Letters from Iceland,* perhaps the most peculiar travel book in English, is more than anything else a book about books, mostly a poem about poems.

In a bus lurching over the lava desert east of Mývatn, Auden "had a bright idea about this travel book. I brought a Byron with me to Iceland, and I suddenly thought I might write him a chatty letter in light verse about anything I could think of, Europe, litera-ture, myself." Auden being Auden, it is mostly about books. "This letter in itself will have very little to do with Iceland, but will be rather a description of an effect of travelling in distant places which is to make one reflect on one's past and one's culture from the outside." He finds—and would still find sixty-four years later—most travel books boring, an endless repetition of events "extremely like each other—meals—sleeping accommodation—fleas—dangers" He claims to be "neither clever enough nor sensi-tive enough" to write the alternative: "essays [like D. H. Lawrence] on life, prompted by something seen." Auden saw words and lines on a page very clearly; for a man of his habit of mind, books *are* life. I share his predilection, and in this we are both being thor-oughly Icelandic.

Auden and MacNeice's real tour guides are Grettir, Gunnar, Njal, Egill—the old saga heroes, who haul the two young travelers along from perception to perception. At Hólar, the old bishop's seat of north Iceland, Auden encounters Hermann Göring's brother and Alfred Rosenberg on pilgrimage. Auden comments that "the Nazis have a theory that Iceland is the cradle of the Germanic culture. Well, if they want a community like that of the sagas they are welcome to it. I love the sagas, but what a rotten society they describe, a society with only the gangster virtues." Iceland swarmed with Nazis in the '30s; Hitler, who didn't know

Icelanders very well, intended to turn the island into a religious shrine for the Aryans. Auden, who had read more than one book, knew romantic foolishness when he encountered it.

"Journey to Iceland," one of Auden's finest poems, compresses into a few of its stanzas a compendium of the most famous Icelandic books—teachers of "prose and conduct."

> Then let the good citizen here find natural marvels:
> The horse-shoe ravine, the issue of steam from a cleft
>> In the rock, and rocks, and waterfalls brushing the
>> Rocks, and among the rocks birds.
>
> And the student of prose and conduct, places to visit;
> The site of a church where a bishop was put in a bag,
>> The bath of a great historian, the rock where
>> An outlaw dreaded the dark.
>
> Remember the doomed man thrown by his horse and crying;
> "Beautiful is the hillside, I will not go";
>> The old woman confessing: "He that I loved the
>> Best, to him I was worst,"
>
> For Europe is absent. This is an island and therefore
> Unreal. And the steadfast affections of its dead may be bought
>> By those whose dreams accuse them of being
>> Spitefully alive . . .

Whether Europe was absent in 1936—or ever—or whether islandness dooms one to unreality are questions that would provoke most readers to an entertaining quarrel with Auden. Islands are not continents, thank God, and I have often felt a vague intuition that North America was the unrealest property on the planet. By 1940 Iceland would be circled by German submarines and occupied first by the British, then by the Americans. The NATO base at Keflavík and the radar tracking station at Höfn are visible ghosts of the presence of Europe and its wars.

In 1964 Auden, by now a gray eminence, returned to Iceland for the first time since 1936. During the intervening twenty-eight years, World War II had brought sudden prosperity to Iceland, devastated Europe, and made Auden into an American. MacNeice was dead, the automobile had replaced the horses Auden loved so much, Reykjavík had turned from a corrugated-iron hamlet into a modern city of concrete buildings, and Iceland had finally regained its independence again after seven hundred long years. Like any old traveler (and like me) who returns to visit a magical experience of youth, Auden is both nostalgic and suspicious of change. "For me personally, it was a joy to discover that, despite everything which had happened to Iceland and myself since my first visit, the feelings it aroused were the same. In my childhood dreams Iceland was holy ground; when, at the age of twenty-nine, I saw it for the first time, the reality verified my dream; at fifty-seven it was holy ground still, with the most magical light of anywhere on earth. Furthermore, modernity does not seem to have changed the character of the inhabitants. They are still the only really classless society I have ever encountered, and they have not—not yet—become vulgar."

Not yet. Not even in 1999. In an interview Auden said that Iceland had proved its capacity to endure poverty with grace and civility, but no one was yet quite sure whether any civilization could survive prosperity without becoming vulgar—and stupid. What would Auden have thought of Kringlan mall—canned muzak and all—or the vision of fifty automobiles parked in a row with fifty drivers babbling on their cell phones, ignoring the light on Mount Esja or the terns crying overhead? Sensible Reader, beware nostalgic fulmination, but keep in mind, particularly if you are American, that sometimes vulgarity lays its head down next to your sleeping body at night and, by morning, like the ominous exploding seedpods from *Invasion of the Body Snatchers,* has occupied the soul.

The soul of Iceland looked healthy to me that summer. Whatever the progress of urbanization—or, to be more precise, suburbanization—of Reykjavík and its environs, the Icelandic countryside was still inhabited by dreamers, eccentrics, poets— whether in language, music, carpentry, fish, or whatever obsession possessed them. After two or three experiences—epiphanies—the idea came to me that poetry need not be made only of language, but that human beings were capable of a poetry of gesture: some act of imaginative generosity (or generous imagination) so full of feeling, metaphor, spontaneous wisdom that it metamorphosed into a kind of behavioral poetry.

The roots of this poetry of gesture lie deep in Icelandic history and culture. The *Hávamál,* the ancient "Words of the High One" in the *Elder Edda* still remind Icelanders—and indeed the rest of us—that:

> It is always better to be alive,
>> The living can keep a cow:
> Fire, I saw, warming a wealthy man,
>> With a cold corpse at his door.

There's no afterlife or glorified body in the *Hávamál;* and you, Sensible Reader who mumbles the liturgy, how certain are you? We live on only in language and memory, the stories of us alive.

Cattle die, kindred die,
Every man is mortal:
But the good name never dies
Of one who has done well.

Does this mean that only generals, plutocrats, politicians, sports stars, and serial killers can hope for stories to be told in the high hall? The *Hávamál* is smarter than *People* magazine or the Dow Jones.

The nitwit does not know that gold
Makes apes of many men:
One is rich, one is poor—
There is no blame in that.

You gain immortality not by amassing money, but by some act or gesture that captures the imagination.

I'll give two examples of the poetry of gesture and how it operates in ancient Icelandic literature. Both stories deal with unexpected gifts. *Njal's Saga*, Iceland's *Iliad*, begins with the story of a man named Hrut traveling to Norway to prosecute a lawsuit over an inheritance, and also to make his fortune and reputation as a successful Viking raider. He leaves a fiancée behind in Iceland, a beautiful woman named Unnur. In Norway he falls into a hot affair with the queen mother, Gunnhild. When he leaves her to return to his betrothed in Iceland, Gunnhild puts a witch's curse on him that he should be unable to consummate his marriage. The curse works; the furious Unnur divorces Hrut, reclaims her dowry at the Alþing, and in the process, of course, humiliates him. Hrut refuses to accept the financial penalty and challenges Unnur's father, Mord Fiddle, to a *hólmganga*—going out to an island to fight it out. Mord, who had no death wish, refuses to fight Hrut—

a famous warrior who isn't in the habit of losing such battles. Hrut and his brother, Höskuld, ride home from Þingvellir after the disastrous legal proceedings but are stopped by heavy rains so they stay the night at the farm of a man called Thjostolf. The saga continues:

> Thjostolf sat between Hoskuld and Hrut. Two boys who were under his care were playing on the floor with a little girl; they were chattering loudly with the folly of youth.
>
> One of the boys said, "I'll be Mord and divorce you from your wife on the grounds that you couldn't have intercourse with her."
>
> The other boy replied, "Then I'll be Hrut and invalidate your dowry-claim if you don't dare to fight me."
>
> They repeated this several times, and the household burst out laughing. Hoskuld was furious, and hit the boy who was calling himself Mord with a stick. It struck him on the face and drew blood.
>
> "Get outside," said Hoskuld, "and don't try to ridicule us."
>
> "Come over here to me," said Hrut. The boy did so. Hrut drew a gold ring from his finger and gave it to him.
>
> "Go away now," he said, "and never provoke anyone again."
>
> The boy went away, saying, "I shall always remember your noble-mindedness."
>
> Hrut was highly praised for this. Later they rode off home to the west, and so ends the episode of Hrut and Mord Fiddle.

In "Audun's Story" a dirt-poor west-fjords farmhand spends "all he has" to bring a polar bear he captured in Greenland as a gift to King Svein of Denmark. He takes passage and lands in Norway, where King Harald is at war with Denmark. Harald asks him for the bear. Audun says no. He intends to give it to Harald's enemy, Svein. Harald offers to buy the bear. Audun still refuses.

Harald then says, "I think it'll be best to let you get on with your journey—it could be good luck will come your way. But I want you to do me a favour: let me know how the journey turns out." By the time Audun lands on the Danish coast, both he and the bear are close to starvation. He meets Aki, a steward of King Svein's, and asks food from him. Aki refuses to give him anything but offers to sell him food for a half share in the bear. Audun has no choice, but considers his gift spoiled. After Audun and the bear fatten up a bit, he and Aki bring the bear to King Svein, Svein asks Audun where he's from. An Icelander, he says, "I've just arrived from Norway, and before that I was in Greenland. I'd hoped to present you with this bear I bought with everything I had. I met King Harald, and he gave me leave to travel where I wanted after he made me an offer for the bear that I wouldn't take. But, my lord, when I came to see this man Aki my last penny had been spent; I was dying of hunger, and so was the bear. Now the gift's been spoiled. Aki wouldn't help me or the bear unless he got a half-share in it." The king is furious with Aki. He says, "You were a little man, Aki, and I made you great . . . yet you thought it proper to stand in the way of this man who wanted to give me a priceless gift which he'd paid for with all he had. Even King Harald, our enemy, saw fit to let him travel in peace. You deserve to be put to death. Leave this land at once, I never want to set eyes on you again. But as for you, Audun, I feel just as much in your debt as if you'd given me the entire bear. You're a welcome guest and you must stay here for a long time." Audun becomes the king's retainer, makes a pilgrimage to Rome, but after a while asks Svein's leave to return to Iceland. Svein, at first angry with what he senses as ingratitude, demands the reason. Audun must go tend to his poverty-stricken mother back home. Svein says, "You must be a lucky man. It's the only reason you could give for wanting to leave, without offending me." He gives him a ship, a bag of silver, and finally a bracelet off his arm—in case he should lose everything else.

On the way home Audun visits Harald in Norway and recounts his adventures. Harald asks what gifts he received from Svein. Audun lists them from the bear forward; after each gift Harald says he would have done the same. When Audun arrives at the royal bracelet, Harald sighs, "That was really generous, and more than I'd have done," so Audun takes the bracelet off his arm to give it to Harald in thanks for his safe passage. The saga ends with the news that Audun came home to become a man of great good fortune with many progeny—maybe W. H. Auden himself among them.

These princely gifts—bear and ring and bracelet—come from a full soul or a full ego—no niggardly calculation for future profit or advantage underlies them. These are not the gifts of the timid or small hearted, but of the madly impetuous who give everything—on a whim. The gold ring stops a bratty child better than a cuff on the ear, and, unlike the cuff, it will last. The poor farmhand behaves like the equal of kings, and the kings recognize the gesture of a natural aristocrat—their equal. Only a nitwit values gold as a marker of spirit, echoes the *Hávamál*.

The practical value for any culture to possess a literature that stays alive in the national consciousness is this: it feeds the soul stories, images, gestures as a mere recitation of dry historical fact can never do. It teaches us how to be human beings, what is our right relationship to land and nature, to other members of our peculiar tribes, and finally to the whole of mankind. Emerson and Mark Twain do a better job of making Americans than high-school civics class, stock options, or real-estate papers. Those old stories of grand aristocratic gestures and the gnomic wisdom of

the *Eddas* weigh down every Icelander firmly on his cubic yard of
lava better than his new laptop or cell phone.

Strangest of all, the Icelanders, who were never afflicted with
much enthusiasm for orthodox Christianity or any literal readings
of the Bible are, at bottom, literary fundamentalists. If you propose that God created the world in seven days, Christ was born
of a virgin and a bird and rose from the dead after three days,
almost any Icelander gives you a quizzical look, then mutters:
well, while Christ may have been a wise teacher, these myths violate both science and reason and common sense. But if you ask
whether Grettir Ásmundarsson, the greatest Icelandic outlaw,
was born at Bjarg, a farm in the north, fought a Swedish ghost at
a neighboring farm, wrestled a polar bear, lifted a ten-ton rock
and moved it, was killed by a sorcerer's spell on top of an island,
swam four miles through the ice-cold fjord to get fire from the
nearest farm (he was afraid of the dark), or that his head is buried
deep under a boulder at Bjarg, the Icelander says of course and
wonders why you are puzzled. Literature is true; religion—maybe,
maybe not. If the story has lasted a thousand years, been elegantly told in a famous and ancient book, and if half your neighbors claim descent from Grettir, then who could doubt?

The old saga of Grettir became, in fact, the instrumentality
for my return to Iceland in 1999, and, as he did for Auden and
MacNeice sixty-two years before, Grettir himself served as the
real tour guide despite being probably legendary and certainly
long dead. The dead cling to an uncanny power of remaining
lively in Iceland—maybe on all islands.

I taught Grettir to a class of undergraduates in what is called
in the Minnesota state university system "global studies semi-
nars." Students take three classes about a place—always a warm
place in the winter semester—then trot off to have a cultural

experience. It was spring, so we went to Scandinavia traveling like the terns to find light and grass finally turned green. Student travel these days in middle-class America often sinks to shopping and discos, so I determined that at least a handful of Americans would make a try at connecting landscape and culture with literature and myth. The Icelanders had just retranslated their crown jewels, the five massive volumes of sagas, into handsome and accurate English prose, and I knew and admired the editors of the edition, two smart fellows named Viðar Hreinnsson and Örnólfur Thórsson. Örnólfur agreed to do a cheap offprint of the new Grettir translation with maps, glossaries, and useful background scholarship. Viðar, who knows the sagas as an evangelist knows the Bible, offered to accompany the students north to fill their heads with saga lore. I suggested that Grettir was a better guidebook to the real Iceland than the Lonely Planet tour book. Grettir mapped not only the mountains but the soul. When you say such sentences to students, they examine you strangely.

Grettir, the last of the great Icelandic family sagas, may be the closest of them all to the hearts of Icelanders. It is an epic tale of failure, bad luck, endurance in the face of massive hardship, a hero born out of time or in a time with no use left for heroes. The anonymous author, a contemporary of Chaucer, wrote it down in the late fourteenth century, describing events four hundred years earlier. He begins, like all saga writers, with the settlement of Iceland in the ninth century and the family history and genealogy of the hero: descended from Onund Tree-Foot, Ofeig Hobbler, and Ivar Horse-Cock. All great stories are rooted in history, family, and landscape from Homer to Tolstoy or Faulkner. Television and new fiction deceive us these days with their mindless present tense.

Grettir is a bad egg from the beginning. The saga says: "Grettir was their second son. He was very overbearing as a child, taciturn and rough, and mischievous in both word and deed. His father showed him little affection, but his mother loved him dearly. [The great warriors and killers in the sagas, like Egill Skallagrimsson, are always mama's boys.] Grettir was handsome, with a broad short face, red haired and fairly freckled, and as a child he was slow to develop." He is lazy and disobedient. His father asks him to care for geese. Bored and irritated, he flies into a temper and kills all fifty of them. He is ten. He flays his father's horses alive. Asked to rub his father's back, he grates it to bloody shreds with a wool comb. When he's criticized, he grins and answers with a sarcastic obscene poem—in perfect form, of course. All this before puberty when his real trouble starts.

Grettir, on the surface, has all the heroic Viking virtues—strong, arrogant, stoical, fearless—but Iceland after 1000 is a country of farmers, mostly peaceable sheepherders and at least nominal Christians. Grettir accepts every challenge; he fights trolls and berserks, crawls inside a haunted grave mound to wrestle with the undead—and bring back money. Insult him or goad him and you are as good as dead. Bad luck, fear, and jealousy follow him, even on his Viking expedition to Norway, and he finds himself—still a teenager—outlawed.

To be an Icelandic outlaw was somewhat different from the old West notion. The legal code, fixed since 974, prescribed many offenses sentenceable by outlawry but provided no means of enforcement. To be outlawed meant literally to be outside the protection of the law; your membership in the community of civilization ceased. What did it mean? That you could be killed by anyone at any time under any circumstance without consequence or penalty. Any house that harbored you could be burned with you inside it. Few dared even to feed outlaws. You were condemned to live in the most uninhabitable places on earth, in the interior lava deserts, next to glaciers, and on impregnable cliffs. If anyone found you sleeping, you were dead game. You were alone and unprotected, no food, no shelter, no friend. Killing you was another notch toward fame in some young hot-shot Viking gun—or ax, to correct the contemporary technology. Most went to Norway for their outlawry, but even there Grettir's bad temper and bad luck dog him, and he is soon on the run everywhere. For twenty years he survives this misery—still a record in Icelandic history, a grand achievement to have stayed alive so long. He remained fierce and brave, but gradually his temper mellowed and a kind of compassionate resignation grew inside him.

Grettir, the bravest man in Iceland, slayer of trolls and bears, is afraid of the dark. The malignant ghost of a Swedish swineherd named Glam terrorizes a farm in a nearby valley. He crushes horses to bone splinters, leaves human corpses flayed and broken. Grettir, against good advice, takes him on. After a harrowing battle in which a house frame is pulled apart, rafters torn, door frames shattered, Grettir pins the undead monster down in the snow when the moon scuds out from under a cloud and he sees Glam's eyes. They unnerve him as nothing else ever will. Glam, dying, utters this curse: "You will be made an outlaw and be forced to live alone and outdoors. And this curse I lay on you: My eyes will always be before your sight. This will make it difficult for you to be alone. And this will lead to your death." And then, the saga tells us, "Grettir drew his short sword, chopped off Glam's head, and placed it against his buttocks." And Glam's curse comes exactly true.

After sixteen years of lonely wandering, Grettir finds the perfect impregnable fortress: the island Drangey, four miles out into the middle of Skagafjörður in north Iceland. Drangey is a six-hundred-foot-high sheer-sided flat-topped tuff island, the ghost of a 700,000-year-old volcanic eruption under a glacier. It rises sheer from the sea. It is virtually unclimbable without ladders, but on top you find yourself in a rich grassy meadow of a half-dozen acres, with freshwater springs. The cliffs are a cupboard full of seabird eggs and nests. Local farmers, even a thousand years ago, hoisted sheep to the top and fattened them there in the deep grass. You can drop a line six hundred feet into the sea for cod, halibut, haddock. If you pull up the ladders behind you, you are safe. Only the gulls and puffins can pay you an unexpected call, and they don't mean to kill you.

Grettir is joined there, high in the air, by his younger brother, Illugi, and a comic servant, Glaum, whose job is to tend the eternal fire that protects Grettir from the long dark of the Icelandic winter. The careless Glaum lets the fire go out. They have no boat, so Grettir swims four miles through the forty-degree fjord to the nearest farm, Reykir. He bathes his cold bones for a long time in the hot-spring pool and then, exhausted, goes into the farmhouse to fall asleep next to the fire. The next morning the women of the house find him still sleeping. A servant girl can't resist a peek at the snoring hero. "'Upon my word, sister, Grettir Asmundarson is here, lying naked. He looks big-framed to me all right, but I'm astonished to see how poorly endowed he is between his legs. It's not in proportion to the rest of him.'" Grettir wakes at the girl's giggling and chases her while reciting a boastful poem:

> I bet my bollocks are twice the size
> that other spear-thrusters boast,
> even if their shafts
> can outstretch mine.

He snatches her up on the bench with him, and the saga reports that "when she left Grettir she did not taunt him again."

The farmer gives him fire, but cannot give him life. Soon after this charming anecdote—expurgated from nineteenth-century translations of the sagas: a hero's balls? Indeed!—Grettir returns to his fortress in the sky, but is mortally wounded through the sorcery of an old witch and finally ambushed and killed by his enemies. His outlawry ends only with death, but his ghost still haunts not only Drangey, but the consciousness of every Icelander. Mattias Jochumsson, the nineteenth-century poet, sings out at the end of a long poem praising his exploits and character: "You, Grettir, are my nation." The literary fundamentalists prefer for a hero a brave man with no luck, a witty failure, a mixed character who learns forbearance from misery and loneliness to the more conventional generals and millionaires. This choice speaks well for them, I think.

Örnólfur Thórsson speculates about the outlaw sagas that "the viewpoint and narrative follow the exiles out into the world of nature and look back at society with the outlaw's own eyes. 'No man is an island'—but these outlaws are, thrown at the mercy of nature itself, and in a symbolic way they find temporary sanctuary on islands." Auden and MacNeice meet Grettir's ghost on Arnarvatn Heath just south of his old farm Bjarg. Grettir asks MacNeice:

> Memory is words; we remember what others
> Say and record of ourselves—stones with the runes.
> Too many people—sandstorm over the words.
> Is your land also an island?
> There is only hope for people who live upon islands
> Where the Lowest Common labels will not stick
> And the unpolluted hills will hold your echo.

Not only do Icelanders remember Grettir's words, no one driving around the bend in the mountains to see the first sight of Skagafjörður to the north with the straight-sided cylinder of

Drangey in the middle of it, floating in the sea mist, forgets that
it is still Grettir's island and that great and tragic things happened
there one thousand years ago and will go on happening till some
unimaginable sandstorm covers up the words. Till that sandstorm
happens I thought it a good idea for a pack of Minnesota students
to climb that island to see if the poetry of gesture still kept company with Grettir's wraith.

The Minnesota students and teachers arrived in early May, an
uncertain season for Icelandic weather, one claw of winter still
clinched into the neck, but perennial light now till late August
when the first pure darkness comes back for a few hours. Most of
the students were young women from the small-town Midwest,
pale Norwegian milkmaids. The blustery winds outside the airport blew their blond hair into horizontal saw blades. The sky
was the color of layered lead. Fat cold raindrops blew past them
from west to east, not up to down like more timid continental
spring rain. I watched their faces on the thirty-mile bus trip into
Reykjavík as they watched the bare craggy lava, hardly covered
by tan lichens, the black sea foaming onto the rock, a few damp
sheep searching out a stray grass blade. "My God, is this country habitable?" they must, like so many innocent tourists, have
thought. They had read Grettir and Halldór Laxness. Did they
imagine the outlaw skulking in one of the lava caves next to the
road, damp, shivering, hungry? At six o'clock on such a morning
after a long plane trip over half a continent and Greenland, no
one talks much.

After brief recuperation at a Reykjavík guest house, they put
on their fancy clothes for a trip to Bessastaðir to be welcomed to
Iceland by the president, now a political scientist and professor
named Ólafur Ragnar Grímsson. How many academic groups are
welcomed to a country at its version of the White House? It was

the first grand gesture of the Icelandic imagination that they saw. Some had been to Washington, where they had been welcomed by armed soldiers, metal detectors, security checks, and traffic barriers. They drove to Bessastaðir on an almost empty road, and when they arrived they knocked at the door as civilized people do when they come calling. The president, his secretary, and a lady carrying a silver tray of champagne glasses welcomed them. No police, no buzzers, no guards, no IDs. Ólafur Ragnar, an elegant man with a fine head of wavy presidential hair, eloquent in four or five languages, escorted them through the old manor house, giving them a good tour of its history and antiques, pointing with particular pride to his office where foreign dignitaries are greeted. The visitor faces a wall-sized bookshelf stuffed floor to ceiling with *some* of the editions of the works of Icelandic poets. There is not a single line of prose in the office where the nation's bills are signed into law. As it should be elsewhere. In the drawing room, the housekeeper passed glasses of champagne for a *skál;* no IDs were checked—certainly some underaged daughter guzzled a flute of her first bubbly on an official school trip. Ólafur welcomed and toasted the Americans. We toasted Iceland and the presidential hospitality. Ólafur gave a fine small speech to the students on the egalitarian, democratic tradition in Icelandic history. Pictures were taken, then Ólafur shook their hands at the door and wished them a pleasant trip north to Drangey. "You must be very careful when you climb it. It is dangerous," he said.

The next day they boarded a bus to begin their real adventure on the trail of old Grettir. Viðar sat at the front of the bus, telling story after story of the landscape we passed, Hallgrímur Pétursson's church in the whale fjord, Egil Skallagrimsson's farm at Borg, a mountain where Grettir hid for a winter, the turn to Þingvellir, the parliament plains, a haunted mountain pass, the birthplace of a great poet, the distant gleaming of two glaciers to the east. The weather alternated between shafts of sun for fifteen minutes, then blustering rain trying to blow the bus into the sea for another fifteen. We stopped at Bjarg, Grettir's birthplace, where we were met by the young farmer, Axel Sigurgeirsson, a flaming red head and beard with the face of an Irish elf or a young D. H. Lawrence. He escorted us to the grettistak, the enormous boulder Grettir lifted up and moved. It is the size of a pickup. He showed us the stone in front of his house under which Grettir's cut-off head has slept for a thousand years. Do you believe it? asks one of the girls. Of course, says Axel, as if you had asked him whether water ran downhill. The students were beginning to get the drift of literary fundamentalism. They stopped at the Hegranes plain where Grettir bested all comers at the neighborhood games. They stopped at the old turf farm, Glaumbær, where Grettir lived for a while. One young blonde sighed, "My God, we're on a Grettir Hajj." We were still about an hour from Hofsós, a tiny town on the west shore of the fjord where their beds waited for them. Now they became cranky and tired of saga lore, as might be expected of jet-lagged American students. The sky cleared and a stiff north wind with an ice bite in it rocked the bus. Drangey was now visible in the fjord, a giant stone slab lit up by the arctic sun. One girl said it looked like a birthday cake. Their minds probably turned to pizza, e-mail, their absent boyfriends, and warm beds.

Hofsós, their destination, is a tiny old market and fishing town where for centuries Danish merchants bought hides and stockfish and kept the local farmers in debt for coffee, flour, sugar, lumber. The Hof river flows fast out of the mountains and rushes into the sea at its *ós,* "mouth." Sweet water and saltwater have been noisily fighting it out there since the last glacier melted, but until a few

years ago, that was almost the only noise in Hofsós. Iceland, like
the Midwest of the United States, has been steadily losing its
small towns and remote farms as the young crowd into Reykjavík
for jobs and excitement, and the local economic life dries up.
Hofsós almost died at the end of the nineteenth century when
bad times fueled an enormous emigration from north and east
Iceland to America and Canada. It got a brief new lease on life
from mid-twentieth-century prosperity and good fishing, but now
its undersized harbor and declining population couldn't keep it
alive despite the grandeur of its physical setting and the charm
of its old cottages. You can't eat charm and pretty views. The old
Danish store and the pack house for fish and hides, both antique
timber buildings, were collapsing into ruin. The fishermen's cottages stood vacant, rotting in the salt spray.

Valgeir Þórvaldsson, a farmer's son from north of town,
couldn't bear to see Hofsós die. While working as a carpenter for
the Skagafjörður Folk Museum's project to restore the old Danish
pack house, he fell in love with history and the physical refur-
bishing of old buildings. Endowed only with a dreamily impractical imagination, his great skill as a carpenter and refurbisher,
and what money he could raise from anybody crazy enough to
invest in his schemes, he spearheaded the restoration of the old
cooperative store, to transform it into an elegant museum of the
western emigration with a genealogy center and library. Here descendants of emigrants could come find their nineteenth-century
relatives who stayed home and the location of the farms they had
left. Genealogy is, after all, the Icelandic national sport. Then
Valgeir helped remodel a broken-down old cottage into a charming restaurant serving Icelandic food: thin pancakes, *vínarterta*,
smoked salmon and lamb, fresh fat trout seined from the lake on
his farm. Then he went to work on the old fisherman's cottages

to remodel them into little guest houses. He bought a flag factory, which employed local housewives so that Iceland would not have to suffer the disgrace of flying imported flags. All this in a town of 250 at the end of the world, forty or fifty miles south of the polar drift ice, in a country with a population of 250,000 and a market so small that every Icelander who has ever lived in the last thousand years (800,000 should you be able to resurrect their bones— Grettir and the whole lot) would not be able to fill Tiananmen Square for a communist party rally. Valgeir is a dreamer and, of course, completely crazy to have done this—to save his dying hometown. He is also a man of great sweetness of soul, with the generous impetuosity of a Renaissance prince, a farmer who thinks he is a Medici. I had met him and seen the museum the summer before, and thought the students would like him and be charmed by the beauty of Hofsós. It was also the launching spot to take the boat to Drangey, visible now all night from anywhere in town, a stone birthday cake sleeping in the fjord.

The busload of cranky tired students rounded the bottom of the fjord and turned north. A mile or two south of the turnoff to Hofsós, I saw Valgeir parked along the roadside. The bus stopped. Valgeir got on and welcomed the students in his Icelandic burr: "Velcome to my hometown. It iss a great plesure to grreet you." Valgeir is a big sturdy man with ruddy cheeks, a reddish goatee, and a wide smile. The students were a little surprised, a little pacified—first the president, now this affable man. "I have a little surprise," he whispered to me.

Hofsós is a mile and a half down to the sea from the main road. At the turnoff I saw Valgeir's "little surprise." Four splendid Icelandic horses topped by four riders in full regalia: blue and red blazers, white britches, shiny black boots, black helmets, carrying four large flags—American and Icelandic. After eight tedious

literary hours on the bus the tableau shocked the students back
to life. This was not going to be an American evening. The horses
turned to lead the bus slowly into Hofsós at a *tölt*, a gait peculiar
to the Icelandic horse, the four feet prancing like delicate pistons,
the rider sitting stock still and erect like a frozen statue in the
saddle, no bounce and sway to bruise your hind end. It must have
looked like some grand medieval ceremonial procession being led
from the city gates to the cathedral for a coronation. "Where the
hell are the trumpets?" I asked Valgeir. He smiled.

When the horses arrived at the bottom of the hill in the center
of the old village, the bus disgorged the students, who were
handed small glasses of Brennivín for a *skál*. "Wait a moment,"
said Valgeir and glanced toward the riders, who cantered back up
the hill. At Valgeir's signal, they demonstrated the five gaits of
the Icelandic horse up and down the hill five times, ending at a
full speed ahead, damn-the-torpedoes raging gallop. The horses
stopped short in front of the students, nostrils foaming, sweat
gleaming on their flanks, shaking out their disheveled manes.
Everyone raised their shots and *skál*ed one another: *Velkomin.*
"That was a class act," I said to Valgeir. "Ve are wery happy to see
you." said Valgeir. In these days of triple-bolted deadlocks, purses
full of mace, strangers shot dead as burglars by suspicious house-
holders, Valgeir had just made a poem about hospitality, an ancient aristocratic perfectly formed poem without a single word
of any human language, fabricated entirely out of air and spirit,
a gesture elevated to high art. I'm not sure that such a gesture is
even possible in the United States now—it would require public
permits, police escorts, liability insurance, complaints from neighbors about steaming piles of fresh horseshit. And for strangers?
Foreigners? For your daughter's wedding maybe, but for college
students? Valgeir had just given a polar bear to the king of

Denmark for the hell of it, and had in the process proved himself a poet, not only with his imaginative recarpentering of the entire town but with this grandiose equestrian gesture of welcome. *"Skál,"* we all said, downing one more shot of caraway-flavored firewater.

After dinner, old teacher Holm demanded that his students go to bed early in anticipation of good weather and an early climb up Drangey. Thank God, they ignored him completely. Your first night next to the sea in the endless arctic summer light after an afternoon with horses is no time for prudence. Continents love prudence, the favorite virtue of puritans, but it is always overrated. It gains you nothing but a drudge job and a long slow death. Extravagance, on the other hand, is an island virtue—and if you take your life seriously, it is often demanded of you. Blake, an island man, said "The road of excess leads to the palace of wisdom" and "Enough! or Too much." The midnight summer light in Skagafjörður is remarkable; the mountains turn pale orange and lavender, the sky pink and gold. The water shines as if the light polished the surface with a lemon cloth. The cliffs both north and south of town are symmetrical columnar basalt full of fine perches for fjord contemplation; the seabirds cry all night; seals pop their oily black heads up out of the tide to examine you. The first wildflowers are up on the grassy hillsides: poppies and violets and aromatic angelica. There are no mosquitoes in Iceland, nor have there ever been. If your body can't do a little howling and singing and cavorting on a night like this, there's probably not much hope for you as a human being. The Minnesota students rose to the occasion. Duty-free bottles of Brennivín were drunk; cigarettes and cigars smoked (a wonderful moment of sin for Americans); long deep talks that veered toward vexed questions of philosophy took place; there was kissing and fondling,

I hope, and outdoor lovemaking and who knows? Some may even have fallen in genuine love! Stranger things have happened in that magical light. Some saw fish. Some saw horses. Some, very likely, saw God. They did not sleep much, if at all. Sleep is for the prudent, not for those possessed with the extravagant joy of being alive in a magic place on a magic night. *Salúd,* my students! You performed well your first duty: disobedience.

The next morning the Drangey boat arrived in pale half-gray light, no wind, an unusually calm warm day at this latitude, the fjord placid as a Minnesota stock pond. The "Earl of Drangey," as farmer Jón from Fagranes across the fjord is affectionately called, guides most novices to the top of the island. He is in his early seventies, has an unruly thatch of gray hair, spectacles, a sturdy still-strong body, legs thick and tough from climbing uphill for a whole lifetime. He's climbed Drangey two thousand times at least, he says. His face is full of wit and humor, sentences punctuated with the rising and falling of his bushy gray eyebrows. He collects bird eggs on the cliffs, hanging from a sling. He fattens his sheep in the grassy sky meadow, hoisting them up from a rolling boat. He's built a little shack on top. No, he's never met Grettir. Must be a shy fellow, dead so long and without his head. Valgeir comes along, and his assistant, the beautiful Vigdís, who serves as host and genealogist in the museum. A few students confess to vertigo and go hiking by the sea instead. Most seem a little frightened as the boat nears the sheer straight-sided cliffs rising up to the height of five or six grain elevators. No one is more wobbly than old fat wheezy Holm, the apotheosis of sloth and bad habits. But some responsibilities in life can't be shirked. Drangey is one.

Drangey grew larger, more forbidding as the boat neared it. The dark cliffs were piebald with bird shit; they looked like some giant had clawed them with great gashes and fissures. The air grew loud with a cacophony of birds, their flaps and squawks bouncing off the cliff like shots in an echo chamber. There seemed more birds overhead at Drangey than there were Icelanders alive and dead. The dark may have troubled Grettir, but he was unlikely to be annoyed by silence. This was the noisiest solitude on the planet. Around the back of the island appeared an indentation in the cliff for a boat to come close to shore, then a jumble of wet boulders that served as a beach. Jón squired his charges off the boat and over the slick boulders, then pointed at a steep path going straight up the cliff. Except for one spot halfway up where the path disappeared and you had to cling to a chain for balance on a narrow ledge over a sheer drop-off, the path up was not dangerous—but it was straight up. The young and vigorous proceeded quickly and old Jón veritably danced up the mountain without drawing a heavy breath. He looked like Nijinsky about to imitate the firebird. Old panting Holm brought up the rear, huffing and puffing his fat way upward, the exact opposite of old Jón and fifteen or twenty years his junior. Valgeir and Vigdís hung back to make sure the old graceless bear didn't manage to stumble a hundred feet downhill on his noggin. A few hundred feet from the top, Valgeir bounded off the path. "Where the hell is he going," Holm inquired of the beautiful Vigdís, who was keeping an eye on him. "He has spotted an egg," she said. Back he came with a brilliant blue oversized egg, still warm. "A *svartfugl* egg," said Valgeir; "very delicious." The three of us sat on the hillside contemplating the magnificent egg—and me catching my breath. Just before the last ladder going straight to the top sits a rock ledge four or five feet wide. Jón stopped the climbers and ascended the ledge. "At this point," he said—in Icelandic of course—"it is customary to stop and pray the Lord's Prayer aloud in thanks for a successful

trip to the top." He prayed in Icelandic, even crossing himself in
the old papist manner. I doubt he had been inside a church for
fifty years, but Icelanders, while not overtly religious, are superstitious to a fault. He had very likely prayed there two thousand
times and was not about to break a winning streak. Still not
breathing heavily, he scampered up the iron ladder (installed in
the nineteenth century—too late for Grettir) to his fiefdom high
above the fjord. The students followed, their geezer teacher coming last, his gasps melding with the bird squawks.

At the top, a rolling meadow, rich soft grass a few feet high,
folded over on itself, a perfect mattress for a summer nap. Jón
showed off the places where Grettir built his hut, where he was
killed, where he hauled up driftwood and cast his fish lines, the
fresh-water spring where he drank and washed. All these descriptions were punctuated with wry jokes, old poems, folklore. Vigdís
translated for the students. I labored mightily to follow half his
Icelandic. He came to a little mound with a depression in the grass
behind it. "And here Grettir brushed his teeth," he said, lifting a
gray eyebrow. The whole crew gathered in the grass and we read
the story of Grettir's death from the saga passing the dog-eared
copy from reader to reader. Someone grabbed all the cameras and
took group portraits, the mountains lowering in the background,
the sea far below stretching off endlessly to the north. A light mist
started to fall. We all thought of the long slippery slide down the
cliff to the waiting boat.

Everyone arrived safe at the sea again, some muddier than
others. A good deal of my downhill trip was made not with feet
but buttocks. On board, Valgeir and Vigdís unpacked sandwiches,
vínarterta, coffee. We retraced Grettir's swim four miles east to
the hot spring, Reykir, and the farmhouse where the servant girls
mocked his cock. Later in the summer another Icelandic madman

swam it in Grettir's memory—though he cheated slightly by
wearing a wet suit. The old rock-lined hot-spring pool is still
there, still hot. Underground volcanoes don't lose their poof in
a mere thousand years. We stood in a circle around the pool reading the story of Grettir's swim. We had all turned into literary
fundamentalists by now, driven bonkers by the eerie light and
the odd power of that island refuge. A real rain started to fall.
The damp and exhausted clump of students boarded their bus for
the long drive to the other side of the fjord. Vigdís tried to goad
the students into singing. Icelanders are compulsive bus singers,
drunk or sober, and they all know the words to a hundred songs,
but the Minnesotans wanted only to rub their sore feet and warm
up a little. It's not every day you pay a call on a thousand-year-old
ghost.

One old story from the top of Drangey still haunts me. For
nine hundred years after Grettir, Icelanders used the island as a
larder—like Valgeir gathering eggs, catching birds, climbing up
and down on rope ladders. Many died on those cliffs. Drangey
cannot be made into a safe place. In the thirteenth century Bishop
Guðmundur the Good from Hólar, the northern episcopate just
across the fjord, decided to reduce the death rate by consecrating
the island. Guðmundur intended to sail around the island to
bless the whole circumferance. Just as he was about to complete
the circle, he heard a voice calling out as if from the cliff face itself: "We wicked ones have got to be somewhere. Leave room for
us too." What psychological and ecological truth there is in that
story! Humans try to moralize nature, to tame and pacify it, to
corral it inside the straitjacket of the single truth, but nature is
large and various. Our timid ethical and religious ideas don't mean
very much in places like Drangey. If you imagine perfection,
salvation, the triumph of whatever your hobbyhorse—religion,

democracy, good health, politically corrected lives, the voice will slither out from the heart of the cliff and remind you that both humans and nature itself include everything: room for the wicked as well as a small corner for the good, the virtuous, the ideal. You don't need a whole continent for a microcosm of nature. A few acres of grass in the sky will do.

I believe all the stories, the rock, the buried head, the voice and the claw, the poor man's polar bear, the swineherd's eyes. I am, whether by DNA or inclination, an evangelical literary fundamentalist. Stories are true. Poems are true. What lasts for a thousand years in the consciousness is true. Music is true. The impulses inside your own body and head are all true—all reliable. Horses at a *tölt* are true. The sea never lies, and the thicker the mattress of grass grows on top of Drangey, the more truth in it. A *kría* will never lie to you, nor will a codfish, not even a trout. But every word spoken by a government, a church, an army, or anyone who has any interest in selling you anything or giving you orders or who promises to make you rich or eternal is a damned, vile, rank, putrid lie. So there. Would you let someone like *me* teach your children?

The students soon disappeared into the more cosmopolitan cities of Scandinavia: Copenhagen, Bergen, Lund, then back to Minnesota just when the first mosquitoes hatched. I came back to Iceland where two of Marcy's and my old friends from teaching in China ten years ago met us. Andrew and Min are adventurous Brits and decided (like their countryman Auden) to have a look at the island that went to war with their empire over the fate of the codfish.

The four of us rented a car and started east retracing the route I drove with Howard Mohr on my way to my summer farm job so many years ago. Like Reykjavík, the south of Iceland had been

hauled into the twentieth century, maybe the twenty-first pre-
maturely. The road is paved, punctuated by American-style con-
venience stores—gas stations peddling fast food, comic books,
road snacks, rental videotapes, souvenirs. As in, say, rural Ohio
or Colorado or Georgia, these stores are full of lurking teenagers,
traveling families with howling babies, bored old folks, all drinking fountain cokes, eating hot dogs, wiping rémoulade off their
shirtsleeves, enjoying the whiff of diesel fumes and burnt sugar.
But the falls at Skógar still fell dependably, Vatnajökull still
spewed its icy tongues almost to the road, calving blue icebergs
into glacial lagoons, lambs still grazed on the roof of the turf
church at Núpsstaðir, the sea still thundered up from Antarctica
onto the black beach at Dyrhólaey, the sheep had not begun to
look like intellectuals, and Höfn was still as beautiful and as enjoyable to pronounce with a hiccup as it ever was. Even modern
technology and consumerism can't do much to shake the bedrock
foundation of islands; saltwater seems to stave off the slide to
absolute corruption.

We stayed at a little country hotel outside Höfn owned by a
man who told me a very interesting tale. I'd noticed when we arrived that the wall of his parlor was lined with a thousand odd
books in several languages, including a fine collection of editions
of Halldór Laxness. Ásgrimur remarked that Halldór came close
to being his father. His mother, in the late '20s, studied domestic
science at a country school outside Reykjavík, working in the dining room to pay her way. There she met the young Laxness who
was staying there while he worked on his first long novel. Laxness
fell swimmingly in love and courted her in the grand manner. She
understood even then that he was a genius and she liked him, but
she finally rejected his courtship. "Halldór," she said, "you are a very
sweet fellow, but you talk like a fifty-year-old professor reading

an ancient book. When you speak to me, it's like hearing the voice of my grandfather, not my husband." She sent Halldór on to his Nobel prize and married Ásgrimur's father, Gísli, who presumably spoke Icelandic as if he lived in the twentieth century.

When you round the southeast corner of Iceland you arrive at the first of the chain of fjords that corrugate the east coast: Berufjörður—at whose tip sits the tiny old market town Djúpivogur. Six miles out to sea lies Papey, the island of papists—*papar* in Icelandic. Is this the island where Catholics were banished from this legally Lutheran island, there to eternally genuflect, douse themselves in holy water while chanting Latin hymns to the virgin far from the reformed mainland of Iceland? Not quite. It was for almost a thousand years a prosperous farm. My great-uncle Josef married a girl from Papey, and a whole tribe of my hometown Icelanders claimed descent from the island. Rather than Catholics, the whole lot of them were thoroughgoing agnostics except for a few Swedenborgians and theosophists. Papey instead was by legend, and probably by historical fact, the first inhabited chunk of Iceland, discovered by Irish monks who seemed, in the Middle Ages, always to have searched out isolated islands or bleak stony sea cliffs as sites for their beehive oratories, where they could pass this earthly exile in contemplative meditation and prayer. The west coast of Ireland is full of their relics: the Arans, the Blaskets, the Skellig rocks, the cliffs at Slea Head. The Irish were skilled seamen in their skin boats. Saint Brendan probably beat Leif Eriksson to the North American coast. Sailing northwest from Ireland, Papey might have been the first land sighting. Plenty of stone, plenty of birds, plenty of fish, plenty of grass, plenty of silence. *Ave Maria, gratia plena* and off you go to happy meditating. And there you are halfway through lauds, gearing up for primes, when the surly Viking outlaws pay you a

call in the ninth or tenth century, just as they made their unwelcome calls up and down the coast of Ireland: thieving, pillaging,
rampaging, and worst of all, upsetting your celibacy by leaving
their seed behind them everywhere, then settling down to raise
sheep and daughters. As the old Irish poem goes:

> There's a wicked wind tonight,
> Wild upheaval in the sea;
> No fear now that the Viking hordes
> Will terrify me.

The Irish are gone now, disappeared into the Icelandic gene
pool, but my own theory is that they left behind the most powerful ghost of all: they turned the lunk-headed illiterate Norwegian
pirates into a tribe of poets, scholars, storytellers, boozers, dreamers, believers in fairies and elves. I propose that the Icelanders
are nothing more than escaped Celts, fallen off the bar stools
of west Ireland, the Orkneys, the Shetlands, with their sheep,
their schemes, their wild imaginings. Not a smidgen of pious
Scandinavian stolidity in the whole lot of them! Prove me wrong!
Or fight the sea with your broadsword.

I knew no one, Icelander or tourist, who had set foot on Papey.
Two of my father's cousins, descendants of nineteenth-century
Papey farmers, once rented a car to drive around Iceland, but
when they got to Djúpivogur, noted the existence of their grandmother's birthplace in a gray mist and drove on. I imagine that, as
Minnesota farmers, they didn't fancy a sea trip. But I had come
to Iceland by sea, and now I intended to leave it by sea, even if
only for an afternoon.

It was a sunny warm day in early June, a light wind, a calm sea.
We drove down to the harbor past the old turn-of-the-century

timber Hotel Framtíð (the future)—the right name for an old
hotel with creaky floors. A white boat named Gísli í Papey swayed
in the water, the only boat without a fishing rig. I cranked up my
primitive Icelandic and asked a pretty blonde girl walking up
from the harbor if she knew how to get hold of Már Karlsson, the
name of the skipper printed on the Papey flyer. She blinked twice
before answering me in English: "He's my father. He's home having lunch, but he'll be back at two o'clock. I'll tell him to look for
you." We ate warm *kleinur* (Icelandic cardamom doughnuts) and
drank coffee at the hotel of the future till Már emerged. The four
of us were the only passengers, and Már, having been given a
foreigner alert by his daughter, brought along a retired schoolteacher, Ingimundur Sveinsson, to speak English to us. The Gísli í
Papey bobbed up and down in the long North Atlantic rollers so
that Búlandstindur, the big perfectly cone shaped mountain behind Djúpivogur, rose into view, then fell out of it, as if it existed
only inside a steadily turning kaleidoscope. After forty minutes
sailing we arrived at the little harbor of Árhöfn to be greeted by
thousands of puffins who lined the small cliffs and hilltops like
a dignified assemblage of senators, bishops, and financiers. What
a grandly odd bird with its bulbous bright orange and black beak,
its orange waddly feet, and its enormous fat white breast and
black back; it looked like a squat banker in a tight tuxedo about
to burst his shirt buttons after a heavy dinner. They move awkwardly and stiffly on land and seem to be always at full attention
lacking only a pince-nez and a cummerbund to complete the
portrait. Puffins are the only birds I know that make you laugh
when you first see them assembled—and they are professional
assemblers. They induce gaiety; can you possibly be weighted
down with dark thoughts of cosmic misery while looking at this
amiable and ridiculous bird, imagining its ripe fish breath? These

thousands of them in their island puffin town make you giddy—silly as a teenager in love.

Ingimundur, who was in his early seventies, belonged to a tribe whose numbers are legion in the Icelandic countryside: the local historian and genealogist, the keeper of a thousand years of lore. We left the puffins to circumambulate the mile-and-a-third-square island—just the right size for a few human beings and a multitude of puffins—and gulls, guillemots, murres. Papey shares with Drangey only its mattress of rich lush grass folded softly over on itself. It is not grand and craggy, but a gently rolling meadow, a prairie plopped down in the open Atlantic, a suitable place for farmers, a bad hiding place for outlaws, whose only protection here would be the heavy seas that the Irish prayed for. Probably a bad place for anchorite monks, who instead of devoting themselves to ascetic denial probably scribbled poems during vespers and dined on fat tasty puffin breasts and fresh poached haddock. Ingimundur took us to the presumed ruins of an Irish oratory, a hill called Einbúi, the Loner (the fairies church), over the Írskuhólar, the Irish hills, past Papatættur (the pope's knob), and up Hellisbjarg (the highest mountain on Papey, about a hundred and fifty feet), then up the fifty-foot bright orange lighthouse tower that crowns it, where Vatnajökull's tongues and the serrated ridges on the mainland become your true backyard.

The old farmer Gísli, whose descendants still own the island, built an asymetrical farmhouse out of driftwood at the turn of the century. The rooms are the size of whatever washed up on the beaches of Papey. He built a lot of bookshelves. A hundred yards from the house sits a tiny wood church, built in 1807, probably the oldest and smallest church in the country. It is ringed by the graves of the farmers who've lived there.

Unlike Drangey with its history of tragedy, violence, and black
magic, you sense on Papey the sanity and continuity of human
life, the benevolence of nature even here in this northern ocean.
In this grass human beings have lived for a thousand years, making dinner, hauling water, cutting hay, stealing eggs from seabirds,
fishing for cod and haddock, pitching manure onto a field, reading
late at night by whale-oil lamps, making love, raising children,
burying children, lying in the soft grass on warm summer days
staring at the sea and the sublimity of the landscape ten or fifteen miles away on the mainland, and thinking of nothing at all
but that the world is sometimes a sweet and mysterious place
and that it is good to be alive in it and to know that you are alive.
And if after these deep thoughts you nap a little, you will be
guarded in your sleep by an assembly of puffins lined up like your
benevolent great-aunts and uncles to keep you safe as you dream
of God knows what.

Though I doubt any of my own ancestors ever had any connection to Papey, I would, if offered the chance, gladly come back to
camp out in Gísli's driftwood house in my old age with a pile of
books and a decent bottle of cognac, to die here in my sleep at
123 to the noise of the sea and the birds crying, to be praised for
twenty minutes in the tiny church, after which my ashes would
be dumped off a cliff, a company of dignified puffins acting as
pallbearers and mourners, and a family of seals barking away to
sing me back into the tide. Iceland is a good island, but Papey is
the right island—the island by which to judge all others. It took
me only till my mid-fifties to try it on for size and discover, much
to my delight and astonishment, that it fit. A perfect fit.

From Papey it is a long winding trip by road to Vopnafjörður
in the northeast corner of Iceland. Try pronouncing this roll call
of fjords, Sensible Reader. Remember to trill the *rs*:

Berufjörður
Breiðdalsvík
Stöðvarfjörður
Fáskruðsfjörður
Reyðarfjörður
Eskifjörður
Norðfjörður
Seyðisfjörður
Mjóifjörður
Lögmundarfjörður
Borgarfjörður

Don't they have a wonderful archaic look on the page? If you
learn to pronounce them all and recite them in a rhythm, they
become a geographic poem, a mantra to induce in you a height-
ened spiritual state. Since the roads around them are mostly still
rough gravel tracks clinging to ledges along the sea, the trip will
also include sore kidneys and a throbbing sacroiliac. But never
mind. You pass slowly through some of the most sublime scenery
on earth, rough crags plunging to narrow inlets, scree tumbling
down to torture your tires, and in every fjord a little village, a
few gaily painted houses, a fishing harbor, a freezing plant, a
store, a gas pump, a sign to mark the birthplace of some distinguished local poet, and over all the perfume of fish: fresh, dried,
rotted, frozen, drifting through the salty air. What the middle of
continents most lacks is fjords. Is civilization possible without
them?

To get to Vopnafjörður, where most of my grandparents were
born, in summer means going up the highest mountain pass in
Iceland, Hellisheiði, over the Butter Mountains, Smjörfjöll. The
gravel road rises steeply from the tidal marshes of the Hérað to

near four thousand feet. At the top, more fjords: Vopnafjörður, Bakkafjörður, the forty-mile-long peninsula, Langanes, and then north of that in the far distance Þistilfjörður, and then if the day were clear enough and your eyes sharp enough, the polar ice. I've stood on many wild grand places in my life, but the top of Hellisheiði takes the prize. The road, needless to say, closes in early fall. But today we go down as steeply on the north. The four of us have come to Vopnafjörður not to genuflect at the farms of dead ancestors but to visit my cousin Cathy Josephson, a Minneota girl who decided to perform a reverse immigration—a rewind of her grandfather's journey—to become an Icelander again in the same neighborhood her grandparents left in 1893.

It's a good story, as you might expect. Cathy, now in her late forties, was born on a Minneota farm, the oldest daughter of her grandfather Sigfus's oldest son, Frank. Her grandfather, born in Iceland, remained in most ways an Icelander his entire life, though he was a veteran of the First World War and didn't return to see his birthplace till he was in his sixties. Though a farmer like most of the immigrants, there lingered about him a kind of old-world elegance and refinement. "Sigfus Frank was a real gentleman," my mother and his cousin always said, "and he speaks the best Icelandic of all of us." Cathy was the apple of her grandfather's eye—to resurrect an old cliché almost unavoidable in describing the symbiosis between them. She was from childhood one of the rare young who seemed more comfortable with old people than with her own contemporaries. She had all the classic bad habits of immigrant Icelanders—she painted, she wrote poetry, she liked the farm better than the town, she was a passionate and energetic genealogist who collected family lore and could describe your connection to Uncle Arngrímur's second wife's stepson's third daughter. She seemed to herself adrift in urban bourgeois America.

She married without enthusiasm and took dull jobs to get money
while she guarded her private passions. Six or seven years ago,
after her grandfather's death, her family decided to have a reunion in Vopnafjörður to visit the site of Sigfus's birthplace and
honor his memory. Forty of them bought tickets to Iceland, but
since no one spoke more than a few words of ungrammatical
Icelandic, they hired a guide and translator from Vopnafjörður, a
stepson of one of their cousins: Haukur Hreggviðsson. Haukur, a
big sturdy hearty fellow, was an itinerant mechanic, a passionate
stamp collector, a caretaker for the falcon-breeding grounds in the
Mývatn wilderness, and, like so many small-town Icelanders, a
jack-of-all-trades. He had learned fluent American English working at the Keflavík NATO base. He made sure the Josephsons had
a good time. They all fell in love with Iceland, all forty of them,
but Cathy outdid her relatives. She fell grandly in love with Haukur
too. Suddenly the dull world seemed full of possibility and joy.
Maybe it was the June light just south of the Arctic Circle that
drove them slightly crazy. It has happened to others. Cathy flew
back to Minneapolis, closed up her life there, said toodle-oo to
her job, and flew back to winter in one of the most isolated fjords
in Iceland. She and Haukur married in the old church at Hof,
where her grandfather was baptized in 1893. They were, so far as
any observer could see, blissfully happy, a life short of money but
full of fun, jokes, affection, adventure. I met Haukur many times
and liked him enormously. We traded stamps like oversized
nerds brandishing our perforation gauges. Haukur, like so many
Icelanders, was a gifted storyteller and mimic who could do a
riotous description of a country dance, imitating the voices and
gaits of all his neighbors. Laughter entered a house when he arrived. What a mad gesture—and what fine luck for cousin Cathy,
I thought to myself when I met them together. She is a tiny blond

woman, half Haukur's size, but the two of them had the look of an even match. They played each other well.

But the universe sometimes inflicts brutal revenge on those who presume to spontaneous joy. After a few years of marriage, Haukur was diagnosed with terminal stomach cancer, a common disease among Icelanders, perhaps because of a diet heavy in smoked foods, perhaps because of DNA, perhaps for no reason at all. He was given a few weeks to live and told that it was impossible for him to return to Vopnafjörður, even to die there. Haukur was hardly fifty, a big vigorous man full of life. Cathy, though a small woman, inherited her grandfather's fierce stubbornness. She was not about to let Haukur go so soon. He rallied and didn't die on schedule, so he and Cathy returned to Vopnafjörður where, though dreadfully sick, he enjoyed life for the better part of a year. Cathy nursed and tended and goaded him with great affection and humor—and stoicism. Within the year he was indeed dead, but not before most of his pleasures were restored to him for a while.

How sad for Cathy, said the Minneota neighbors and relatives. Such a happy marriage ended, but I suppose she'll be home soon to resume her real life. But they underestimated her toughness. She had fallen in love not only with Haukur but with Iceland. "I'm staying," she announced. "I'm an Icelander now." She and Haukur had intended to find one of the many deserted farmsteads in this valley of declining population to remodel it into a little guest house for fishermen and tourists. And so she did. With the help of Haukur's old friends and relatives, who respected her devotion to him, she moved to a farmhouse eight miles north of town with five cozy bedrooms, a couple of baths, and a front yard that looked over the panorama of the whole fjord and the mammoth ridge of the Butter Mountains. And here, at Hámundarstaðir, the four weary travelers found her.

We dined on fresh boiled haddock—a gift from one of Haukur's cousins; you do not *buy* fish in Iceland—and boiled local potatoes, all swimming in proper high-fat Icelandic butter, washed down with shots of landi—quality moonshine in a Sprite bottle, contributed by one of Haukur's brothers. While the rest of Iceland basked in sun, Vopnafjörður was shrouded with thick black clouds. Snow flurries predicted for tomorrow—June 10. Polar winds rattled the windows. We all toasted Haukur, then we toasted the landi, then we toasted Grandpa Sigfus, then the guests toasted the hostess. After we had toasted the Icelandic dog who sat in the corner looking hopeful, we were ready to talk. Cathy's Icelandic was still shaky, but improving daily. An English-speaking husband was no boon to her language skills. Desperation was proving, as it always does, a better teacher. She had the usual Icelandic panoply of jobs, necessary in out-of-the-way places on this expensive island. She worked at a nursing home; she coached local ladies in English; she did light housework for a handicapped woman; she had a job coming up in the fish-freezing plant in town. Fishermen from Reykjavík were renting rooms from her while they pursued trout and salmon from the three local rivers. A few Minneotans had traveled through in pursuit of relatives. She loved Vopnafjörður because it reminded her of the Minneota of her childhood, a close-knit, neighborly community of farmers, where people shoveled each other's driveways, baked brown bread and *vínarterta* for each other, shared their pheasants and ducks during hunting season, and lived without locked doors, on either houses or cars. She liked having lots of cousins. She liked going to country dances to dance all night and then soberly drive her neighbors home at dawn. She liked the summer light on the sea and the Butter Mountains. She liked Haukur's overstuffed stamp-collecting and novel-reading chair sitting in the middle of the parlor next to a

dish of his favorite German butterscotch. She liked sometimes imagining Haukur sitting there doing his stamp deals on the phone.
She liked living in a time warp, for that's precisely the right name
for Vopnafjörður. Give or take electricity and a computer or two,
the valley was three generations behind the United States, and,
she thought, more power to it for staying that way. It was the soul
of the island woman talking, who had been born out of time and
place in the middle of a continent that was too big, too fast, too
money crazy, with too little saltwater and too little neighborly
decency. I think my tough, small, clear-eyed cousin, Cathy, may
be the wisest of all my relatives, and certainly wiser than me. We
finished off the first bottle of landi with one more round of toasts,
but for the life of me, I can't remember what the hell we toasted.
The Bulgarian geodetic survey of 1947? The presidency of Grover
Cleveland? The inventor of the sewing machine? *Skál.* Góða nótt.

The morning we left, it was, as the Icelandic weather bureau
predicted, snowing—only lightly, hardly enough to cover the
brave early wildflowers. But snowing. On June 10. The road west
from Vopnafjörður is terrible, bone-cracking washboard one-lane
gravel, and it runs straight for fifty odd miles through the bleak-
est desert in Iceland—and that is bleakness of a very profound
kind. Some of that gravel desert is part of my great-grandfather
Björn's farm, Hauksstaðir. I always wondered what his sheep ate
in summer: fifty square miles with fifty blades of spindly grass—if
you are persistent enough to find them—bare gravel hills without a human being alive, most frequently traveled without meeting another vehicle at all. And in snow. On June 10. I couldn't
face it. I handed the keys to Andrew, the stoic Englishman, and
huddled in the back seat with a sweater over my head trying to
brood my way into a proper depression. When finally we arrived
at Mývatn, the center of Iceland's volcanic activity—and likewise

of the tourist trade, today mostly Germans in earnest looking hiking boots—I thanked Andrew for driving the one stretch in Iceland I dread. "It was a bit lifeless, I suppose, and I wouldn't be keen on driving it often, but it had its own kind of eerie beauty— the snow and all. I rather enjoyed it. Actually I expected terrible weather, a bit bleak and arctic. It's been much too sunny and pleasant." There are good reasons why some people prefer to travel with the English. It takes more than disaster to bring them down. There are fleeting moments when I think they deserve to have their empire back.

Now we were bound for Hofsós again, so that Andrew and Min could see this charming and lovely place before heading back to Saffron-Walden. Marcy and I were staying a few extra days so that we could meet our old friend Wincie when, along with the cathedral choir from Reykjavík, she came north to sing a few concerts. We took a small side trip to the other side of Skagafjörður to the country town of Sauðárkrókur—sheep river hook—to meet another Icelandic eccentric, a schoolmate of the novelist Einar Már Guðmundsson, who was raising Mediterranean sea bass— the most expensive fish in France—in fjord water. We found Gúndi Ingólfsson tending his fish at his downtown hatchery. He was another witty storyteller, full of sly irony and completely mad schemes. He warmed the icy fjord water with hot-spring water, larded the tanks with bass food, and had twenty-thousand warm-blooded Mediterranean fish fattening happily sixty miles south of the Arctic Circle. He intended to fly them off to four-star restaurants in Paris where a scarcity of bass had skyrocketed the price. Why is a perfectly sensible biologist doing this? He liked life in Sauðárkrókur, his hometown, and wanted to raise his children there, but like midwest small towns, Sauðárkrókur was collapsing into economic death. The old timber houses were being demolished to make room for concrete bunkers, the children drifted to Reykjavík or abroad, farms were being abandoned yearly. So Gúndi bought a 1900 timber house, once the town doctor's office, made it livable, found an old warehouse next to the water, and began farming sea bass—a little business to keep the children at home. He had acquired an abandoned fish farm north of Hofsós and intended to expand his bass stocks—and create new employment in a moribund corner of the district. His greatest pleasure though, he confessed, was to sit on a winter night in his homemade hot-spring hot tub listening to his naked old friend Einar read him chapters out of his newest novel over a bottle of whiskey—"Now that is work for a human being, to write those wonderful books." Where are the Gúndis in America, these mad impractical idealists with heads full of literature and schemes who want to risk everything to save their hometown because it is a decent place? Are Valgeir and cousin Cathy and Gúndi—and a half dozen more I met—possible only on out-of-the-way islands? Can't we have a little energy and imagination without greed and ambition in the middle of continents too? Gúndi sent a bag of bass with us to Hofsós. They were delicious, firm sweet flesh, grilled with plenty of garlic and wine and lemon.

Andrew and Min left for the airport at Keflavík; Marcy and I returned to Hofsós to await the Dómkór, the Cathedral Choir from Reykjavík. "Cathedral" is a grand word, but Sensible Reader should keep in mind the size and religious enthusiasm of Iceland. The cathedral is a small old church—perhaps the size of a rural Minnesota Norwegian Lutheran or German Catholic Church. It might seat three hundred, sardine style. Still, it is the seat of the Lutheran bishop of Iceland and sits next to the parliament building (Alþing) and the Reykjavík city hall. Except for Christmas and funerals, attendance of worshippers is thin and irregular, but the choir—like so many in Iceland—is regular, enthusiastic, and skilled—a few trained musicians, even a few professionals, but mostly ordinary people with decent voices who love the noise of human beings making harmony and counterpoint together. The rock and roll, New Age, or country twang liturgies have not yet arrived in Iceland. I prefer to think that taste rather than customs regulation ensures that happy fact. The choir sings standard choral repertoire: Bach, di Lasso, Brahms, Mozart, Palestrina, Bruckner, garnished with modern Scandinavian pieces and most of all the surprisingly rich and imaginative tradition of Icelandic choral music from its beginnings to the present. One modern Icelandic composer of liturgical music, Þorkell Sigurbjörnsson, has composed hymns already so beloved by singers that the Icelanders have forgotten he composed them. They have been sucked up into the music of everyday life. It's a high honor for a composer or writer that his work should be taken into the consciousness of his audience while his name disappears. "Anonymous" is the most prolific human genius of all.

The Dómkór tours twice a year, once abroad to bring gems of Icelandic music to places like Budapest, Leipzig, Lisbon, or Madrid, and once to the Icelandic countryside, this year to Skagafjörður, where they intended to perform at Hólar, the old bishopric, then ten miles north at Hofsós in the community hall, and finally for a birthday party in Siglufjörður at the northern tip of Iceland. The choir singers are a jolly lot who have become good friends while singing together and, like most Icelanders are as devoted to a good time as they are to high art. You probably can't have one without the other. Dour singers cannot break the heart. In Iceland they travel by bus, presided over by their beloved director and organist, Marteinn Hunger Friðriksson, who tries to keep them calm and dignified till after they've sung.

I had told Wincie the story of the student reception at Hofsós.
She mulled over the thought of horses. "Damn Valgeir! Horses!
And for foreigners! The choir had better damn well have six horses
when we arrive." She called her old friend Vigdís who conveyed
the news to Valgeir, who must have smiled wickedly when he
hatched his plan. I knew what was going to happen when the
choir rounded the bend to Hofsós. They didn't. I intended not to
miss this small moment.

The choir arrived on their bus late Friday afternoon. Six magnificent horses, this time with riders resplendent in red blazers,
holding six billowing Icelandic flags awaited them at the turnoff.
I wasn't on the bus, of course, but Wincie reported a good deal of
gasping.

After the *tölt* into town, the choir—faces of stunned delight—
got off the bus as Marteinn poured them a Brennivín. The horses
did their five-times-up-and-down routine with, if possible, even
more thunderous noise and foaming nostrils than I had seen before. When the horses came to a stop, Marteinn poured the riders a Brennivín, but before anyone *skál*ed, Marteinn gave a pitch.
Standing by the sea at Hofsós, the choir serenaded the horses
with first a heartfelt melancholy old Icelandic folk tune and next
a vigorous joyful leaping one. Then everyone raised their glasses,
and while the music disappeared over the chilly water of the fjord,
we *skál*ed. Here's mud in your eye, universe. I knew one of the
songs and tried singing along on the tenor part, but I found my
voice clutching and my eyes watering. Sentimental fool! This is
the end of the twentieth century. Check your stocks and shut up.
What do these hayseeds know about life? Horses and folksongs
indeed. What a waste of time. Doesn't anybody do a day's work in
this godforsaken backwater?

The next day the choir rode thirty miles north to Siglufjörður, the northernmost town in Iceland and for much of this century the richest. Americans understand oil booms and gold rushes, towns rising from wilderness in the blink of an eye like thistles watered and fertilized by money, even rumors of money. When the fertilizer stops, the thistle wilts, dries up, leaves only a withered stalk that cracks in the wind and disappears. In Iceland, the boom was not oil or gold but herring.

The Norwegians, who had a mechanized fishing fleet at the turn of the century, struck gushers of herring off the north coast of Iceland. They used drift nets, then purse-sein nets to literally scoop up herring out of the sea. Icelanders soon acquired the technology themselves to cash in on the herring. Hundreds of vessels plied the north and east coasts. Siglufjörður exploded almost overnight into Iceland's third city—a boom town—its harbor full of hundreds of masts, new buildings up overnight, three shifts of "herring girls" working twenty-four hours a day beheading, salting, embarreling the wet gray gold nuggets, boat after boat dumping its hold onto the docks, herring deals cut in back rooms, dormitories full of deckhands and herring girls grabbing a quick nap before their next shift, more herring, more barrels, more tons, more salt, more labor, faster, faster, clouds of acrid herring smoke fogging the air downwind from the factories where herring were melted into fish meal for the pigs of Norway, fortunes made overnight, fortunes lost even faster, then made again, then lost again, another boat arriving spilling slippery herring onto the dock, next shift, collect your pay here, pass the salt. And then, in 1969, it stopped. The herring simply disappeared, or better yet failed to arrive for the party and left no forwarding address. After fueling Iceland's first burst of modern prosperity during the First World War, keeping Iceland the only country in Europe to have profited from the depression of the '30s, and paying the tab for Iceland's surge into twentieth-century technology in the '50s and '60s, the herring went toodle-oo. No barrels, no herring girls, no fish meal, no money. And while Siglufjörður still existed, it did so—as the polite euphemism goes—in much reduced circumstances. Though it surely smelled better now at the end of the century, the ghost of old fish-meal fragrance still lingered in the air. The boisterous cackles of the herring girls as they whacked off heads and pulled out guts probably still echo off the steep closely packed mountains that delay dawn for an hour or two, then truncate the glorious sunsets still going on thirty miles away.

You don't pass by Siglufjörður on your way to anywhere. It is the end of the road. If you arrive here, you must have needed to be here, for no wrong turning is possible. During most of the century there was hardly a road to Siglufjörður at all. The mountains at the end of the peninsula both west and east plunge straight to the sea. The only other road down to Sigluförður went over a high, steep, and exceedingly dangerous pass. Till the '50s you walked up a few thousand feet to the top of the pass to meet the bus that would carry you to Reykjavík, then out into the world of oceans and continents. Finally, after the herring were long gone, the Icelanders tunneled through a mountain and cut a fine paved road out of the cliffs over the sea so that you could arrive safely in Siglufjörður, not to truck out your herring fortune, but to sing.

Our old friend Wincie was, as Icelanders say, of Siglufjörður ætt—descent. Her grandfather moved here a century ago to open a bookstore—presumably to capture the fisherman trade. What else to do between herring runs but read poetry? While others amassed fortunes in fish, he made a modest living in the book trade, enough to raise three sons and a daughter and send the sons out over the pass for an education and a life in the wide world.

I knew two of the sons. Wincie's father, Jóhann, was a school-master, lexicographer, and poet. His books of bilingual limericks are still in print long after his death, delighting Icelandic lovers of witty light verse. Imagine having to sparkle in two languages! Her Uncle Þorsteinn, when I met him, was the director of music programming for Icelandic State Radio, but had been in his youth a tenor of size and magnitude who had a budding career both in opera and as a recitalist. You might expect Iceland to produce barrel-chested bellering Wagnerian tenors who can overwhelm an orchestra of fortissimo trombones. They do not. Icelandic tenors tend to sweet-voiced soulful lyricism, Irishmen à la McCormack or Italians à la Gigli trapped in those oversized Icelandic chest cavities. So it was with Þorsteinn. Wincie gave me a copy of one of his old recordings made in the '50s, mostly Icelandic songs. I never heard him sing, and Wincie said that after beginning his work in radio, he stopped singing—entirely. Jóhann and Þorsteinn were both men of great charm and intelligence, both full of Siglufjörður stories.

The fjord was so isolated in the '30s that neither brother had ever seen a banana. Jóhann recalled the excitement of the local children when the Christmas freight boat rounded the turn into the short steep fjord. "You could smell apples all the way in," said Jóhann. They saw their first orange in the mid '30s as almost grown men. The brothers packed cardboard suitcases just before World War II to climb the pass and meet the bus, and, aside from family visits, their lives now moved far outside the little kingdom of herring. Their sister, Kidda, who never married, stayed in Siglufjörður and kept a shop until her death; there also she tended her nephew, Gunnar, Þorsteinn's natural son, born in 1938. Gunnar was born deaf and autistic, and continued after Kidda's death to live in Siglufjörður, though now in a sheltered home with a half dozen others. And now, on June 15, he was celebrating his sixtieth birthday, and the cathedral choir, whose members included his cousin Wincie and his half brother and sister, Hannes and Kristín Björg, were coming to Siglufjörður through the tunnel to sing a little concert for him.

It was a day on which you forgive Iceland everything, its long winter dark, its gales of cold rain, its shroud of leaden fog, its eternal wind: not a cloud, not a breeze, everything blue, still, bright, warm—but only by local definition—maybe seventy degrees. I had waited twenty years to see Siglufjörður, refusing to do so except in the company of a local: Wincie. She'd been to Minneota with a local tour guide: me. I insisted on the same service. We took a car, an hour or two before the choir left, driving north from Hofsós around the north end of Skagafjörður, then north again on the cliffs over the sea. Such roads, though no more dangerous than a county road in flat North Dakota—if you stay *on* them—provoke some tiny shiver of excitement for midwesterners. Sea below, cliff above, snow high above, sea again stretching north endlessly till it becomes loose ice, then fast ice. Travel to Siglufjörður and you have northed out; you have run out of island in every direction. You stare at a flat blue horizon.

Lights on through the little tunnel, then down sharply along more cliffs and there you have it: Siglufjörður. It's good to get a first sight of any town on a fine day in the company of someone who knows and loves it, whose history and DNA are grappled to it by ropes of memory, lore, the very stones and boards of its houses, the holes in its streets, the voices of its dead. "There's the old road, see it, winding inland up to the pass—my God, I remember coming down that horrible road in a jammed ramshackle bus when I was a teenager, fresh from America with hardly a word of

Icelandic; there's the old *bíó* where we went to the movies; the
herring docks were full of ships unloading then, and the smell—
my God the smell; the fish-meal plant was back of those ware-
houses; they've torn down Gísli's old shop, but look at that
monstrosity they've put up; we used to go to that valley over
there for picnics, nothing there but a deserted farm now; there
are the company offices—there was a dormitory upstairs—it's
the herring museum now; I was a herring girl too, my first summer
job—we worked endless shifts, shouting at each other, joking;
it's the best way to learn Icelandic; turn down this street—there
it is—my grandfather's house. We sold it years ago, but they've
kept it nicely—what a lovely paint color; his bookstore was downstairs, the kitchen was tiny, the bedrooms tinier; imagine four
children in that little house. Of course take a picture here—I'll sit
on the stoop."

  We met the choir at the herring museum—what other kind of
museum would Siglufjörður have? What other town on the whole
planet has got another one? If you want to know herring, you
must come here. It's a fascinating place crammed with old photographs: of the harbor jammed with hundreds of masts, the barrels
of salt herring stacked by the acre waiting to be loaded for export;
the teenage herring girls of 1920—now great-grandmothers if
they are alive at all. The museum puts on a tableau of what used
to go on night and day; local people act the parts. One wheels in a
load of herring, dumps it in the wooden trough, the herring girls
in red shirts and babushkas, brandishing heavy knives, behead
and gut the fish, then pack them tight in barrels head to tail with
handfuls of salt, faster, faster, paid by the barrel not by the hour,
the barrels wheeled out to the end of the dock. It's a noisy and
enjoyable spectacle, followed by the obligatory shot of schnapps

and a few herring cutlets on rye bread, then off to sing, with
a little fish breath like puffins who have learned to read music,
breathe from the diaphragm, and round their vowels.

Gunnar's birthday party is being held in the dining room of
the hotel, the fanciest place in town. Icelanders love ceremonial
birthday parties, particularly as they age; fifty is big, sixty bigger,
after seventy pull out all the organ stops. Who wants to be a
teenager in a civilized place like this where humans are rewarded
for growing old because they are expected to grow wise?

The choir assembles outside the front door; Marteinn gives a
few instructions, tells them what they are about to sing; someone
asks who's got the flowers for Gunnar, always flowers for birth-
days. Wincie and Kristín Björg survey their makeup; you have to
look good for Gunnar. Hannes straightens his tie. Wincie hands
Marcy her camera, asks her to take snapshots for the family. I've
got my push-here-dope camera ready too. Marcy and I hang back
while the choir files into the foyer to wish Gunnar a happy birthday. I can, of course, see nothing yet, but I begin to hear strange
noises, a kind of pitchless groaning and grunting that crescendos
steadily. I had momentarily forgotten that Gunnar had been profoundly deaf from birth. Never having heard language, he made
in his throat the eerie noises of those who have no idea what
noises they are making. I felt a little fear, a little dread of going
inside, some strange interior hesitation. So did Marcy. We came
in last to shake Gunnar's hand and say with active lips: "Til hamingju með afmælið, Gunnar." Happy birthday.

Gunnar was a big sturdy barrel-chested man with thick spectacles and a short brush of iron gray hair. He was duded up in his
best suit, a crisp white shirt, and a gay yellow tie. He held an
enormous bouquet of flowers with his left arm; offering a powerful handshake with his right. His face shone with pleasure—a

huge grin, delighted eyes, his crow's feet almost dancing. You felt jolly shaking his hand, seeing that pleasure in him. He groaned in response—ooo, iii, ummm, ahhh—it sounded like Icelandic poetry to me. *Til hamingju* again.

The dining room was set for the grand occasion, cut flowers in vases on pink table cloths, a silver coffee pot, the serving women in pink aprons lining the walls holding cream cake after cream cake on silver platters, the smell of coffee brewing, the first local well-wishers already assembled at the side of the room, anxious to outwait the concert and have the first go at the cream cakes. The choir lined up on one side of the room facing Gunnar who stood at attention, still holding his birthday flowers, an audience of one. Marcy and I readied the cameras, but I sensed trouble coming. Marteinn gave the pitch and the choir began singing, an old Icelandic folk song probably about the mountains and the blue sea and the longing in a young man's heart. They sang as beautifully, as tenderly as I have ever heard them—or for that matter any choir—sing. The sound broke the heart, but the other sound broke it even more. Gunnar sang along in his strange pitchless voice, still smiling from ear to ear, full of joy. I tried to focus the camera—my eyes streamed with tears, fogging the view finder. I blubbered like a fool. I handed the camera to Marcy. Her face was a waterfall of tears; she handed me Wincie's camera. I staunched the flow for a second to look at the choir: every one of them weeping while they sang. I looked at Marteinn—conducting with one hand, wiping away tears with the other. The serving women wept. The locals wept. The mice must have been weeping in the wall holes, and the handful of flies laid down their wings to weep, ignoring the cream cakes that ought to have been their target. The whole universe wept except Gunnar, who went on grinning, having as good a time as it is possible for a human being to have

on this sometimes grief-filled planet. The choir took pitches and
sang again, another old Icelandic song—and again they sang and
again and again. This was no dummy concert. This was the real
thing: human beings making beauty for one another with every
shred of energy and intelligence inside them. And all weeping—
avalanches of tears, a Skógafoss of tears, a melted glacier of tears,
a fjord of tears, a whole ocean, a Milky Way of tears, a cosmos
of tears. And all the time Gunnar grinning and singing, clutching
his flowers, having a fine sixtieth birthday, a little hungry now
himself for a slice or two of those lovely cream cakes and a nice
cup of strong coffee.

After Gunnar thanked them, the choir filed out to return to
their bus and Hofsós, a party tonight, a concert tomorrow. Marcy
and I rode home with the choir, leaving the car for Wincie, Kristín
Björg, and Hannes, who, of course, stayed for cream cakes with
their brother and cousin and their old friends and relatives from
town. The choir was strangely silent on the drive back, unusual
for such a jolly and talkative bunch. Mostly we all stared out the
window at the sea stretching off endlessly to the north, as if by
looking hard enough we might understand the grandeur of the
afternoon and—what the hell?—maybe even the meaning of life.

That night Wincie explained Gunnar's singing. A teacher who
came round to his house had been teaching him to breathe like a
singer and hold his own hand to his throat so that he could feel
the vibration of his vocal chords as he tried to change pitches.
The tickling in his hand pleased him. He was disappointed not to
have gotten a fiddle for a birthday present. He liked the feeling
of the trembling strings too. Gunnar is actually a splendid dancer,
said Wincie. Unlike many lead-footed Icelandic men, he has
rhythm. He feels the pulse of a dance beat in his feet through the
boards of the dance floor whether waltz, polka, or tango—and he

learned the steps well. A pleasure to dance with Gunnar, said his cousin. Music arrived at his body, as it arrives at the ears of ordinary audiences. Maybe the soul of a great tenor passed into his DNA from his father, Þorsteinn, but through the circumstance of deafness he was left to discover music in another way.

Why did we all weep? What lies at the bottom of this remarkable afternoon in this remarkable ruined herring town at the absolute outer limit of the civilized world? Was it pity for the poor handicapped man? No. Was it a desire to do social-worker "good" and enhance your "self-esteem"? No. Was it soap-opera sentimentality to weep over poor Gunnar the tenor's son who would never hear Schubert? No. Was it social obligation, a duty to sing at the birthday parties, weddings, and funerals of choir relatives? No. Was it some heroic craziness programmed into Icelandic genes? No. Then what the hell was it?

It was a concert, pure and simple, human beings singing for each other as they ought to. It is called civilization, and our sometimes flea-brained tribe of mankind has worked long and hard to get even a little of it. Mostly we have stumbled, but sometimes we move forward a fraction of a millimeter. We did so at Gunnar's birthday party, all of us. It was a good afternoon for civilization, for a change. It was giving a polar bear to the king of Denmark for the hell of it. It was shutting up a bratty child with a gold ring. It was surprising strangers with horses and flags. It was dreaming up mad schemes to save hometowns. It was falling into middle-aged love at a family reunion. It was a shelf full of poems in a president's office. It was the wind blowing over the grassy remains of Irish monks on a sunny afternoon. It was the ghost of the herring that kept a country alive and afloat. It was the wisdom of islands given a body. It was the face of all the dead either you or I have ever loved. But it was still a concert, lovely music for a man turning sixty. Happy Birthday, Gunnar. Happy Birthday, civilization.

SIGURÐUR TWENTY YEARS AFTER

After my trip back to Reykjavík in 1998 to introduce Minnesota students to Iceland, then climb Drangey, a local newspaper called me for an interview and a photograph. Though Icelanders were used to American Express tourists, they thought literary pilgrims newsworthy. *Dagur* arrived on a sunny day; they photographed me in a Reykjavík backyard, looking like a crotchety old bear, then we had coffee and I gave them a little digest of the students' adventures, throwing in my idea about literary fundamentalism in the native stock. Iceland being Iceland, the paper also wanted to know the names and dates of emigration of my grandparents. What farms were they from in what district? "Oh, so your grandmother was from Þingeyarsýsla? My grandfather too. Perhaps we are. . . ." The Sensible Reader who has plowed so far through this long essay will have no difficulty finishing these sentences. We finished our coffee, said farewell, then I went on to Copenhagen with students, and never saw the news story. By the time I came back to Iceland a month later, I had forgotten that it took place. But that small news story and picture turned out to be gestation for the most touching and nostalgic afternoon of my return to Iceland.

A few days before my final return to Minnesota to go back to work as a school teacher, the phone rang in Wincie's downtown Reykjavík flat, whose back room I had been occupying. Nobody home, so I answered the phone. It was an oddly familiar voice asking if the Bill Holm whose picture had been in *Dagur* was still in Iceland. "My God, Sigurður Björgvinsson," I erupted.

"Oh Bill, do you remember who I am after so many years?"

I began quoting his own wisdom to him, in his own English, sentences spoken twenty years ago still lodged firmly in my head. "Then you must be the Sigurður who, when asked why there were five newspapers from five political parties in a country with a population smaller than Dayton, Ohio, said: 'It is very difficult to govern a country which is inhabited by two hundred thousand gods.' And by the way, Sigurður, are the trout still so fat in Mývatn?"

"Bill, you have not forgotten me"—as if I could forget that the sun rose in the east. "But now I am an old man. I don't go to sea anymore."

"The red hair you remember, Sigurður, is now almost white. I too have grown into an old coot. But the part of me that went on Bakkafoss is still young and foolish and full of schemes. But against your good advice, I have forgotten all my Icelandic."

"And my English is still terrible, too. You must come have lunch with Magga and me. We live in Reykjavík now, not so far from the house where you stay."

Sigurður had called *Dagur* to find the location of the interview in order to track me down. Icelanders still give names and addresses when asked, assuming that their fellow humans are not serial killers and international terrorists to a man. We fixed a lunch date just before I had to leave.

Wincie came along to lunch. She had heard Sigurður stories for twenty years and wanted to meet him. Sigurður and Magga lived in a block of concrete flats not far from the middle of town. How odd to visit Sigurður two stories in the air, no pitching and rolling underfoot, no slap of breakers against the hull, no crying of gulls.

When I first met Sigurður he was in his late fifties, about my age now. He was still a regular seaman, and, during my Fulbright year, he would have been home only for a few days to wash clothes, greet his family, pay his bills, then pack his duffel for the next run to Portsmouth, Brazil, Rotterdam, Nigeria, wherever. So despite our clear affection for each other, we hadn't seen each other for two decades. Sigurður would now be somewhere around eighty years old.

His broad smile, his alert eyes, his boyish enthusiasm for the world were unchanged, but his hair had thinned and grayed, and he was, if anything, bonier and more gaunt than twenty years ago as if some malady had taken fat and energy from him. But he was still Sigurður—excited to see me (as I was to see him) and anxious to tell me what had been on his mind for twenty years.

We walked past his parlor—full of books and pictures of his children—past the kitchen where Magga (whom I'd never, of course, met) was tending to the haddock for lunch, to Sigurður's private lair. "And this is my study."

One wall was covered with books, the other with maps of the world, of Iceland, of the oceans, a detailed map of the wilderness north of Vatnajökull, a map of Cuba, of the old Soviet Union before it collapsed into warring states, portraits of Gorbachev, Fidel Castro, Sigurður on board a ship. At his work table he had recreated the radio station in a ship's control room. His old globe sat there, now even more full of markers showing the biography of his life at sea. Sigurður began opening drawers under the bookshelves: nautical charts, radio charts, city maps, topographical maps, even old tourist maps—all the places on the planet where Sigurður had set foot, breathed the air, and explored, each with its own drawer. But here were the new projects too. Sigurður began a passionate excoriation of the bullying moneyed class of capitalist Icelanders who planned to dam the powerful glacial rivers running north from Vatnajökull—through Mývatn of course—to sell hydroelectric power, build factories, destroy the natural water courses and the salmon that migrated up them, corrupt the environment, all to steal bread out of the mouths of working Icelanders. Sigurður had charts, statistics, articles to provide evidence. He used his cane as a classroom pointer, whacking the wall map to point out lakes, natural reservoirs, water drainages, river sources.

Magga stood watching at the study door with a worried face, pointing out in Icelandic to Wincie that Sigurður had had some small strokes and that she tried to keep him from getting so excited. Probably useless. It was bred into Sigurður, probably with DNA, to think hard and passionately about the large world and to do his best to bring it to its senses. He caught me looking at Gorbachev. "He was a great man. He brought perestroika to the Soviet Union. Now the capitalists have taken over. But I think that socialism is not dead." Soon he was showing me a book he was reading, by Benedikt Gíslason frá Hoftieg. "His family is connected to Minneota, as I remember." Time had not dented Sigurður's memory. He pointed to a map of the Westman Islands. "They are rich fishermen, but it is the only place in Iceland where you go into a house and find no books. They cannot be real Icelanders." He showed me the books of poems by his brother, the Mývatn poet. "It's too bad you don't read Icelandic. He is one of our best poets. All Mývatn men." Suddenly he looked crestfallen. He whacked the hydrological map again. "Because they have fooled so much with the rivers, the trout in Mývatn are not so fat and sweet as they should be—or as they were." Sigurður would save the rivers for the honor of the Mývatn trout. Is there a better reason?

In the twenty years since we'd seen one another, I'd published seven or eight books of poetry and prose. Twenty years ago I'd told Sigurður of my passion to be a writer, to see my name on a book spine or two. He said, "Of course, you are an Icelander—by descent. What else would you want? Money? Fancy clothes? To write books! That's best."

I brought a couple of books—the only ones I had with me: a book of poems and a book of essays about Minneota characters, mostly old Icelanders. Sigurður fingered them fondly, then read the little inscription to him. "This is good. I am very proud of you." I had the peculiar feeling that the ghost of my own father was pronouncing a sort of benediction on the kind of life I had chosen for myself. Magga announced lunch, and we assembled in the kitchen to eat haddock and potatoes with a plate of tomatoes and cucumbers from the Hveragerði hothouses. "Now you must eat what real Icelanders eat," said Sigurður, and so we did.

After lunch it was time for me to leave to pack for the airport, the long dull flight back to continental life. "You can't go quite yet," said Sigurður. "Come with me," and I followed him into his bedroom. "An Icelander must always keep a book pile by his bed. You are never reading just one book but many." We sat on the edge of the bed and Sigurður gave me the annotated tour of his book pile. Stephen Hawking's *A Brief History of Time:* "This is a difficult book, so much mathematics, but he is very brilliant man—no body left at all, no voice, only a brain and a talking computer." Aristotle's *Politics* in Icelandic: "He understands so well what public life does to human beings." *Anglo Saxon Poems* with glossary: "They are so close to Icelandic I can read them almost without a dictionary. Do you know 'The Seafarer'?" A novel by Laxness: "I've read it many times before, of course." A Steinbeck novel: "Do you know his book on the Sea of Cortez?" And more. It was a bottomless pile. Sigurður, small strokes and all, clung to his inner life and his mental life with tenacious interior claws. He would be himself or nothing till he disappeared back into the sea on which he'd lived so much of his life. He would, by God, think till the lights went out, and the whole world was his province—oceans, ideas, capitalist plots, the state of trout, the mystery of the origin of the cosmos itself, human nature, poems. If you are a human being, it is *all* your business. Until you die. No letup. No slacking. The answer may lay in the next book, or the location of paradise on the next map. Maybe this is the mentality of islands—to take the whole universe as your personal province, your personal responsibility. A continent man owns a farm, or a building, or if he is silly enough, a company. An island man owns the stars and what is behind the stars, and then what is behind that.

"When you visit an Icelander's house, you must take a book home with you," said Sigurður, rummaging in his pile. "This is the book for you—the biography of a Mývatn farmer, Jón Jónsson frá Vogum. He wrote it in English in the 1860s to teach himself the language, though he had never heard it spoken."

"Sigurður," I said, "I have owned this book for twenty years and treasure it. You gave it to me when we left Bakkafoss."

"Well, so I did. It was a good choice. Wait just a minute. I have the right book here." He came back with a slim book of photographs. "This is my son Kjartan's book. He makes composite panoramic photographs of Iceland with a computer. I don't completely understand the technology, but the photographs are lovely. I'm very proud of him." Sigurður signed the book in a firm strong hand. We thanked Magga for lunch while Sigurður slipped on his outdoor shoes to walk us down to the car. Out on the street I could almost believe he was eighty years old. He moved slowly now, as if the ocean swells inside still made him a little uncertain on land. At the car, he embraced me and kissed me on both cheeks. "It was wonderful to see you after all these years, and wonderful that you remembered your old friend Sigurður. Blessaður, Vilhjálmur." I think he did not see me weeping in the front seat as we drove away. So many tears in Iceland, and all so joyful.

Diégo-Suarez

Madagascar

Antananarivo
Antsirabe

Fianarantsoa
Ambalavao

Tuléar

℘ Madagascar
The Red Island of Music

FIANARANTSOA: THE PLACE OF GOOD LEARNING

In the fourth week of January 1997, an Indian Ocean cyclone of serious magnitude pounded the central east coast of Madagascar with a sudden foot of rain, one-hundred-fifty-mile-per-hour winds, and huge tidal surges. Eighty miles inland and almost five thousand feet up the steep escarpment that rises quickly from the sea through dense jungle to a mountainous red savanna sits Fianarantsoa, the place of good learning, Madagascar's third-largest city. The tail of the cyclone knocked out all Fianarantsoa's water and electricity, closed all roads to the coast, and completed the work of making an uncertain telephone system inoperable. A few days afterward, I arrived by car from the north to give a lecture on American poetry garnished with old ragtime and stride piano at a place called the Business English Center. Our little traveling party of cultural emissaries consisted of the handsome, charming, and trilingual Lanto Hariveloniaina (who worked for USIS in the capital, Antananarivo), Gabriel, our driver (who managed to be wryly witty in English without speaking a word of the language), Marcy, and me. We checked into the Hotel Soafia at the north end of town. It was not quite what one expected in the middle of an

island in the west Indian Ocean 250 miles off the south coast of
Africa. Hotel Soafia was a rambling Chinese temple and monastery
with bedrooms, moon gates, asymmetrical corridors easy to be
lost in (you had to go up to go down), carved dragons, double happiness signs in old characters. On the way into the lobby we passed
a French patisserie smelling of croissants, chocolate, and strong
coffee. The electricity had just come back on but was uncertain,
the telephones were out cold, and no water had entered the pipes
anywhere in town for two or three days. We were issued a pitcher
of water for keeping the empty toilet bowl calm until it could be
flushed again—who knows how long? The front-desk clerk was a
lovely young girl with golden Malagasy skin and high cheekbones,
long straight black hair, and the ghost of an epicanthic fold. I
immediately liked the Hotel Soafia, which housed, of course, a
Chinese restaurant—serving Malagasy pork stew—next door to a
French bakery. If you are going to travel a long way from Minnesota
in a blizzardy January, you may as well arrive in a place that doesn't
remind you much of home. The balcony off the hotel room overlooked a landscaped pool, a half acre of bougainvillea, roses, God-
knows-what blooming flowers, and, in the distance below us, the
peaked medieval-looking roofs of Fianarantsoa. The faucet belched
out a dry raspy cough. No washing off red road mud for the cultural travelers. A lamp flickered out, then on, then off again. No
matter. The sun shone fiercely in a huge cloud-strung sky here
almost astride the Tropic of Capricorn, high summer, high rainy
season in the southern hemisphere.

Only a tiny minority of the fourteen million odd Malagasy
citizens will ever experience the pleasure of a night at the Hotel
Soafia—too expensive, the best in town. The tab for the night, as
I remember, was about a hundred thousand Malagasy francs—
twenty dollars. It was probably less since the franc had already
been devalued once since I'd arrived a few weeks before.

Depending on which official statistician you choose to believe, Madagascar is either the fourth poorest country on the planet, among the ten poorest, or in the bottom percentile for per capita income—about two or three hundred dollars a year, give or take small change. It is poor, certainly; no genius is necessary to discover that. What minuscule fistful of cash the ordinary citizen clutches at any given time is not worth much anyway—over five thousand francs to the dollar when I left and probably worse now—but it is very beautiful, very sane cash. The banknotes are pale green, lavender, soft pink, tawny gold, teal blue, adorned with heads of poets, musicians, athletes, wise old men and women, beautiful girls on the front—nary a dictator, general, or central banker among them. On the back face: famous mountains, zebu with their herders, pirogues (the graceful native fishing boats), lemurs, tropical birds, butterflies, tortoises, a man carving a *valiha*. My favorite, the blue one-thousand-franc note, is adorned with the head of a handsome young man. "Do you know who that is?" asked a *valiha* player in Tana after I'd listened to a concert from his remarkable orchestra. I didn't. "That is our flute player's grandfather. He was the most famous flautist in Madagascar, a great virtuoso." I thought wistfully of Alexander Hamilton, Andrew Jackson, U. S. Grant. One thousand francs is worth twenty cents—or less—a good souvenir for your musician friends, eh? Whatever the hard-currency value of the franc, that note is worth an enormous amount in real value, for what it reveals of the Malagasy soul.

An American visiting the poor—usually on holiday in warm places: beach, sun, sand—usually has to fight off two thoughts, both probably useless. First, why don't they do something about it? Get organized, work harder, throw the bums out, join the free market; and second, why don't we do something about it? Surely some foreign aid, a program or two, the peace corps, AID, loans, debt forgiveness will solve this. We veer madly between social

Darwinism and pious do-goodism, bouncing fast from left to
right inside the same brain in any given quarter hour. These notions are both beside the point. We go wrong because of our fundamental puritan mistake: equating money with the grace of
God. We (and old Island is as mired in the quicksand of our too-
rich behemoth as you, Sensible Reader) mistake poverty for an
abnormal human state. Poverty, on our sweet earth, is the order
of the day, and the order of our history with its measly half-
dozen millennia of consciousness. Poverty is normality incarnate
for us poor bare forked animals.

A casual tourist seeing the bare feet of so many of the
Malagasy—their tattered rags, mud houses, old ladies selling
empty scotch bottles, dead batteries, and bent nails, begging
children, lepers, open sewers, bony dogs sprawled out comatose
in the mud, women sifting through street garbage for salvageable
morsels for their children—sees—as he sees in Mexico, China,
Nigeria, New Jersey, downtown Minneapolis—the bas-relief of
poverty, a frozen image, a cliché. He does not imagine that such
human beings might have cultures, histories, souls, poems, and
songs nobler, more alive, than his own. He does not see the faces
of his own ancestors or their equal poverty. He does not see that
while human beings are often geniuses at the art of poverty,
they generally grow steadily stupider and more brutal under the
might of money—at least too much of it. Do not misunderstand,
Sensible Reader. I do not mean to romanticize poverty. It does
not ennoble; it kills, finally. But poverty, though it may be caused
by the deliberate greed of some who ought to be stopped from
propagating it, is for those who suffer it only a matter of chance,
a turning of the wheel. With or without money, the soul lives
until the body dies. Whether it lives afterward is a matter not
for essayists but for theologians.

No water, no power, no phone, no toilet, no highway, no train in Fianartsoa, the place of good learning? *Mei guanxi,* as the Chinese say on such occasions: it doesn't make any difference. Off we went to the Business English Center for "American culture," poetry and music still encrusted with the unwashed dirt and sweat of a few days on the road. The hall was packed, everyone dressed to the nines, both young and old, suits, ties, dresses, hose, even in the muggy heat. We moved in a Yamaha electric piano that we had brought from Tana, my one concession to the absence or complete inoperability of pianos in rural Madagascar. The power charged through the contraption's umbilical cord. All's well. I met my introducer, a Chinese Malagasy, the country's most successful vintner. "Do you still speak Chinese?" I asked. "Of course," he said, "but only Cantonese." "So English is your fourth language?" "Fifth. Back in our socialist days, I spent three years in Cuba on work brigades for Fidel. Fluent Spanish. Now I must learn English for the wine business." His English was fine, almost without accent. He welcomed and introduced me. I began. The audience looked alert, as if they could follow my English with ease. I was warned in Tana that sometimes "on the road," English skills might be more good intention than fact. The piano was my ace in the hole for such occasions. Everyone understands Scott Joplin and Jelly Roll Morton whatever their language. I read William Carlos Williams, Walt Whitman, Emily Dickinson, Carl Sandburg, Robert Bly, Louis Simpson, poems by my own contemporaries, a few of mine, interspersing them with anecdotes about American life, comments on language.

I had driven to Ambalavao in the afternoon, a small town twenty miles south of Fianar. The road crosses a high mountain pass and travels through the equal of the most gorgeous scenery on the planet. Long brilliant green valleys, terraced rice paddies,

red hills and cliffs, every rise crowned with the handsome stone
ancestral tombs that decorate all Madagascar. The boulders on
the pass were pockmarked with garishly painted political slogans
for a half-dozen presidential candidates. Madagascar had just had
a lively election before Christmas, but had no president as yet.
The ballots were being endlessly recounted under armed guard in
the ministry office in Tana, every recount producing a different
result. Didier Ratsiraka, who brought Maoist socialism and complete economic destruction to the country from 1975 to 1991, was
trying to reclaim the leadership against Albert Zafy, a professor
who had let the economy slide even further into chaos for seven
years. The last recount headline I'd seen in a Tana newspaper read:
"Ratsiraka 57 percent, Zafy 53. Another recount called for." Local
wags loved it. The country seemed to be doing perfectly nicely
without a leader, as I suspect most countries, including this one,
would. Now if we could just get rid of the army too. The beauty of
the countryside and the absurdity of politics moved me to write
a little poem. I thought the audience might like it because it used
the few Malagasy words I'd learned.

THE PRESIDENT OF ROCKS, JANUARY 1997

Boulders on the pass to Ambalavao
all painted with politicians' names:
Zafy, Ratsiraka, Ratsiraka, Zafy,
waiting to preside, but still
no president in Madagascar.
Far below, lime green rice paddies
rise like a stepladder out of the valley.
Farmers stand ankle deep
in rice water, weeding. A blue painted cart
pulled by two black zebu wobbles

down the road, loaded with grass.
An old lady walks by with a basket of bread
on her head, long tan loaves like fingers.
Children wash in water tumbling off a cliff.
Do these rocks need a president?
Will rice elect a leader?
Does water want to be governed today?
Does bread long for law and order?
The old king's name was long and grand:
Andrianampoinimerina, but the names
of rice, water, cattle, bread
are short and quick: *vary, rano, omby, mofo,*
and no one remembers the president
of any place at all.

The clock on the wall was haywire, but it felt to me like time for music. I sat at the electric Yamaha, said a few words about ragtime, then started a piece by Joplin: "Elite Syncopations." Out went the power. Down went the piano. Dry thumping on dead circuits. The power flipped back. Two and a half bars of Joplin. The gadget hissed at me, expired again. I talked a little more, waiting for power. I started again. This time the room lights stayed on, but the piano died with a whimper, sounding like a car horn going over a cliff. The hell with you, then. I stood up, sang them a Woody Guthrie song, told a joke, read one more poem. Time up? I looked at Lanto. More, said the Fianar folk. I sang, talked, babbled, improvised poems. Finally I thanked them for coming in four of my eight Malagasy words and said good night. They applauded. I'd gone two hours. In a foreign language. With a dead piano. The red light beamed on the Yamaha one last time. I played them a Malagasy dance tune I'd found in a book. I had no clear idea how the rhythm went, but hoped for the best. They bounced in their

Afindrafindrao

dedicated to Rajery

Bill Holm

transcribed for left hand alone

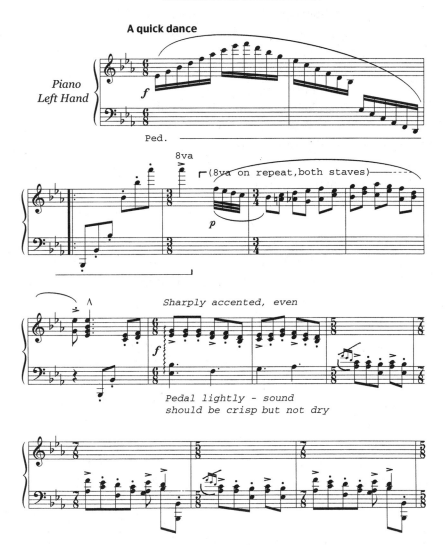

(End 8va on repeat) *No ritard*

chairs, asked a few questions, then rose to depart. One couple in
the front row who had looked particularly alert came up to pump
my hand and thank me—in French. I summoned Lanto. He translated. They enjoyed your speech and singing, even your anger at
the piano. They thought you a skilled orator. But their English? I
asked. They neither speak nor understand a word of it, said Lanto,
but they love oratory, watching face and gesture, listening to the
music of speech—even in a foreign language. Well, I'll be damned.
I shook their hands back, then fired at them my four words of
French: *Merci beaucoup. Bonne nuit.*

We all adjourned afterwards to Papillon, reputedly the best
restaurant in Madagascar, an outpost of Paris and haute cuisine
for the old colonials. We were guests of the Chinese vintner, a
grandly hospitable fellow. The waiter, an immensely dignified,
white-haired, red-coated, gold-skinned gentleman of about seventy took our orders—in French. He looked to me like a version
of the old headwaiter in *My Dinner with André.* After we had ordered aperitifs and surveyed the starters, I asked them about
the non-English-speaking couple. How could they bear it for two
hours? The Malagasy prefer long speeches laced with poetry,
proverbs, elaborate rhetorical tropes. It is not a laconic culture.
It values public speech—the music of words. All Malagasy are
used to the sometimes enormous orations delivered for the turning of the dead—the *famidihana*—when ancestral bones are exhumed, rewrapped, toasted and praised, danced seven times
around their tombs, and then orated over—for many hours. If
you learned Malagasy maybe you could become a funeral orator,
joked one. How close did I come on the last piece, I asked. Oh,
"Afindrafindrao," they all nodded. It was composed in 1879 for
the *valiha,* by Razafindriantson. It has been the national dance
for a century and a third. Too slow, said one. Too Lutheran, said

an American who lived in Fianar. The rhythm must have more bite, said another. It's in fives and sevens, not march time. But did you see the audience? said another. If you had played one more chorus, they would have risen to dance. The Malagasy can hardly resist rising from their chairs to move in the presence of good music. They were honored to hear a *vazaha* (foreigner) here so briefly play that tune, said another, even if you played it so damned badly. I'll practice, I promised, but fast fives and sevens are hard for Minnesotans. The martinis and Camparis, DuBonnets and oysters and paté arrived. Now we all faced a decision: tournedos, canard à la kirsch, osso buco, langouste Thermidor. The old headwaiter examined us sternly: foreign riffraff. Who needs Paris when you've got Papillon?

When, after five or six wrong turns in the maze of corridors in the Hotel Soafia, we arrived at our rooms, the water was back, the toilets flushed, soap and towels waiting. I opened the balcony doors to let the night wind blow the bougainvillea into the room. While I showered, I hummed "Afindrafindrao" a little, practicing on my fives and sevens, still not quite getting the swing. I thought to myself, who's civilized on this planet—us or them? The poor or the rich?

ANTANANARIVO: RATOVO AND RAJERY

In 1996 western Minnesota was in the midst of its worst winter in over a century. A procession of seventeen full-scale blizzards began in October, one smashing in on the heels of the last, the roads now only narrow tunnels through the drifts. Those roads closed whenever the wind blew, snapped shut like sclerotic arteries. People left for work five miles away in calm weather only to arrive home three days later. Wind chills often plunged to a hundred degrees below zero in the howling arctic gales. The thermometer hardly rose above minus twenty degrees. The radio warned you not to leave your car if you were caught suddenly by one of these assaults. You would die within two or three minutes. All the churches canceled Christmas. No one felt much like worshipping anyway. They felt like cursing, or moving. Enough was enough.

During one fall blizzard, the phone rang. It was difficult to hear anything because of the rattling windows, thrashing branches, the house creaking on its foundation. Outside the frost-crusted windowpanes, the world was invisible, a maelstrom of wind-blasted snow. A distant operator asked if this was Meester Holm. It was Antananarivo calling. I knew who it was. I'd met Paul Saxton when I had a Fulbright lectureship in Iceland. Paul worked at the American Cultural Center in Reykjavík, and his Peruvian wife, Eliana, often saved me from boiled fish with doses of green chilies. We had remained friends these many years. Now Paul was director of the USIS Cultural Center in Madagascar. Could I come for a long trip to give lectures on American culture and literature to English-language groups scattered through the country? January and February maybe? As it happened, I was on sabbatical from my teaching job in Blizzardville. I think my delighted "Yes Indeed!" was audible ten thousand miles away without benefit of telephone.

You do not arrive in Madagascar without a few rituals reminding you that you are not going to New Jersey. First you fill your arm full of fresh holes: innoculations for cholera, typhoid, tetanus, hepatitis B, then prescriptions for Mefloquine to ward off the worst consequences of malaria, Imodium for your inevitable dysentery, a huge and colorful visa entitling you to enter Madagascar once for sixty days, and the heaviest plane ticket I had ever held in my hand: Minneapolis, Detroit, Paris, Rome,

Nairobi, Antananarivo, thirty hours in an iron tube. Marcy and I intended to go to Minneapolis five days early to shop for the trip, see friends, go to a grand seventieth-birthday party for an old friend, forestall the possibility of being trapped by yet another blizzard and missing the plane. But the granddaddy blizzard struck five days before, just as we walked out to the already packed car for the normal three-hour trip. Five solid days of relentless hurricane-force winds and swirling snow, all roads closed going anywhere. On the morning of the fifth day, the highway patrol informed us that the roads north (a hundred miles out of the way) might be open—a single lane—if we were lucky and they hadn't blown shut, and Highway 12 might be open from Willmar to Minneapolis if the plows had been out. We arrived at the airport after two hundred twenty icy miles, an hour before the plane left. We needn't have hurried. The airplane sat on the runway for another hour having its wings de-iced before it could fly to Detroit. We almost missed connecting with the flight to Paris. A day and a half later, an Air Madagascar jet banked over an Indian Ocean reddened far out to sea by the red soil eroded from Madagascar's hills. We landed early in the morning at Ivato Airport. Eighty degrees, more red dust, flowers everywhere, a sea of gold faces.

The Northwest Airlines stewardess on the plane to Paris asked where we were going. Madagascar? Is that the little island by Africa? She is not alone in her ignorance. Ordinary citizens know almost nothing about Madagascar, and what little they think they know is mistaken. It is a hard place to pigeonhole. It is—from the evidence of science, culture, history, geography—almost sui generis; one of a kind. The one fact the poor stewardess thought she had grappled was completely wrong. Madagascar is, if nothing else, not small. It is an enormous California-sized island,

1,000 miles long, 350 miles wide, sitting in the Indian Ocean,
250 miles east of Mozambique. It broke off from Gondwanaland,
the prehistoric theoretical concatenation of all the continents,
120 million years ago, after which it drifted east to its present anchorage. It remained uninhabited longer than any other large
habitable landmass, until maybe fifteen hundred years ago when
immigrants from Borneo, Malaysia, Indonesia crossed the Indian
Ocean in small boats, probably stopping first by the east coast
of Africa, then settling down on this strange island. They found
peculiar neighbors, man-sized lemurs, twenty-foot-tall two-ton
flightless birds—like Jurassic ostriches—enormous mongooses,
but no cats, dogs, poisonous reptiles, or hoofed grazing ungulates.
They spoke Malagasy, a Malayo-Polynesian language related to
Hawaiian but not to any neighboring African language. Evolution
and history passed by Madagascar in peculiar forms.

Madagascar is still home to most of the world's lemurs,
chameleons, and orchids. Its fauna and flora are the great antique
shop and museum of nature, everything ancient, strange, unexpected, one of a kind. The most numerous animals are the imported zebu, African humped cattle.

Anthropologists love Madagascar for its funerals. The family
tombs that dot the countryside are full of the wrapped bones of
many generations of ancestors. When a family member dies, zebu
are slaughtered, orchestras hired, new silk wrappings for the old
corpses sewn, the tomb opened, the ancestors exhumed and rewrapped; there is wine, dancing, celebration, sometimes for days.

The Malagasy are paddy rice farmers in the tradition of their
Polynesian ancestors. They are the most enthusiastic rice eaters
in the world, but the French who colonized them left their mark
on the table too: croissants, strong coffee, goose-liver paté,
baguettes, proper sauces.

The only people I ever met who could instantly identify Madagascar were stamp collectors and Norwegian Lutherans. Philatelists continue to prize Malagasy stamps for their beauty of design, for the exotic images that decorate them. Since the middle of the nineteenth century, Madagascar has been the prime missionary project of Norwegian Lutherans, whether here or in the old country. American Lutherans in my boyhood annually collected money to convert the Malagasy. They still do. Few parishioners could find Budapest, Caracas, or Bangkok on a globe, but their fingers moved automatically to Madagascar while singing "From Greenland's Icy Mountains to Afric's Coral Strand."

Aside from an occasional clip on endangered lemurs, Madagascar has never been much on the mind of the *New York Times* or the television networks. The United States has never even sent troops to Madagascar to save anyone, protect freedom, or guard property. Perhaps that's why Madagascar is one of those rare places where Americans are still welcomed with affection. Sending a middle-aged writer from Minnesota to read poetry and play the piano in January is probably as close as we've come to an armed invasion.

I collected stamps and knew Norwegian Lutherans, but, aside from that, existed in as great a state of ignorance as most of my fellow citizens. I looked first for literature, books to read. I knew a few poems by two poets, Jean-Joseph Rabearivelo and Flavien Ranaivo, both translated from French, not Malagasy. I called a Lutheran seminary to talk to a teacher who had spent forty years of his life in Madagascar and reputedly owned a vast library. "It won't do you much good unless you have fluent French, Malagasy and Norwegian," he said. "There's little in English." "What is their music like?" I asked. "Extraordinary."

The reverend did not exaggerate. I found in a Saint Paul music

shop a tape of what the cover described as "The Robert Johnson
of Madagascar. The Famous *Valiha*, Rakotozafy." The cover drawing shows a mustachioed gold-faced man strumming what looks
like a mailbox with vertical strings. One end rests on an old section
of tailpipe. Rakotozafy's "Famous *Valiha*" is actually a *marovany*,
built square rather than, like a true *valiha*, a round tube of bamboo with a slit in the middle for sound. The strings in both are recycled bicycle brake cables. Rakotozafy, like most players, made
his own instrument—partly of wood, but partly scrap sheet metal
added to increase the instrument's resonance, like the steel guitars of the old bluesmen. It is made essentially of junk and scrap—
the orchestra of the poor. On this detritus, Rakotozafy plays what
sounds to my ear like a combination of baroque counterpoint and
virtuoso blues guitar, which nevertheless remains entirely itself,
unmistakable as Malagasy music on a Malagasy instrument. It
melds the ping of a good harpsichord with the cascading arpeggios
of a harp. The songs are mostly in triple rhythms—no thump, two,
three, four here—but with ingenious syncopations and hemiolas,
and rhythms of five and seven. The rhythmic hiccups fill the
music with dance energy, and the tuning of the *valiha* in alternat-
ing thirds gives the harmony a great sweetness and charm. I'd call
Rakotozafy the Fritz Kreisler of the *valiha* as much as the Robert
Johnson, but he remains past all such comparisons, an entirely
individual musician. How I work to avoid the word "unique"! It is
nonsense, a trifle, a filler, an ad word. Everything is one of a kind.
Yet this music, and the thousands of Malagasy virtuoso players
who operate out of this same live tradition, is only itself, though
the tradition steals blithely from Indonesian, African, and western
music, Bach, French waltzes, Norwegian hymns, Black American
blues, ragtime, and jazz, anything that strikes its ear. It is an
island of its own music. It does what a live tradition is supposed

to do, eat everything in sight, then digest it into something else with new and original energy.

It's six o'clock in the morning in early January, and I am riding in a United States government van into Antananarivo, capital of the red kingdom. The city sprawls over twelve steep hills, densely packed with tall narrow houses adorned with second-floor balconies. Those houses snake up and down the twelve hills on serpentine roads. At the crest of the highest hill sit the burnt-out ruins of the Rova, Queen Ranevelona's palace from the mid-nineteenth century—no skyscrapers here, only the fifteen-story Hilton hotel sticks up above its neighbors. It's a city built to human scale, a kind of toy city children would imagine if left to fabricate a town plan. Between the hills farmers still work their rice paddies on the flat. Scrawny chickens wander freely up and down the streets. Almost everything needs a coat of paint or a repaired foundation— too little money here for a long time. The streets are narrow, steep, sometimes still cobbled, everywhere pocked with vast potholes, mud swelling up through cracks in the tarmac. Too many people here; like every third-world capital, half the farm population has swelled into town creating slums and chaos. Too much poverty, uncollected garbage heaps being investigated for treasures, few feet with shoes at all, mostly sandals made from old tires, but every head—male, female, child—jauntily be-hatted. Clogged, immobile traffic even so early, every car trying to squeeze into the same scrunched lane; in New York City this would be cause for bloody fights, cursing, probably shooting, but here a driver who cuts into the traffic offers a genteel wave of thanks, and the other driver waves back, only one example of the instinctive delicate sense of courtesy that seems the birthright of every Malagasy. It certainly isn't ours. It says: We're all broke, all frustrated, all desperate, so let us carefully observe civility to our fellow sufferer. Tana, the town's nickname, must once have been one of the most eccentrically beautiful cities anywhere on the planet—before overcrowding, poverty, corrupt government, too many cars dented its charms. But in first morning light, or at sunset looking down from one of its many hills over the sea of multicolored roofs, standing next to the bougainvillea, the heavy banana leaves shivering overhead, the far vista of the rice farms spreading out for miles past the edge of the city, everywhere red ground and pale green rice paddy as far as the eye can penetrate, its magic is not yet gone.

The most famous institution in Tana is the Friday *zoma*, the public market, locally reputed to be the second largest in the world, though no one can ever tell you which one exceeds it. It is vast, many city blocks jammed with thousands of white octagonal umbrellas. Dayton's, Macy's, Harrod's, Sears and Roebuck, and Wal-Mart all jammed together outdoors. Food, furniture, crafts, drugs, clothes, junk—whatever you need or want. Haggling is required; the market is a noisy, joyful frenzy of voices, smells, music, shouting, a mass of bodies squeezing through the narrow channels between vendors' umbrellas. I went, wanting to buy nothing but to memorize everything internally to help me get through the next American errand to fetch Hamburger Helper or microwave-safe cookware. Goods in the market moved not by truck or conveyer belt or even wheelbarrow but by loaded baskets balanced on the head. A famous tourist photograph of Madagascar shows an old lady with a long goose neck curling up out of her basket. I went to the goose market and there she was: a dozen of her, carrying a dozen geese. The Malagasy (in the central highlands at least) are generally small, fine-boned people, but such weights their heads carried! I saw nothing drop. I stepped out of the traffic for a minute to write this poem.

BALANCE

At the Friday *zoma* in Tana everything
goes in a basket on the head:
five kilos of tomatoes, a goose,
two chickens, fish, flowers, rice,
avocados, mangoes, plums.
With balance, everything is possible:
carry the Bible, Shakespeare, Homer,
the new physics, the old philosophy.
Carry anything but money.
Money tips over.

Through these narrow lanes between
white umbrellas move
five-foot humans topped by two feet
of woven reeds, and they all move
like dancers on point: head erect,
toes ready, eyes ahead, rhythm even.
You're ready to feel it!
Now a whole line of dancers, bodies
fine tuned and balanced, move from
one end of the universe to the other, but
drop nothing, with the neck of a goose
curling up above the reed basket,
like radar to check the air for enemies,
maybe opportunities.
This balance goes all the way down
to the toes, then deep into the red earth
to keep you upright.

I did most of my work in Tana at the USIS Cultural Center, an
old three-story building halfway up one of the twelve hills, a library

and meeting room on the ground floor, narrow wood stairs up to classrooms and offices. It was a cozy, unofficial-feeling place. A day or two after I arrived I had a meeting with Sandatra, a group of fifteen or twenty local writers. Some wrote in French, most in Malagasy, one fellow even tried poems in English. I read to them, Lanto translating what he thought they might have missed, then they read to me, a poem apiece. We talked about rhythm, the sounds of vowels in different languages, the right subjects for poems, the difficulty of finding publishers or an audience. They asked about American writers; I asked about who was hot in Madagascar. It's an oral culture, they said. People love spoken poetry, most carry old *hainteny,* the old Malagasy oral poems, in their head, but not so many readers, still much illiteracy in the countryside. I reiterated that it was mostly in the colleges, corporations, and government offices where you could find illiterates in America. I gave away several copies of Minnesota books, mine among them. They gave me a handsome anthology their group had published. I couldn't read a word of Malagasy. English was not easy for them. Still, there's something wonderful about a gift of poetry—even if all you do is admire the exotic look of the words and pet the page. My shelves are full of slim volumes of poetry— in Icelandic, Swedish, Chinese, Khmer, Azerbaijani, Ukrainian, Finnish, now Malagasy—all treasures, gatherings of the true work of the oversoul.

Since I had been advertised as a lecturer on old American keyboard music and, as a Rakotozafy convert, had expressed my desire to hear more *valiha* players—in fact to see one played— the clever Lanto was put in charge of conducting a search and organizing a few informal concerts at the cultural center. "Ratovo and Rajery," he said. "They are the best in Tana, maybe the best in the country. Ratovo (or to give his full Malagasy name,

Ranaivovololona Ratovonirina) appeared at three o'clock on a
sunny January afternoon with his orchestra and their assemblage
of instruments—*valihas* of various size and design, a couple of
kabosy (Malagasy guitars), gourd rattles, reed brushes, a three-
string fiddle *(lokanga basa), sodina* (end-blown flutes), skin drums,
an accordion. Marcy and I and a handful of employees made up
an audience. And they played—Lord, how they played! Wild
Malagasy dances, folk tunes from various corners of the country,
delicate ballads full of subtle counterpoint, American jazz (even a
Thelonious Monk tune), virtuoso flute solos played by the grandson of Rakotofra (whose head is on the one-thousand-franc note)
French, Viennese, and local waltzes, an accordion polka, and the
dance "Afindrafindrao." They passed instruments back and forth,
shifting from gourd to drum to guitar to *valiha* to singing so that
despite their meager numbers—a half-dozen musicians—it felt
like a full-scale symphony concert. It was an afternoon of daz-
zling musical skill, even genius; had these gentlemen been born
in Budapest in the Western tradition, we would now have a string
quartet that could match the last one of that name. Ratovo, the
orchestra's leader, an elegant curly-haired fellow in his thirties,
was equally well known as a maker of instruments, and as inventor of new variations on the old Malagasy traditional forms—a
local Stradivari or Guarnari del Gesu. He himself played a chromatic *valiha* he had concocted. The simple folk version is strictly
diatonic, twenty-two notes arranged in a major scale. On a chromatic *valiha*, Ratovo explained, you can play modern jazz, Bach—
even Arnold Schoenberg. I ordered a chromatic *valiha* from him to
take back to Minnesota. To plunk a scale on the *valiha* is simple;
to *play* a *valiha* requires years of grueling practice, plus probably a
DNA code disposed to music, the same demands exacted by a violin or a piano. I began that afternoon to get the sense that I was

in the presence of a musical tradition of size and magnitude—a planetary gem—that had survived missionaries, colonizers, and unimaginable poverty intact, alive, full of energy, beauty, and intelligence.

Rajery was on tour with his orchestra when I arrived so I had to wait a week or two to meet and hear him. Lanto tracked me down one afternoon in the cultural center library after I had finished giving a talk to local English teachers. I leafed through *Time* magazine looking for blizzard news from Minnesota. Temperatures had sunk to sixty below in International Falls, a new state record. It was only forty-five below in my hometown—almost summer. "Rajery is back in town. Let's go to his shop and see him." We left, snaking through the narrow cobbled streets in the USIS van. Rajery's shop, a modest room in the middle of a dusty working-class block, was open to the afternoon sun. A row of handsome *valihas* sat on a table against the wall, a few *jejy* gourd basses leaning against it, a row of drums below. Rajery, too, was an instrument maker, like most Malagasy musicians. On an island with no money, if you want music, you must sing it or build it yourself out of materials gathered for little or nothing; cut your own bamboo, go to the bicycle junkyard, dry the gourds from your uncle's garden, trade a little music for a strip of cowhide from a neighborhood farmer. This is comparable to beginning violin lessons by being presented with a pile of wood, catgut, horsehair, and a jar of varnish. How lazy the rich become! Energy and ingenuity drain out of them as the NASDAQ rises. Can anything bought for mere money ever be truly valued—or loved?

Rajery came out from the back of the shop to greet us cordially. He is a small wiry man, a fine-boned delicate pale-gold face, humorous eyes. Like most Malagasy, he is soft spoken and elaborately courteous. I was not entirely surprised when he pulled off his rubber right hand with his left, set it on the counter, picked up a valiha, checked the tuning, listened with ears alert as a fox, and without fuss started an intricate—and lightning fast—version of "Afindrafindrao" which must be a *valiha* player's classic warm-up piece to get the blood running into the fingers. But there were only five of them and a stump playing this music. Impossible. I did my best not to watch, but curiosity overwhelmed me. This simply could not be done, yet I was hearing it not only done but done brilliantly. I must now disappoint the Sensible Reader. I watched and heard Rajery many times; I even jammed with him one night at the house of an embassy official who was an enthusiastic guitarist. Rajery is the most skilled improviser of ingenious counterpoints that I have ever heard. He hears a piece once, finds the key, listens a little and proceeds with counter melodies in contrary motion, adding harmonic piquancy—pungent and unexpected dissonance to perk up the lines. This modest and courtly man may be the greatest natural musician I've ever met. Lanto had told me a bit of the story of his life. He wanted nothing as a boy but to be a musician but lost his hand in an accident before he was a teenager. He fell into despair, thinking his life ruined, the music gone out of it forever. Gradually the unkillable interior music came back to life and he started practicing again on the *valiha*. He invented a way to play using the calluses on his stump, but he won't talk about it or describe it. It is his business how he plays the *valiha,* and not yours. It is your business to listen—and that is an extraordinary pleasure. I wrote that afternoon a prose poem about Rajery and his instrument, but mostly about the interior artist in human beings, the best part of us.

VALIHA

I

Start with a hollow tube of wood—maybe bamboo, three feet
long. Make a vertical slit for sound to escape. Nail twenty bicycle
cable strings in a circle. Cover the nails with a strap of zebu hide.
Arrange twenty melon-gourd pegs under the strings for tuning.
To make the scale: left, right, left, right. Do re mi fa sol la ti do
and again. Strum with either hand: you make thirds. A cascade
of cuckoo calls. The sound should be sweet and sharp together—
half harp, half harpsichord. Hold upright between your legs.
Pluck whatever music it is in you to make. These, like all directions, are not quite so simple as they seem.

II

In a dusty little music shop in Antananarivo, a man selects a
valiha from a row of instruments he's built. He takes off a rubber
hand, sits on a stool, begins playing with five fingers and stump,
as if that were as normal as the sun rising. He starts with a dance
tune in fives and sevens. Another man nearby picks up a reed
brush and adds rhythm. Done with that, he segues into the next:
"This one comes from Tuléar, where the tunes are wilder." The
other fellow hauls down a carved drum. I count thirteen beats
in the pattern. Someone tells him I play hymns in ragtime. He
smiles wryly, strums a jazzy "What a Friend We Have in Jesus,"
then adds the first strain of a Joplin rag. Bach too? "Jesu, Joy
of Man's Desiring." He chuckles. "Here's one from Minnesota—
your home." He sings Bob Dylan's old song "Blowin' in the Wind."
How many roads does a song walk down to travel from Hibbing
to Antananarivo? He plays for an hour, tunes from everywhere,
ears alert as antennae for new counterpoints inside whatever he
plays, a smile crossing his fine-boned face as he thanks us for
being his guests.

III

Three quarters of a century ago, Josef Hoffman played a
Beethoven concerto in Boston. Afterward, a rich lady squeezed
his small, fat-fingered, cigar-stained hand and said, "How wonderful that you play with those hands!"

"Madame," snorted Josef Hoffman, "surely you don't imagine
that one plays the piano with one's hands!"

Nor dance with the feet, nor carve with a knife, nor kiss with
the lips, nor paint with a brush, but with something else inside
a human being that fuels that longing for beauty and order—
something that rears up in the oddest circumstances, anywhere,
anytime, anybody, with a bamboo tube and a bicycle spoke.

Early in 1997, his relatives "turned the bones" of Rakotozafy,
thirty years after his early death. His *famidihana* provided an occasion for national celebration—to honor the bones of Madagascar's
greatest twentieth-century *valiha* virtuoso. Thousands came to
dance his silk-wrapped corpse seven times around the family
tomb. Rajery played the *valiha* for the occasion. I think Rakotozafy's
bones must have been pleased with the music.

Colonized countries all over the planet lost their music and
their stories and poems during the heydey of imperialism. It is
one thing to lose your raw products, your freedom, your independence, sometimes even your language, but to lose your music
and poems means to have a chunk of the soul carved away. Much
of the native music of east Africa is gone, though much survives
in the west. Where is Mayan music, Haida music, Filipino music?
Madagascar was either lucky or fierce. Its music is intact, and
thus, whatever its poverty, misery, public chaos, the weight at
the bottom of the soul is intact. Money can always arrive again,
the trains can be made to run on time, the children all to own ten

pairs of shoes, even the forests to be regrown. But the extinction of music has more serious consequences for the human race than the possible extinction of Madagascar's extraordinary collection of lemurs. Even among the lemurs, the largest, strangest and per-haps most threatened, the indri, is famous primarily for its own singing—loud tunes that carry a mile away from the treetops where they live. Lose the indri and you lose the music. Lose the music and you lose the soul. Madagascar's soul is in very good shape, whatever its statistical poverty. Mr. Ratovo and Mr. Rajery will provide testimony for that.

DIÉGO AND TULÉAR

I took four trips to the various corners of this huge island to give lectures and readings at English-language centers, the first by car through the central highlands to Antsirabe and Fianarantsoa. The roads in Madagascar, particularly those from Tana to the coasts, are seas of mud and ruts—holes large enough to swallow a pickup, disappeared bridges, in some places only tracks through damp sand. A hundred miles could take a week—or a month. In order to actually arrive, you fly. So we did—to Diégo-Suarez in the far north, and to Tuléar on the southwest coast, facing Africa, and finally by car to Tamatave, Madagascar's chief port on the Indian Ocean. I'll try to give the flavor of these places, none of which could be mistaken for each other. Madagascar is geographi-cally an island (the fourth largest in the world) and in its peculiar separateness from both Africa and Asia is certainly a psychologi-cal and cultural island, but it is itself so vast and various that it seems a separate continent—"A World out of Time" as the TV special series described it.

Every Malagasy town has two names, colonial and native—à

la Saigon and Ho Chi Minh City. Most Malagasy still use the old names. This exhibits neither love nor nostalgia for their colonial past, but a secure calm in the presence of history and habit. Diégo-Suarez (Antsirañana) is named for two Portuguese sailors who first saw Madagascar around 1500. It has always been a port, a fortified navy town, first used by the French, then during World War II by the British, who occupied it to keep its fine harbor from falling into the hands of the Vichy government or the Germans. Today it is a sleepy place, not fought over by anyone. As the northernmost town in Madagascar, it is closest to the equator, here eight degrees north. In February, high summer, and rainy season, the old ramshackle colonial buildings—second-floor balconies with shaded walks under them, looking like New Orleans' French quarter without paint—seemed to be sweating as much as the citizens. Not much air-conditioning, instead many slowly turning ceiling fans languorously churning the damp air around.

We arrived in gray rain. This was not Tana! Faces here on the coast were darker, more African, adorned with Muslim skull caps, long robes, a mixed brew of languages and physiognomies. Hanitra Rabetokotany, our USIS escort, came from an old and distinguished family of intellectuals and poets around Tana, pure highland Merina stock, and she looked as much a foreigner here as Marcy and I. "I can hardly understand the dialect," she confessed, with the tone of a traveler from Kent in Newcastle. Port towns always attract fine mixtures of humans—immigrants, ship jumpers, mysterious travelers who never leave town, sailors from half a planet away who marry local girls. But Diégo had lost its strategic value for the navies of the world, and the impassable roads south meant that local goods could not be easily transported or sold to the rest of the island. Now, at the height of mango season, fruit rotted on the trees with no handy markets. I joked that

I could do a lively business selling fresh mangos in blizzardy western Minnesota on February 5. "You can buy a whole treeful for five hundred francs"—about ten cents. I thought long thoughts drenched in mango juice as Jérémie, our rakish driver—a firm believer in "Damn the potholes: full speed ahead!"—surged on-ward to meet the town dignitaries. In 1997 the university system in Madagascar had fallen into almost complete collapse: teachers unpaid for months, buildings untended, schedules nonexistent, no budget. As with the absent presidency, the country seemed to be carrying on nicely without it, but ultimately a country must have a decently functioning school system even if it decides to live without a president. The little university in Diégo seemed calm, efficient, trim, well tended—a contrast from the chaos in Tana. We met the rector, who announced his name: Said M'ze. "You have the shortest name of anyone I've met in Madagascar." "It is the shortest name in Madagascar. My grandfather came from Zanzibar." M'ze, a soft-spoken handsome man, was indeed not a highlander, rather a dark African face—no Indonesians in his woodpile. He invited us to dinner later at one of Diégo's fine fish restaurants but said we would have to wait till sundown. It was Ramadan, so he fasted all day. Most of Diégo was Muslim—fifteen mosques to three churches—the result of Arab traders and proximity to the Comoro Islands and Zanzibar, both Muslim outposts. In the rest of the world, Muslims and Christians (and throw in the animists) were mired in bloody fights fueled by harsh rhetoric and fanaticism, but here in Diégo, all these immigrant stocks and religions coexisted calmly while the five-hundred-franc trees heavy with mangos fermented in the saturated air.

Next we met the mayor in his new marble city hall. Lucien Zasy was a gregarious, expansive man, witty and quick in English as I assume he is in his several other languages. He welcomed us to town—and to the enormous auditorium in the city hall where I was to give my reading. We walked out of his fourth floor office to a huge tan marble slab of a balcony. He made a sweeping gesture at the horizon, misty green mountains, the bay, the roofs of the town, the Indian Ocean stretching off to the north. "From here, every day in Diégo you can see the rain coming from this direction, then arriving here, and finally leaving town for those mountains. By that time, more rain has arrived from over there. Enjoy the rain. Enjoy Diégo."

In the afternoon, I met two of Said M'ze's teaching staff, an engineer and a chemist, Mr. Randrianampianina and Mr. Ramaroson, who played guitar and *marotaly*—the Malagasy harp. I was furnished a small electric piano with four octaves that sounded like a calliope, not quite the instrument for Beethoven or James P. Johnson. First they played for me—starting again with "Afindrafindrao"—then I played for them. We jammed together a bit on "Saint Louis Blues" and "When the Saints." Then Mr. Ramaroson soloed on his magnificent harp—"I built it," he said. In addition to its lovely tone, it was a fine piece of cabinet work, an instrument that looked as elegant as it sounded. We shook sweaty hands—no air-conditioning in a humid ninety degrees—and they left to teach: chemistry and math. At the door, Mr. Ramaroson asked if I would send him a jazz reed for soprano sax—his other instrument. Unavailable in Madagascar. In America you can buy plenty of reeds, but many other things are in shorter supply.

The next morning we left to tour a little of the Ankarana Reserve in the mountains outside Diégo. Gray fine drizzle alternated with hazy shafts of sun. We traveled again with the rakish Jérémie at the wheel, and Hervè Bakarizafy, another elegantly soft-spoken man with a dark African face, as our guide—our

Sakalava Henry Thoreau. Ankarana is one of a dozen reserves
and parks where the Malagasy, with the aid and encouragement
of scientists all over the planet, try to keep intact their extraordinary museum of fauna and flora. Because of its ancient separation
from other land masses and island isolation far enough from a
continent to make species exchange almost impossible, evolution
proceeded strangely throughout Madagascar. Its largest snake
is the tree boa, cousin to South American snakes but not to any
African species. Lemurs provided no competition for the more
aggressive and intelligent monkeys, so have almost disappeared
from Africa or elsewhere, but here, without serious predators
or competitors, they branched out grandly into many varieties
and flourished. Over one thousand orchids, found nowhere else
on earth, bloom here. With no large predators of the cat, dog,
or reptile variety (only a few imported crocodiles, whom the
Malagasy regard as sacred), the mongoose and civet evolved to
perform their functions, so that the largest lemur eater on the
island, the fossa, though it is the size and rough shape of a small
panther, is in fact the giant of the civet family. The primitive,
insect-eating spiny tenrec, found only here, looks like a small
porcupine, but isn't. The most numerous reptiles are the slow
moving, comical, mitten-footed, lightning-tongued chameleons.
The largest, Parson's chameleon, can reach close to two feet
long—including its fine spiral tail—and weigh up to ten or
twelve pounds. Even now scientists continue to discover new
species, new plants, new delights in the remaining forests of
Madagascar. Biologists, from Alfred Russel Wallace onward, vi-
brate with joy at the thought of its treasures—all, alas, threatened by growing population, slash-and-burn farming, and the
oppressive poverty that can turn even rare species into edible
protein.

Hervè had x-ray eyes. Riding at sixty miles per hour, he spotted chameleons in roadside trees. As we climbed a hill, he told us
to look back just over the treetops to see the tsingy-limestone
pinnacles so sharp and narrow that humans are still trying to figure out how to penetrate and explore them. Ankarana sits on a
limestone plateau underlaid with caves and subterranean rivers.
Hervè had explored most of them. He knew this difficult wilderness as a farmer knows his fields, foot by foot. With only an afternoon, we couldn't see much. We drove up a muddy path as far
as possible, with fine mist making slick mud. While Hervè grace-
fully ambled downhill, the rest of us half slid through a dense
muddy tangle of forest. The lemurs were hiding today, though
we scared up a few more varieties of chameleon. At the bottom
of the hill, under a collapsed limestone ledge, a lovely waterfall
fumed and gurgled before disappearing underground. After enjoying it for a while, we grunted back uphill. What we had not
seen, Hervè conjured in the mind's eye with his stories, even poetry of this wild landscape. Isn't that a naturalist's real work: to
feed the imagination?

Halfway home a bald tire blew out. A broken spare. The first
taxi *brousse*, an overloaded rusty wreck of a Renault, stopped to
give us and our sad tire a hitch to the next market town. The
vazaha, Marcy and I, provided our rescuers much merriment and
curiosity. While we sat across the street from a little market
square, two young fellows tried to sell us local emeralds. A gaggle
of children decided that I was Père Noël. All of us—even Hervè—
were caked with drying mud, so we bought a few ripe mangos
to keep ourselves moist till we could limp back to Diégo on our
freshly patched tube.

The next night I read in the marble town hall. Someone found
a piano. I shared the program with the two musician-teachers,

and a chorus and dance line of students who had worked up a
program of folksongs and local dances. I remembered the warning that most of the audience would understand only a little
English. As in Fianar, everybody dressed for a good time in their
Sunday best. What do I read? I puzzled. I tried a little humor. Not
a murmur, though polite attentiveness. What next? I grabbed a
poem by Etheridge Knight, a distinguished American poet, recently dead, who was a genius of sound, his own readings almost
symphonic. I read "Ilu, The Talking Drum," a poem about the
Nigerian drummer Olantungie, who brings calm and fellow feeling to a bunch of nervous people with his drum. Here's the poem:

ILU, THE TALKING DRUM

The deadness was threatening us—15 Nigerians and
    1 Mississippi nigger.
It hung heavily, like stones around our necks, pulling
    us down
to the ground, black arms and legs outflung
on the wide green lawn of the big white house
The deadness was threatening us, the day
was dying with the sun, the stillness—
unlike the sweet silence after love / making or
the pulsating quietness of a summer night—
the stillness was skinny and brittle and wrinkled
by the precise people sitting on the wide white porch
of the big white house . . .
The darkness was threatening us, menacing . . .
we twisted, turned, shifted positions, picked our
    noses,
stared at our bare toes, hissed air thru our teeth . . .

Then Tunji, green robes flowing as he rose,
strapped on Ilu, the talking drum,
and began:

kah doom / kah doom-doom / kah doom / kah doom-
doom-doom
kah doom / kah doom-doom / kah doom / kah doom-
doom-doom
kah doom / kah doom-doom / kah doom / kah doom-
doom-doom
kah doom / kah doom-doom / kah doom / kah doom-
doom-doom

the heart, the heart beats, the heart, the heart beats
slow
the heart beats slowly, the heart beats
the blood flows slowly, the blood flows
the blood, the blood flows, the blood, the blood flows
slow
kah doom / kah doom-doom / kah doom / kah doom-
doom-doom
and the day opened to the sound
kah doom / kah doom-doom / kah doom / kah doom-
doom-doom
and our feet moved to the sound of life
kah doom / kah doom-doom / kah doom / kah doom-
doom-doom
and we rode the rhythms as one
from Nigeria to Mississippi
and back
kah doom / kah doom-doom / kah doom / kah doom-
doom-doom

After the first kah dooms, the audience joined in, maybe three
hundred of them, a huge verbal drumming echoing in a marble
room. They may not have understood English perfectly, but
they apprehended that poem. They wanted it again. I read it,
wishing I had Etheridge's powerful, resonant voice beside me.
Maybe he was. He certainly must have enjoyed—from the spirit
world—the effect of his poem on a hot February night next
to the Indian Ocean, ten thousand miles away from where he
wrote it.

   After the reading, one of the local Peace Corps volunteers
came to the front of the hall to meet Marcy and me. Throughout
Madagascar I met perhaps a dozen Peace Corps folks, mostly
lively young women, but a few of my own contemporaries with
some kick left inside them. A primitive glimmer of a political
idea crossed my brain in Madagascar. The American government
abroad throws its money mostly at armies and industrial schemes.
We love selling munitions, which then frequently get used either
against us or against the most humane citizens of the country
for which we've provided them. But the Peace Corps actually improves the image of the United States by doing intelligent service
to the countries where it operates. Who could argue with hiring
lively and energetic idealists to teach English, public health,
agriculture—while learning something about another language
and culture to boot? Beats the hell out of M-16s and land mines,
which have never done any part of humanity any good at all—
whatever the Pentagon bozos tell you about security threats. The
same thought applies to the closing of American libraries and
downsizing of cultural centers all over the world. The cold war
is over! shout the bozos—no more commies, only Big Macs and
Coke! Now more than ever we need books abroad to save the
United States from its own stupidity. Mark Twain, Willa Cather,

and William Carlos Williams will do us more good than the World Bank or the marines.

I think I delivered an outburst like this to young Marianne Judar, but she overlooked it. We were all starved after a day in the wilderness and a night of culture, so we adjourned to investigate Diégo nightlife. At dinner Marianne told her story, and afterward I wrote this description of what she said:

MULTICULTURAL EXPERIENCE IN DIÉGO-SUAREZ

The young Peace Corps volunteer has learned the Sakalava dialect and brings health news by four-wheel drive to villagers at the end of gumbo roads. Here: no water, no light, no store, not even a toilet pit. *Fady,* she says, taboo to dig a hole in the ground for shit. If you dig, they think the earth will cover your skin with sores. But the Sakalava king bends a little. He decides that while a latrine is not customary, it is permitted.

She found a bright red snake coiled on her pillow, a family of mice hatched at the bottom of her clothes bag, red-footed millipedes—two fingers long—dropped with thuds onto her bed. She saved small tenrecs for the village children to eat when the adults finished the real meat without them. Her pets: lumbering three-inch cockroaches with red stripes who bellow belligerent hisses when you press their backs.

She is from Chicago, she says. At this moment, ten thousand miles away, Buicks and Volvos inch their way down six lanes of the Dan Ryan freeway toward thousand-foot rectangles of black marble and green glass, snow swirling over their towers, over the vast gray lake to the east.

Your first time out? I ask. Not at all, she says. I was born in Iran, lived there till I was eight, speak Farsi. That's where I've seen her face! In the old brilliant colored paintings of houris between the pages of Omar Khayyám; her black hair, black eyes

ready to duke it out with Alexander the Great as he tries to eat
Persia for dinner.

All this mad history vibrates at a café table in Diégo-Saurez,
a Muslim town in Madagascar with a Portuguese name in a
Vietnamese café with a French menu offering pizza and coke and
Tammy Wynette standing by her man on the scratchy muzak
while the February rain keeps falling till the air is clotted with it.

On our last day in Diégo, Jérémie picked us up for a day at the
beach, less exciting than Ankarana, but not a bad experience for
wandering Minnesotans. It was fifty below at home, according to
the news, another blizzard raging. In Madagascar, half fine drizzle,
half muggy sun, a good day for the Indian Ocean. Here's my lyri-
cal portrait of the day:

A RAINY DAY AT THE BEACH OUTSIDE DIÉGO-SAUREZ

In the Oasis café at Ramena Beach, the lady offers langouste but
we only want coffee and the wind that blows up a little squall
over the bay to cool my sweat and sunburn. "No shark attacks
here," says Maurice. The café's pet lemur looks us over with the
big orange eyes that fill half his pointy fox face. We all scratch
him. "So small," one voice. "So soft," another. "He doesn't bite,"
says the waiter at the Oasis.

Two young girls made up with gold and chalk-white flecks on
their cheeks walk by. "Lovely," I say. "May I take your picture?"
They giggle and pose under a coconut palm. "Madames or made-
moiselles?" brings on more giggles. They ask for a copy of the
picture and give me their names: Jocelyne and Natacha.

We finish our coffee and sweet coconut water, continue our
stroll down the beach. The narrow wooden pirogues arrive
through rain and choppy water, fishermen handing off plastic

boxes of plump fish still glistening from the sea. "Good to eat," says one fisherman. "No name in English," says Hanitra. I mention a hunger for fresh fish. "I know the place," says Jérémie.

We pick up shells, tiny fish jaws, sea-polished stones for a half hour, the white sand damp and warm under bare feet.

"Tarondra," says Jérémie pointing as I walk under a wood gate seeing nothing. He chuckles, points again at the top of the gate. A foot-long chameleon sits above my head. "Ugly," says Hanitra. "Nice mittens," says Marcy. *Tarondra* looks nervous, eyes swiveling back and forth in their sockets in opposite directions. He clasps the wood with his mitten feet, pulling along his ancient armored head and too-long tail. He is not built for speed, but patience. Elsewhere he would be eaten by something bigger, fiercer, but here he flourishes, a little reptile newspaper carrying fifty-million-year-old news. We leave this antique to his insect dinner and go sit on the stone verandah in the Bademera café.

I ask what the name means. It's the huge tree we sit under, heavy dark green leaves, fruit just beginning to bud. "Good to eat," says Hanitra. A long-haired man brings cold beer. He looks Chinese. "Vietnamese," says Maurice. He speaks Malagasy to a waitress, French to us, but switches to English mid-sentence when he sees blank faces. Jérémie grabs a weathered guitar from another table and, sitting under the Bademera tree, strums a French tune, singing in a delicate voice. Maurice takes the guitar and strums a bit. "Fingernails too long," he apologizes. The Vietnamese waiter comes back, takes the guitar, puts one foot on a chair, picks a jazz tune with great skill, cigarette still clenched in his picking hand. "Lovely," I say. "I wrote it," he says. "Is this a whole island of musicians?" I ask.

We drink more beer in the shade to more strumming, smell the *angoho* grilling. No name for this fragrant fish in English. A few

lazy flies stroll over my pink sunburn. A breeze comes up to
rustle the Bademera leaves. A hundred yards away the Indian
Ocean sloshes with its own strumming, its own music.

O Madagascar! Sweet island with your soft music, your black
and golden faces, where nature never learned to eat its weak
with bloody jaws, where dancing moves in fives and sevens as if
Pythagoras had never squared the universe, where every throat
I meet, whatever poverty and neglect history scattered among
these trees heavy with fruit, still has song inside it and needs no
money or electricity to sing. Stay anchored in this Indian Ocean
where you live, so far from snow and cannons and marching
armies, and the mad idea that money and machines with heads
more terrible than any *tarondra* will protect us from death or
ever living a whole life in this universe at all.

Tuléar (Toliara), on the southwest coast, faces Africa. The town,
whose name means "tie up here," was invented by the French in
1895, and, in some ways, it is the least "Malagasy" of places—but
in others, the most peculiar, thus most Malagasy of all. It boasts
a climate that rivals Minnesota for nastiness, a humid desert,
little rain, masses of dust, torpid heat, greasy mudflats (on the
space where a beach ought to be) full of sewage and garbage,
stretching out miles west toward Mozambique, broken-down
buildings that, even new, lacked any distinction, poverty, mosquitoes, all the possible charms. It is, in point of fact, an awful place.
I liked it. A traveler who spends his time only in charming and
lovely places risks never seeing anything at all. I learned at least
four things in Tuléar: the nature of weird plants, the meaning of
tombs, the dignity of human labor, and the wisdom of dead fish.

Three of us arrived on a steamy morning at the small airport

in the middle of an almost vegetation-free desert, Marcy and I
and our USIS guide, Hallie Rabenarivo, an American woman of
my generation who married a Malagasy and had lived in Tana
for thirty years—happily. She missed most of the Vietnam War,
Watergate, Nixon, Reagan, the rise of Bill Gates and cyberspace,
everything that slouched toward the United States to be born in
the last third of a century. Curious herself, she took us to a place
she had heard of but never seen: Herman Patignat's garden, a few
miles inland from town. For botanists, southern Madagascar is
Mecca, the Vatican, Valhalla, Olympus—home of spiny desert,
thorn forest, elephant foot, bottle tree (baobab), the whole phy-
lum Didiereacea (plants that look vaguely like cactus but are only
distant relatives). These are the most surreal plants on earth,
an armored landscape of spikes that appear invented by a design
committee of Heironymus Bosch, Salvador Dali, and Edward
Gorey. Here's my description of old Herman and his garden:

HERMAN PATIGNAT'S GARDEN

Herman, the old Swiss gardener, buys a dozen hectares of sand
a few miles east of the Indian Ocean on a humid desert. Dew collects in the cupped fronds of the aloe, the only water for birds.
Herman gathers spiny trees, dwarf baobobs, toxic vines that
bleed milky poison, gray succulents that smell like rotten meat,
tiny orchids, all that's rare and strange and frail in this harsh
place, everything labeled in proper Latin.

In a deep ant hole lives an eight-foot boa who comes out
every three weeks to choke and swallow a chicken. He sleeps
under the spiny trees all night while the chicken dissolves in his
belly, then slinks back down into the dark house he shares with
ants. The natives hate and fear him, says old Herman the gardener. They think he is lord of the ants, who bring him his food,

but I watch him. Always a chicken, only one in three weeks, then
he rests. There were lemurs here, and everyone liked them, but
I moved them out. They ate my best specimens. The snake, a
simple eater, is better company.

Herman watches everything closely, like Jean-Henri Fabre
watching his insects in a scrub field in Provence. This flowers for
only one night. This blooms after dark and drops its flower at
first light. How does he know? He watched in the dark. This elephant foot has grown this far in eighteen years since I first came.
He is seventy-three, half naked, white hair, bushy white eyebrows, a bare bulbous sunburned belly hanging over baggy green
shorts, his back and shoulders scratched by his beloved spines, a
few sores festering on his legs. But he is crazed with love for these
harsh plants, and will go on sweating and pruning till he is one
hundred. That's what crazed love does. I send these to a botanical garden in Tucson; the Smithsonian wants these; these are
named Marnieriensis after the old collector who made Grand
Marnier; these come to me from Australia.

We sign his black guest book, the pages limp and damp. Any
callers from Iceland? I ask, in English. Two, he says, turning to
the page: Sturla and Sigrun. They spoke good French. He wonders why I don't.

We lunch in his little café under a thatched roof, the saturated air vibrating with flies. Zebu steak with green pepper
sauce, a salad of tomatoes and onions in vinegar, lukewarm beer.
No electricity here. No running water. Just gravel and lizards
and spiked plants, and this odd, passionate old Swiss gardener
who invents a world in eighteen years and takes no money for
telling you his secrets. What are they worth anyway? How much
can you afford?

I asked Herman if there were any lemurs in the neighborhood.
Tourists, like scientists, adore lemurs; they are "cute," bright

eyed, furry, cuddly looking; the soft part of us imagines empathy, connection. There is nothing "cute" about Herman's plants. They are botanical savages that would prefer to sting, poison, burn, or wound rather than amuse you with their prettiness.

As in the interior highlands, tombs decorate the thorny landscape of southern Madagascar. Highland family tombs are most often plain and austere, bare stone decorated at most with a painted border and topped with a stone cross or nothing. But here among the local Mahafaly and Vezo tribes, the tombs are elaborate outdoor museums and art galleries, resplendent with upturned zebu horns, carved funerary ornaments, family fetishes, elaborate wall murals, sculptures. One famous tomb is topped with a huge gaily painted airplane—the deceased achieved fame among his neighbors for having once taken a flight. You count zebu horns to determine the wealth and status of the dead.

Projectors intent on "improving" Madagascar, lifting it from its poverty, liberating it from its devotion to taboos, superstitions, traditions that inhibit progress toward joining the modern world, often decry the national obsession for elaborate and expensive funeral celebrations. They bankrupt families, reinforce the power of the past, exhaust the country's resources. These funerals and tombs are not merely a habit, but the real national religion that has survived, like the national music, miraculously intact after centuries of Lutheran, Jesuit, Anglican missionaries, French and British colonials, Portuguese pirates and God knows who else, picking away at its body. These customs last, whatever their impracticality, because they are the true cement that binds a Malagasy to his own land and history; the whole meaning of his interior universe lives inside them. They say: I have lived, been connected to others, occupied a place that my ancestors fertilized with their bones, and their whole carefully tended memory fertilizes my own connection to the world. If I forget, defy, or desert them, my interior ballast dissolves. Ancestors occupy not the next world, but this one; they are my neighbors, my teachers, my mentors. They tell what is forbidden, what permitted. To honor them, I touch them, wrap them, name them, sing to them, dance them seven times around the family house—or in the south, count their zebu to see their honor made visible. Malagasy understand that we do not recreate the world each day on our electric screens; as Robert Bly says, "The world belongs primarily to the dead, and we only rent it from them for a little while." Then we go to join the ancestors where we become the true landlords of Madagascar.

In the United States we euphemize and disinfect the dead to put them out of our minds so that we can progress unimpeded toward we know not where. The loved one passes on to Sunset Gardens where we hire a grief counselor should we be troubled by "inappropriate" memory, then we move on with the first day of the rest of our lives, eating health food, gathering medical data on the internet, buying facelifts, toning up our aging muscles. The Malagasy idea of having a nice day is dancing "Afindrafindrao" with grandmother's dried bones, then pouring her a little shot of her favorite rum while naming aloud her new grandchildren. She is not looking good there in her moldy old wraps so we'll cover her with a new *lamba mena* to keep out the cold and damp till we visit her again in a few years, or even come ourselves to join her on the top shelf, the newest emigrant to the family mansion. Or in the south we count grandfather's zebu—sighing with the joyful thought of what a man he was—is, since his bones always preside over us. Where would you rather be dead—Minneapolis or Madagascar?

Funerals are the great occasion for music, the bread and butter employment of Malagasy orchestras. For days there must be

dancing and singing—not gloomy dead marches but lively tunes
that make you wiggle your hind end and move your feet. And pots
and pots of spicy zebu stew, and plenty of good rum, and a long
flowery speech full of poetry and proverbial wisdom and sharp
wit, then more tunes till the sun comes up and then goes down
again. Invite the priest, too, and the Lutheran minister. Let them
also pray and praise in their own form, then let them eat and
drink and join the dancing and meet the handsome bones of all
our grandparents. Who is sane and healthy, them or us?

Since the town of Tuléar boasted only mud flats, Hallie and
Marcy and I drove north past endless mangroves to find a true
beach. On muddy rutted roads we passed village after village, here
full of African faces and thatch rather than red brick. Tomb after
tomb stood back of the mangroves. Finally we found the open
Indian Ocean where we sat on boulders in the shade all afternoon.
Hallie was a great source of funeral lore—her husband's family in
the highlands had just hired a soothsayer to plan a new *famidihana*. She described the difference between Tuléar and highland
funerals. I wrote a couple of small funerary poems growing out
of that lazy afternoon.

TRAUERMUSIK

In Tuléar the death orchestra plays all night
the same tune, over and over and over
while the old lady waits by the drying body.
When the rich man dies, they kill all his cattle,
hang the horns in a tall tree till the tomb
is ready to receive them. How long
does this go on? A month. Death here
on this hot shark-rich ocean is grander

than ashes to ashes, dust to dust, the body
glorified with music and cattle blood even
as it rots away to its simple bones.

THE USES OF TRADITIONAL WISDOM

When the bones need turning again in the tomb
because a fresh corpse waits to join them,
shrink-drying inside its reed wrap
on the first shelf of the waiting room,
you must go to the soothsayer
so he can fix the bones a proper day.
If you choose the day yourself and it proves
wrong, then you have shamed your family and all
their wrapped and assembled bones.
Besides, if you don't pay the soothsayer,
then what's he to do for food?
It's worth the fee: If the bones had called
for Friday and you foolishly turned them
on Tuesday (Tuesday is always
unlucky but that you already knew
even without the soothsayer's shingle)
or suppose you turn them on Thursday
and the dry bones click together to sign
that you have let them down one more time?
So pay up with a light heart for a little sooth.

In a poor country, the face of death cannot be hid. Death sits
at table with you, lies down to keep you company in the dark.
Death is normal, the most normal of all events. Only birth or
signs of intelligence are cause for true wonder. The job of human
religion—and we have still not figured out to which church God

belongs, if any—is to integrate that normality which is also a mystery, into the tissue of daily life—history, work, family, land— so that we do not all go unhinged at the thought of our own final dissolution. In Madagascar, death and life are a continuum; the funeral connects not this world to the next, but this world to itself in a unity. Why not make death itself the great normality, the bedrock of civilization? It beats private property or pie in the sky as a firm foundation.

I gave my afternoon culture show at the Za-Za club, one of Tuléar's lively discos. Za-Za, a concrete-block dance hall with an outdoor bar, has no air-conditioning. The walls steamed. Local musicians and dancers joined the program. I was presented a three-and-a-half-octave electric keyboard on wobbly stand-up legs, impossible for any music other than rock and roll chording. I read poems.

I tried Jelly Roll Morton to no avail, so I read more. And I sweated. After an hour, there was not a closed pore anywhere on my body from big toe to ear tip—a plump pink hillock of sweat. At the end, thirst and heat drove me to the great mistake all travelers are warned from making in Madagascar, Mexico, most of the world. Ice. I ordered gin, tonic, ice, more ice, a pail of ice, the whole iceberg that sank the Titanic, the whole glacier that calved it. That ice had consequences, but not till later.

That night we met for dinner at the Za-Za—famous for grilled lobsters, gratinée of crab, lively bands, and the wild dancing of its customers. Our hotel was a couple of miles away; since Tuléar taxis are few and undependable, we took a local *pousse-pousse*— "Push-Push"—a Chinese rickshaw, a human taxi. Twenty *pousse-pousse* drivers lined the front of the hotel, noisily offering their best bargains, all high-spirited con artists. If foreigners considered later that they had dickered hard over a dime or a quarter with a man who couldn't afford shoes, who pulled them barefoot through the muddy, dog-shit-strewn, pot-holed streets, it might have stimulated some reflection on unequal income distribution on our cozy planet. I thought of it, then thought of a hot two-mile walk in the middle of the night. I hired one of the *pousse-pousse* gang. I tried to get the flavor of their talk and of our night ride in this little transcription.

THE SONG OF THE POUSSE-POUSSE

> *Pousse-pousse* my fran.
> Very good *pousse-pousse.*
> I take you where you go.
> Where you go?
> Za-Za club?
> Ah, Dance.
> Very good, Za-Za.
> Dix mille!
> Cheap!
> 10,000.
> I take you my fran.
> 6,000.
> Very good dance Za-Za.
> 5,000.
> I wait.
> Take you home.
> *Pousse-pousse* very good.
> Much mud.
> Dark.
> You ride.
> I wait.
> 4,000.

Two way 8.
You take *pousse-pousse*.
Now.

No cars.
Few lights.
A dim oil lamp or two.
Burning charcoal smell.
Grilled goat.
Low talk.
Splash of puddle.
A little trot.
Then walk.
Shoulders like bellows.
Slow sweat.
Hot dark.
Above, the stars.
Southern Cross.
There.
Slap of hard rubber.
Creak of wood.
Moon out now
under gauzy moist cloud.
Singing from a hut.
Soft.
Slow.
Splash.
Trot.
Hotel.

More franc, my fran.
I wait.
Very good *pousse-pousse*.

Even the fish swimming around Madagascar are peculiar, en-
demic, one of a kind, evolutionary anomalies. In restaurants, I
frequently asked what I was eating—having in mind eating another, if I could find them elsewhere. No name in English. Local
fish. Our local host wanted to know if I was interested in the
Musée Oceanographique. Dead fish in bottles. He didn't seem
passionate to call on them himself, but I had heard rumors of
the gem of their collection. I wanted to see dead fish. We went.
The Musée sat back of an oil-storage depot next to the port.
Here's the dead fish I wanted to see.

COELACANTH

In February, tropical summer, we tour the marine museum in
Tuléar, west coast of Madagascar. It's a humid hundred inside
and out. Even the bottles of formaldehyde sweat. Specimen
after vinegary specimen of strange fish: *"Endemique!" "Unique!"*
"Extinct!" Finally, the back room—what everyone comes to see
after enduring the two hundred bottles of briny spines. The
soft-spoken gold-skinned girl flips the fluorescent light, points:
the *pièce-de-résistance* of fish-dom, coelacanth caught in the
Mozambique Channel, the fish that should have been dead for
seventy-five million years, that never evolved, that lives only in
this hot and lonesome ocean east of Africa. He floats in a long
glass tank, facing us. Five feet of mud flaps, a shit-brown, bug-
eyed lump, stumpy double fins, underslung jaw, spiny mess of
a rudder. Was the carpenter of this Platonic form of ugliness
drunk, dim-witted, asleep at the helm of the ship of creation?
　　This . . . this . . . this. . . . How did this breathe . . . swim . . .
survive . . . ? Was this too ugly even for the million sleek and rav-
enous Indian Ocean sharks to eat? Yet live it did—and does at
this very moment—in the gray waters west of this room, this

Quasimodo fish, this phantom of ichthyology, this ghost comrade of the pterodactyl. Does coelacanth broadcast news of what
you looked like before you started your slow crawl out of the
water, dropping your gills and your swim bladder in the tidal
mud to stand upright in the sun, flexing your arrogant opposable thumbs? Bend down now. Press your lips to the tank. Kiss
the coelacanth, offering praise and thanks that he became the
fish of sorrows, the one who stayed behind to atone for your sins
in his flesh. Whatever swims in the Indian Ocean swims inside
you too, all the antique useless parts, the old ugliness, the un-
evolved vitality that says: Stay alive! Stay alive! Stay alive!

That dead fish, itself an isolated island in the sea of evolution, an anomaly oddly connected to the past inside our own
body, came to stand for my whole experience in Madagascar,
the strange red island that keeps singing to me "Stay alive!" as
I muddle through middle age in clean, wholesome, rational,
smoke-free Minnesota. Something older, grander, more terrify-
ing lives inside us than can ever be described on a government
form, or helped by the helping professions, or made to toe the
bottom line of where it's at. In Madagascar, having a nice day
means going to a funeral or staying alive. Same thing.

TAMATAVE AND SOUVENIRS

The fatal ice in Tuléar knocked me low. My interior exploded. I
consulted the embassy nurse who gave me some powerful drug
that was literally audible inside me fifteen minutes after swallow-
ing. My gut sounded like D day, the Battle of Borodino, Agincourt—
catapulted boulders, muskets, howitzers, Gatling guns, modern
chemistry duking it out with ancient bacteria. Take that, you cad!
Chemistry finally won an uneasy truce, so we left by car for the

east coast, down the escarpment a vertical mile, through rain forest to Tamatave, the open Indian Ocean. Our old friend Paul Saxton, the USIS commissar, came along this time to survey the progress of his far-flung English-language empire.

When travelers who have been to third-world countries gather to exchange stories, the talk always goes quickly to shit: Yellow? Mine was green, pure liquid, it exploded like gunshots, I couldn't keep water down, we were on this third-class bus when it hit . . . , no chunks at all, Lomotil didn't faze it, mine was worse, it lasted longer, it looked like paste, I didn't eat for two weeks, you took what? After a while, these conversations begin to sound like a scholarly conference on Rabelais's *Gargantua and Pantagruel*. When I found myself in the middle of them, gleefully describing the consequences of poisoned ice, I often stopped short to think: This is disgusting—and boring to boot. What are we actually talking about? We bourgeois tourists experience a kind of inverted pride when we share the daily miseries of the world's poor. Diarrhea or dysentery and its consequence, dehydration, is, in some form, the order of the day for most of the planet, as normal as poverty or death. We escape for a while our anal-retentive middle-class life, to let everything out at once in a noisy eruption. Few travelers die of it; they suffer only embarrassment, discomfort, an impetus for gruesome road tales. Citizens—and their children—die of it in great numbers, literally shitting themselves to death.

Halfway down the escarpment we stopped for a night at Andasibe—its old French name, Périnet—to stay overnight at a tourist hotel so that we could rise at dawn to hear the song of the indri and have a look at the other wildlife. Much of the dense forest on the escarpment has been logged, even Périnet, but 810 hectares of steep hillside around a lake are intact enough to provide habitat for a colony of indri and many other species. Lemurs branched out and evolved on Madagascar into thirty species. Their numbers are rich with both variety and oddity: the golden bamboo lemur, a three-and-a-half-pound animal, dines on young bamboo shoots laced with lethal doses of cyanide. He swallows daily three times the dose of cyanide required to kill a full-sized man. The nocturnal aye-aye, weirdest of them all, feeds on grubs living under tree bark, pulling them out with an elongated bony middle finger, twice the length of its neighbors. Its teeth, like a rodent's, continue growing all through life. And then the indri, giant of the family, lives in treetops where he bellers out his loud songs to greet the dawn.

We rose just before first light and arrived at the reserve gate about six o'clock, beating either guides or ticket takers. The forest stood shrouded in gray mist. We waited. Soon the singing began. Singing is not quite the right word, though neither I nor the other indri describers can think of a better one. Like whale calls, wolf howls, dolphin chortles or loon yodels, it is music, but not ours. Some system lies under it, but just as we have not managed to explain Johann Sebastian Bach to the indri, they have not managed to explain the order of their songs to us. Mating, pleasure, location, dinner? All or none of the above? We hear a mystery—choose your adjective: lovely, eerie, haunting, unsettling. But every member of the Indri Philharmonic's audience agrees on one quality—loud. You can hear them a mile and a half away, clear and stentorian, God's small furry trombones entertaining you at dawn.

When the guide arrived we followed him into the forest. On the path a pack of neighborhood children presented us with a Parson's chameleon to admire and photograph—for a fee. What a grand and unlikely beast! With his corrugated armored multi-colored head, his nose topped by a row of medieval castle parapets, his vast orange eyes, swiveling in opposite directions—today, tomorrow, she loves me, she loves me not—his branch-grabbing mitten feet, his fat spiral tail that doubles his body size. I'd seen him hunt and eat, his two-foot lightning tongue shooting out in less than a quarter of a second to glue a hapless insect to its sticky tip, followed by the crunching of insect legs and a meditative burp. I'd vote him the comic prince of reptiles. He inspires not ancient terror but gaiety, pure wonder that something so grandly ugly and slow and unlikely could survive so long and prosper.

Inside the forest, my middle-aged tree-blind eyes saw nothing; only damp mist, ferns, mud. Our guide, a small wiry young man who stepped quietly, stopped periodically, held one finger to his lips, pointed with another: a new chameleon, a snake, tracks, an orchid blooming. I'd given up on the lemurs when I heard a peculiar sound overhead—pigs grunting, rooting for their morning slop, the sound of my father's barn. The guide stopped to point upward at the top of the forest canopy: a dozen, maybe two dozen, brown lemurs—who could count?—leaping back and forth from branch to branch, tree to tree, never missing a hold, at ease so high in the air, almost dancing with each other, all the while making the grunting noises of Big Bill Holm's Swede Prairie pigs, a flying herd of acrobatic swine. I listened with pleasure to this aerial porcine music for a while, then we moved on to continue the search for indri. Halfway through the walk we found them, or rather the guide found them. Peering through leaves above, we saw them, quiet now, resting their voices after their vigorous morning rehearsal, perched in pairs or families in the crooks of trees, grooming each other tenderly, probably picking out lice, scratching, patting, nuzzling. Indri look uncannily like small human beings; we've both lost our tail and must travel through the universe singing songs of lament.

As we drove down the rest of the escarpment to Tamatave, the sky cleared and the temperature rose. We could see the Indian Ocean now, an endless turquoise, calm after the typhoon. No mud flats, only big rollers, white sand, palms, bougainvilla. But no swimming, or even wading. In the last generation, sharks had, for some still unknown reason, multiplied and been fruitful all along the coast, where they eat a dozen or two Malagasy every year, children wading in the tide, fisherman knocked out of pirogues. Only inside coral barriers could you put your toes into that hot saltwater.

Tamatave is Madagascar's major port, where most of her vanilla, coffee, meat, hides, whatever the product, leaves for the international market, and the bulk of imports arrive. It is the most Asian of Malagasy towns, full of descendants of Indian traders, Chinese merchants and laborers. Many faces are a blend of the features of all these tribes. Chinese soup appears on the menu of every restaurant, goat kabobs and lentils at street stands. But the chief product of the town became apparent when I turned off the air-conditioning to open the van window. Cloves saturated the hot air, redolent, inescapable. We stopped to have a walk, passing a banyan grove, one tree spreading out over half a city block. We followed our noses to an open square where a flat prairie of cloves, deep brown, baked in the scorching sun. A handful of shirtless barefoot men, themselves the color of cloves, shuffled through the clove heaps, raking them about like autumn leaves, spreading them to dry. So many cloves, an astonishment for a Minnesota farm boy. When I asked later someone told me that these days the liveliest clove trade is with Indonesia, for clove cigarettes. Three years later, whenever I smell a ham baking, the

Indian Ocean rises inside me, the banyan folds its horizontal branches over the house.

Léonie Guerra, the director of the English center, was our hostess in Tamatave. She impressed me with the force and ingenuity she used to accomplish what in much of the country proved impossible. She'd heard that I wasn't fond of electric pianos. A just-tuned Yamaha upright waited for me in the English center. She invited local piano teachers to send their best students to play for me. A flute orchestra of farmers from deep in the bush arrived to blow a few tunes. The English center was packed with scrubbed, gussied-up students waiting first to hear poetry, then to read a little of their own to me. It was a humid ninety-five degrees in that room. Hot cloves perfumed the gusts of air that sporadically blew in past the shutters. I played Bach, Joplin, Brazilian tangos; they played Clementi, Schumann, "Theme from Love Story." One lovely young girl in a bright red dress played a Chopin mazurka flawlessly with great style. She looked cool, unruffled, sweat free, only a few long black hairs fallen out of place—just right for Chopin. I soaked the piano keys with the sweat from my eyebrows alone. The descendants of Icelanders are not properly programmed for the tropics—though they may love them. The flute orchestra—sixteen farmers in matching blue shorts and white shirts played countrified ritual music—in perfect canon. Most of the farmers spoke no French, much less English, only Betsimaraka. The local jazz players hung around to question me about Errol Garner, Thelonius Monk, and Art Tatum. Their curiosity exceeded my powers to satisfy it. I felt sheepish but amazingly happy. I had taught the audience a few small American poems: Williams, Sandburg, Robert Bly, William Stafford. At the end of the afternoon they recited two or three back to me.

That night, Léonie had booked the largest hall in town for a

reading and concert. I shared the bill, as the exotic foreign attrac-
tion, with the Mago group (the farmer flute players), and also
with some of Madagascar's most famous musicians—the match
of Ratovo and Rajery—Daniel Tombo and his family, six players
and seven dancers, and the Berton *Valiha* Orchestra, first and
second prize respectively in a national competition for the per-
formance of Rakotozafy. The rhythm gourds in the Tombo orchestra were made from old Neocide cans with a handful of seeds
inside. I read a few poems, played a set of classic rags, wiped off
the sweat, then went to enjoy the rest of the show. Maybe a thousand people in the auditorium—no air-conditioning. The night
of music carried on and on—the Malagasy fear length neither
in oratory nor in music. They seem not to need commercials.
Tombo's orchestra played "Afindrafindrao." The audience rocked.
After three hours I walked outside to find a sky full of stars. An
Englishwoman who had lived here a long time looked up and
began naming the southern constellations, ending with the
Southern Cross. I thought of Icelandic sailors crossing the equator for the first time and realizing that the North Star had disappeared, only to be replaced by a new set of navigational lights,
provided by the universe. And what a universe it sometimes is
on hot February nights full of music.

Léonie invited the traveling Americans and all the musicians
out to dinner at a fancy seaside restaurant outside of town. The
other customers were gone home already; we had the place to
ourselves. Indian Ocean swells provided the only music. Gold-
jacketed waiters brought out rum, wine, bowls of shrimp to munch,
then the power failed. We sat not in darkness, but in moonlight.
The ocean required no plug to continue its music. Candles appeared. The talk was lively. Somehow, power or not, food arrived,
then coffee, then cognac. I *skål*ed silently, inviting my tablemates,

who had no idea what the hell I meant, to join me. Maybe they thought I was drinking to the sharks in a strange language.

Now the time arrived to leave Madagascar to return for another two months of blizzards ten thousand miles away. What souvenirs do you take home from such a place to remind you, to keep the fragrance of cloves, the chameleon's head, the fine-boned faces full of humor, the flying pigs of the forest, the pluck of "Afrindrafindrao" on bicycle spokes, fresh in your mind? For my last job, I gave a speech to the journalists of Tana, summing up my two months' wander on their island. I decided to show them my five souvenirs.

The first four are a pair of recycled tin cans, a pair of bamboo tubes, a pair of dead insects, and a fierce-looking dried thorn from one of Herman Patignat's beloved trees; no woven rugs, handmade mahogany furniture, silk *lambas*—not even an emerald. Two French tin cans, red Raid and blue deodorant, have been lovingly and cleverly fashioned into miniature Renaults: seats, steering wheel, bumpers, axles, rims, tires, running boards, headlights, all elegantly in proportion and functional, lacking only a motor. What the rich throw away, the poor reimagine. Malagasy children proved perfectly capable of playing for hours with a piece of string, an old washer, a piece of styrofoam packing, a twig, a cow bone. They didn't need Toys Я Us or the newest software for Dungeons and Dragons or Beanie Babies to exercise the play instinct of the human intelligence. Children seemed never bored or unruly in Madagascar. I loved watching them carefully cover their school books from the rain and mud, looking happy in their small uniforms on their way to school. I wanted those two toy cars to remind me of those children.

They will remind me also of the Neocide-can rhythm gourds in Daniel Tombo's magnificent orchestra. Take a handful of

pebbles, an old poison can, and you have music. A Steinway D or
a Bösendorfer Imperial are wonderful machines, but owning them
will not make you a pianist. For that you need imagination and
long labor, and those are not for sale.

I take home a pair of *vahilas*, a chromatic one made by Ratovo
and a diatonic one from Rajery. The customs agent may think
they are shotguns, so I've learned to pluck a scale to disarm him.
He doesn't know that music is more powerful than gunpowder—
sometimes more dangerous. Those *vahilas* will remind me of the
musical tradition and native genius that seem to a foreigner one
of the chief glories of Madagascar, an adornment of true size.

I take home two glass balls, one enclosing a brown-striped,
fat, oversized beetle, the other a pair of brilliantly red bugs with
long stingers. Their eccentric beauty brings to mind the indri, the
Parson's chameleon, the spiny tenrec, the great chirping cock-
roach, the pig-singing brown lemur, the bright green geckos that
guard the windows and ceilings of every bedroom, the red frogs,
the sleepy yellow boa, the aepyornis skeleton at the zoo that
stands ten feet above the ostrich, the basketball-sized fossil eggs
it laid. All the delights of these creatures remind me that life on
this planet is richer and stranger than I imagined.

I take home an armored thorn from the spiny desert to remind me that sometimes nature does not want to be touched by
humans, that life that grows up in harsh places learns to defend
itself—and that includes humans as well as plants. The thorn is
perhaps three inches in circumference, twenty spikes radiating out
from the center, each crowned with a razor-sharp hooked barb. I
do not touch it even now, years later, for its hooks would grapple
me to it. Yet this too is alive, like the coelacanth, my mate, my
comrade. It will remind me to hope that, like it, Madagascar will
retain its spiky individuality, its native genius and resist becoming

homogenous with other places. When prosperity comes and come it will—the great wheel turns—be careful to guard the soul.

Finally, I take home the invisible, the memory of hearing the strangest music of all—my own. On the way to Fianar, we first stopped in Antsirabe, the highest, coldest town in Madagascar. In January the pears, plums, apples, persimmons were ripe and succulent. We visited a Norwegian-run agricultural school, then ate a good dinner with a witty Norwegian cow inseminator, not a missionary, but a World Bank man. I knew from boyhood, of course, about Norwegian Lutherans in Madagascar. Like Mark Twain, I mostly prefer that missionaries of any kind—political or religious—stay home, mind their own business, and let their neighbors arrive at their own conclusions about the great mystery. On one hand, there is Father Damien—a brave man who gave everything with an open heart. On the other hand, Allan Snowball was beaten for speaking his own Objibwa language at a missionary boarding school. Missionaries broke the Mayan goddess statues. Saint Olaf Christianized Iceland with an ax and an army.

In the middle of Antsirabe stands an enormous gray stone Lutheran church built in the nineteenth century. Some of these Malagasy must have been Lutherans longer than my relatives in North America. Since I am still a card-carrying, dues-paying Icelandic Lutheran and occasional church musician, I couldn't resist going to church in Antsirabe. Marcy, who is Norwegian, decided to stay in bed in our charming garden hotel and spend a Wallace Stevens Sunday morning with leisurely coffee and mangos and the green cockatoo in the garden; but Lanto, always ready for adventure, joined me. I put on my best outfit—even a necktie. We strolled to the church half an hour early. I love cognitive dissonance, the mad juxtaposition of contraries, a complete cultural stew pot where the ingredients get to swap flavors and make something new and strange; this may have capped all such occasions in my life.

LUTHERAN SINGING IN MADAGASCAR

In the old stone church at Antsirabe, built by Norwegian Lutherans a century ago to bring northern guilt and gloom to enlighten the tropics, the organ wheezes, the swell shutters clank—a long time between tunings. The Malagasy organist reads from a book of numbers—do re mi fa sol la ti do—but he knows these grim old songs from the Reformation of the north somewhere further inside than any tablature: *"Ein' feste Burg ist unser Gott,"* "Built on a Rock the Church Doth Stand," "What a Friend We Have in Jesus," "Holy, Holy, Holy." Malagasy hymns, says Lanto from Tana. Indeed. I agree. The organist steps out to smoke before the service.

The congregation files in from all directions, gold faces, fine bones, bright dresses, old ladies wrapped in white *lambas* doubling as shawls, white-haired old men in dark suits clutching leather-covered psalmbooks. I sit in the middle to hear, soon engulfed by a thousand tightly packed Malagasy fellow Lutherans. The singing begins a cappella a half hour before the service, an old hymn in three-quarter time whose name and words I've forgotten. All the parts fill in: tenor, alto, tune, and descant, the bass moving in proper contrary motion. It is slow, solemn, huge but not loud, as if this stone house were moving down the road, dancing a largo on its great heavy legs. The sound oozes around like molasses in this humid air, circling the still empty pulpit and altar.

Now it makes no difference what I believe, they believe, Martin Luther or Hans Nielsen Hauge believed about sanctification, grace, faith and works, pregnant virgins, risen corpses. We all believe in one true music—the ninety-five theses of sound.

I stick up above the singers by a foot, pink, plump, and silent, but no one pays any attention. I look around through these surges of hymns. A blond head in the corner sticks up like mine. Later, someone asks: Were the Norwegians there? A few, I say. On the left side by the door? How did you know? They've sat there for a hundred years.

I listen again as the last verse moves onward in solemn motion out into this air a mile above the Indian Ocean, above this gashed red ground, above the black-haired chorus so far from Wittenberg, Trondheim, Minnesota. The real mass is about to start now. The organist, back from smoking, thumps the swell box open. Let us begin. In the name of Andriamanitra, the good-smelling god of all the galaxies.

The Norwegians gave their best, their magnificent tradition of choral singing, and the Malagasy received with grace and genius, digesting the best the foreigners offered down into the stomach of their own culture. The art of receiving is as great as the art of giving. The trick is to give everything. I will hear noises rising above that red island for a long time, singing "Holy, Holy, Holy."

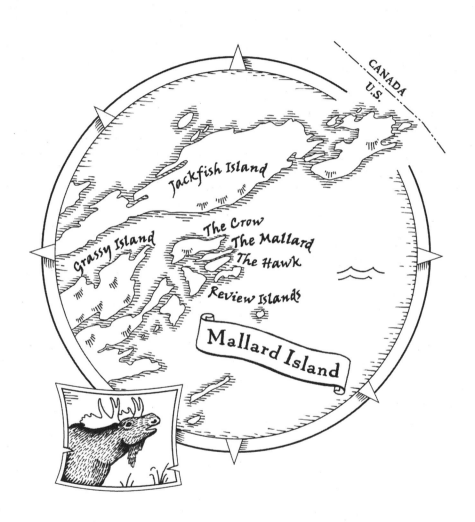

CANADA
U.S.

Jackfish Island

Grassy Island

The Crow
The Mallard
The Hawk

Review Islands

Mallard Island

⁊ Mallard
Island of Civilized Wilderness

ON THE PARLOR WALL OF THE OLD HOUSE where I live hangs what is probably a very bad painting. Whatever its quality as great art, it is certainly eccentric, and equally certainly the work of an amateur painter. Rousseau or Grandma Moses are its true ancestors, not the French academy. It catches your eye—or your heart—not because of its skill in draftsmanship, coloring, or design but because it is of something that catches the eye. This is no abstraction. Its life is only in its subject, not in its design. The woman with whom I share my life is a skilled artist with a keen sense of color and design and, as she often assures me, impeccable taste. She doesn't like the painting, and when I am gone for a few days, I often come back to find it disappeared. I rummage through the hiding crannies in the old house, unearth the painting, and while she is gone on some errand or trip, rehang it in its prominent home on the parlor wall. It is not small, perhaps a yard square. She notices that it has risen from its tomb one more time. This is an old dance. It will continue.

Before I describe the painting for you so that you can make up your own mind who occupies the more just side of this small domestic war, it might be worthwhile thinking a little about the nature of quality in a work of art. Start with the premise that any work of art is a gift given by the artist to his fellow human beings. A true gift has no price; it cannot be appraised. To ask its value is to vulgarize and demean it. Art—whether music, language, or image—is not decoration. The true artist gives everything inside him or that he owns as an act of love. Whatever he withholds diminishes the work of art, whatever the skill or genius of the maker. The true artist sings at full voice for the birthday of a deaf man. The true artist goes gaily off to die of leprosy from feeding holy wafers into diseased mouths. The true artist makes beauty with one hand on an instrument that cannot be played without two. The true artist gives the polar bear he has acquired with everything he owns to the king of Denmark, thereby becoming a king himself. Talent—or genius if you will—is not democratic; William Butler Yeats will always be a greater poet than Robert Service, or Beethoven a greater composer than Anatoly Liadov, but all humans have it inside them to give everything and can therefore make beauty, however clumsy. The function of the very greatest works of art is to make us remember this fact about our own species; every man is his own Leonardo because the Last Supper is already inside him.

Allan Snowball was a true artist. In 1986 he waited on the dock at Mallard Island in Rainy Lake, just a few hundred yards south of the watery Canadian border, for me to arrive on a pontoon boat. When he saw the boat approach, he unwrapped the big square package in his arms to hand it to me as I stepped off onto the island. "A little present for you," he said. "I spent last winter painting it. I took lessons from Gene" (Monahan—a professional painter who lived in Ranier, Minnesota, a few miles away on the mainland). "You'll recognize what it is. It's your poem." I recognized it.

It is sunset on a lake in the northern forest in the middle of the continent, the sky greenish gold, the water already full of shadows, a narrow passage between two islands, both granite slabs covered with a dense forest of scrub pine, spruce, and birch. To the right, a wood canoe with two men, their faces almost invisible—only shadows, the back one wearing a skin hat, paddling, the front man in a jaunty hat with upturned brim, kneeling, holding a violin—awkwardly, under his armpit, not at his shoulder. The artist had not watched Isaac Stern or Yehudi Menuhin very carefully. To the left stands an oversized upright bull moose, huge rack, eyes alert, jaws open as if trumpeting—or perhaps about to sing. Even given the real enormity of a grown moose, this one has assumed heroic proportions in the artist's imagination. He is four times the bulk of the men in the canoe, with the canoe thrown in to boot. The moose stands in shallow water, a few reeds and lily pads sticking out of it, a big dead snag in the foreground. What is this ghostly moose doing there with his Cyrano de Bergerac squared nose erect? What music does the canoeist play for the moose? Does the moose like it? It is a grand painting, and you, Sensible Reader, do not own enough money to buy it, even if you are J. P. Morgan or Bill Gates.

I have been, for many years, a famous hater of trees, particularly when they clump together in numbers sufficient to qualify as a forest. If I drive for a day to escape my house—on an almost tree-less prairie—I go west to the Dakota buttes where trees disappear entirely, rather than north where they grow thickly enough to amputate the sky. I suppose I am a geographical claustro-phobe, but I prefer the long view. Jean Replinger, a colleague at the college where I teach, tried for years to tempt me north to an island in Rainy Lake. She had joined a foundation that administered and cared for the island, and she is herself a great wilderness enthusiast. It's a four-hundred-mile drive through damned trees, I told her. But there are eleven thousand books on the island, two pianos, two violins, wind-up gramophones, wax cylinders of Caruso and Schumann-Heink, first editions of Walt Whitman. Walt Whitman? She had my attention now. A man named Island who loved books and pianos above all things ought to go. I did.

At the end of September 1983, my old friend John Allen arrived south from his job in Alaska with his new girlfriend Susie. We left for the Canadian border in the middle of October, too late for that climate, the first frost long past, the leaves gone, snow possible any day. First two hundred miles of prairie—vast swatches of corn stubble, the last soybeans, farmers plowing furiously to beat the snow—then two hundred miles of forest and lake, the woods growing scrubbier, the land stonier, the lakes colder, Bemidji, Blackduck, Funkley, Mizpah, Big Falls, trees, trees, trees, then bogs, then more trees, International Falls, the stink of pulp—trees melted down to plywood and newsprint—the bridge to Canada over the Rainy River, then the little town of Ranier. Outside Russia, you could not travel so far in Europe without finding an ocean. We had driven from Land's End to the Orkneys, from Paris to Naples, from Budapest to Amsterdam, and we were still in Minnesota, with the snow breathing hard now. But we had come at least to islands, to a lake of sufficient size that you could imagine an ocean—or at least a glacier that had so recently melted after scraping the country clean down to granite bedrock that the land still recovered from its ice weight by each year rising a fraction of an inch toward the sky.

We had directions to Gene Monahan's house, the lady who

would ferry us to the island for a few days to investigate the books, then fetch us back to civilization. I'd never met her. She was a small squarely built woman in her mid-seventies, a face full of humorous wrinkles, thick spectacles, bobbed white hair. Her small bungalow was crammed full of paintings and books, every wall covered, mostly portraits, but some fine northern landscapes. Clearly she was a painter of skill and magnitude. Her faces almost came out of their frames to greet us. The house smelled wonderfully of wood smoke, mothballs, thousands of cigarettes, and warm cookies. She gave the three of us a small tour of the paintings: my daughter Jeanie as a little girl, my son, the ship's pilot, those are my Cree neighbors when I taught painting in the Canadian bush by James Bay, there's my husband. That's Ober, he was about sixty then, such a handsome man, but only a little fellow, short like me. There's Mallard Island, Ober in the kitchen.

Ober, the Prospero of Mallard Island, was Ernest Carl Oberholzer, beloved local eccentric of the Rainy River and Voyageurs National Park country for fifty or sixty years, honored hero of Minnesota wilderness enthusiasts, and now, in 1983, six years dead.

Ober was born in Davenport, Iowa, on the Mississippi, in 1884, the second son of a modestly prosperous German family of bank tellers and real-estate owners. Ober's father deserted Ober's mother, Rosa, just after the death of Ernest's one-year-younger brother, Frank, in 1890, from brain inflammation brought on by an accident. This left young Ernest to be raised by his now single mother and his grandparents. He was a sturdy outdoorsy boy until a bout with rheumatic fever at seventeen left him with a damaged heart. Nevertheless, he went off to Harvard in 1903, where he studied, among other things, landscape architecture, the heritage of Frederick Law Olmstead, designer of Central Park. His mother, Rosa, followed him to Boston where she rented an apartment close to Harvard. With one husband and one son already gone, you can never be too careful. Ernest befriended a young underclassman, Conrad Aiken, the future famous poet, whose past beggared his own for sheer tragedy. Aiken's parents had died in their Savannah, Georgia, house, a murder and a suicide. Ober graduated in 1907 and, with his friend Aiken, spent a long summer in 1908 on a bicycle tour of England and Scotland. He came home to hear once more from his doctors that his rheumatic fever had so weakened his heart that he should expect a short life—and not a strenuous one.

Faced with that Damocles sword, Ober must have decided the hell with it. If I'm going to be dead, I may as well have some fun and do something I love. He came to International Falls in 1909, bought a wood canoe and a pair of snowshoes, and began exploring what at that time (and to some degree still) was one of the last great chunks of wilderness on the North American continent. Most of Rainy Lake is in Ontario, a maze of thousands of islands plopped down in hundreds of square miles of ice water, looking a great deal like the Stockholm archipelago or the clumps of wooded islands from Puget Sound north to Alaska. The lake and the river are the heart of a mammoth drainage system that goes from Lake of the Woods to Lake Superior and north to James Bay and Hudson Bay, a watery tangle of passages used by the French voyageurs to transport furs back to civilization where they could be sold to society ladies or made into beaver hats. It is the home of North America's largest population of wolves, who share the woods with plenty of moose, bear, deer, beaver, all watched over by trees full of eagles waiting to dine on the leavings of whatever the animals kill. It is a properly wild and inhospitable place, afflicted with swarms of voracious mosquitoes and biting flies in season, then in off season frozen solid for eight months during what must certainly be one of the nastiest winters in North America. The high Arctic hardly matches it for severity. International Falls is the coldest town in the United States and often bests sissy Canadian wind chills.

Ober made friends with the local Ojibwa, taking them along as guides and pals on his canoe trips. In the winter he did odd jobs and lived cheap. He was probably an early harbinger of the sixties counterculture, passing the time with his adventurous pleasures before the undertaker had an early shot at embalming him for good. The undertaker had to wait a long time since he died at ninety-three, senile but still decently sound of limb. His life ought to make career-happy Americans checking the Dow hourly on their laptops think hard about not paying the electric bill, chucking the job, and finding a suitably rough place to have some fun for the next odd half century. It beats the hell out of the heart attack at the office, the computer still purring nicely, the mouse poised for action, the suit stone dead in the ergonomic chair.

Ober's greatest adventure came in 1912 when he left for five months with his companion Billy McGee, a local Ojibwa reputed to have shamanic powers. The two canoed and portaged north through partly unmapped wilderness from Rainy River to Hudson Bay. They arrived late in Churchill, where the rivers drain into the bay. Ober, who by this time was functional in Ojibwa, gathered data and stories, both geographical and anthropological (they produced the first accurate map of the region), and, in addition, took an enormous quantity of first-rate photographs with his primitive Graphlex. He collected this material for what I suppose he intended to be his "book" that would make his reputation as an explorer, Vilhjalmur Stefansson with a canoe, but he never

wrote it. His life provided one postponement after another as interesting diversions came up. The next diversion, during World
War I (from which his fever-damaged heart exempted him), was
the rearrival of Mother. Rosa moved north in 1916. Ober still had
neither permanent home nor steady job. He was involved in various local schemes and projects—you can always use a Harvard
man—and one of them finally compensated him with the greatest
gift of his life. He assisted a local entrepreneur named Hapgood at
a Rainy Lake farm resort that Hapgood tried to develop on Deer
Island. For his labors, Hapgood, in lieu of seventy-five-dollars pay,
deeded Ober his own little archipelago: the Review, or Japanese
Islands according to the county map. Ober called his three skinny
sardines of rock and scrub timber with narrow channels between
them by their old names: Hawk, Mallard, Crow.

On the second smallest and surely the skinniest, Mallard, he
began in about 1920 to accumulate his collection of houses.
Mallard is only twelve hundred feet from stem to stern, in places
as narrow as fifty feet from port to starboard. A leisurely stroll
of five minutes will get you from one end to the other. It was not
a vast kingdom physically, so Ober set about making it large in
other ways.

First he built on the east tip a little pavilion he called the
Japanese House, connected to the rest of the island by a wood
arched bridge. He moored an old lumber-camp cook boat—the
Wanigan—permanently to the middle of the island. He bought
cheap an old floating whorehouse and gambling den that had
serviced the lumberjacks, pulling up anchor to cross the border
whenever police arrived either from Canada or from Minnesota.
He christened it Cedar Bark House for its siding. He built a three-
story one-room square tower he called the Birdhouse (named
by his old friend Billy McGee), office on the first floor, bedrooms

with library on two and three. At the west end of the island he built the Front House to watch sunsets—after surveying dawn from the Japanese House. He built a little two-story house across from the Wanigan with an artist's studio and a bedroom—the Cook's House. He built a sturdy boat house behind the Wanigan, but in 1983, after Ober's death, it was lined with shelves and rechristened the Book House. In 1937, after coming into a little cash by selling his mother's house in Davenport, he built the Big House on the highest hill in his Lilliputian domain. Finally in 1950, when he was an old man, he built Winter House, the only insulated space on the island.

He burned kerosene in his lamps and wood in his stoves till he left the island in the 1970s for the nursing home. He pumped water from the lake and shat in a five-gallon pail with a hole cut in a plank sitting on top of it. The little houses are all lined floor to ceiling with bookshelves. They are all full of nooks and crannies, little hidden spaces reached by narrow steep stairs with still more stuffed bookshelves, trap doors leading down to yet more rooms. Inside them stand two old upright pianos stacked with the best art and salon music from the last century: "The Well-Tempered Clavier," "To a Wild Rose," the Beethoven sonatas, Gottschalk's "The Dying Poet," Viennese waltzes, but, surprisingly, the first Bartók and Debussy in early editions too. Two violins hang on the wall, the everyday violin for canoe trips, and the Sunday-go-to-meeting violin for musicales in the Big House. The offices are crammed with thousands of glass plates, negatives, field notes from his trips, transcriptions from Native American languages, drafts of essays, letters, topographical maps. These are play houses filled with the toys of an intelligent but elderly little boy; Ober maintained playfulness to the end.

Outside the houses Ober set about remodeling and civilizing

the wilderness on the model of his old hero, Olmstead. He en-
listed neighborhood artisans, Ojibwa, and immigrant Swedes to
line his island with a rock wall. He tucked nine gardens into tiny
spaces between his menagerie of houses. Since the island surface
consisted mostly of bare granite, pine roots, and lichens, he
barged out topsoil every spring from the mainland for his tulips,
irises, peonies, rhubarb, carrots, turnips, onions, strawberries.
He planted lilacs everywhere—and crab-apple trees, hackberries
from Iowa, even flowering dogwoods. He even tried growing
a corn garden behind the Book House though, not unexpectedly,
it failed. Maybe Ober wanted to admire a little of the Iowa of
his boyhood close at hand. What chance did a native jack pine
have against this onslaught of civilization—order, decorum, an
eighteenth-century garden carved out of wilderness? At night
the old gramophone cranked out Caruso singing "Celeste Aida,"
Fritz Kreisler swooning into "Liebesleid" or "Schön Rosmarin,"
or the steely fingers of Sergey Rachmaninoff rattling out the octaves in a Chopin polonaise. The hell with the loons and their
moony cries of sexual ecstasy burbling over the cold lake. This,
by God, was civilization, Candide's gardens made flesh!

Rosa, herself a musician and a cultured woman, having joined
Ernest on his island in 1916, presided there until her death in
July 1929. Ober was by then deep in the muck of the great political and environmental fight of his life. E. W. Backus, one of the
generation of "malefactors of great wealth," "robber barons," give
them whatever name, invented International Falls by damming
the Rainy River to build a pulp mill, the flagship operation of the
Minnesota and Ontario Paper Company. He acquired timber rights
to an enormous chunk of the Rainy River drainage, had railroad
tracks laid and roads built to transport lumber in and ship it out
as paper or salable timber. But even more money could be made

by selling hydroelectric power to satisfy America's burgeoning addiction to electricity. Backus hatched a scheme to build a series of enormous interlocking dams extending from Lake of the Woods to Koochiching Lake that, had they been built, would have flooded most of what are now the Boundary Waters Canoe Area and Voyageurs National Park, two of the last great stretches of America's wilderness. Those dams would indeed have generated a fortune in lucrative electricity, but they would also have shrunk Ober's islands by raising the level of Rainy Lake from ten to eighteen feet. They would have produced a vast inland Mediterranean freshwater sea, unfortunately frozen solid for seven or eight months a year. And they would have drowned the habitat of the moose and the wolves.

Ober, whose life had been literally saved by this harsh wilderness, launched into battle. He became president of the Quetico-Superior council, testified before legislative committees, bombarded journals and newspapers with letters and essays in defense of wilderness. Partly as a result of his yeoman work, congress had, by the end of the thirties, endorsed the core program that led to the preservation of the Boundary Waters Canoe Area. Backus's schemes had collapsed; Ober found himself, for a while, an environmental hero—a Harvard man who had done something useful with his brains. Lovers of the North Woods still have sound reasons for gratitude for Oberholzer's work.

By now he was sixty—long past his predicted span. Rosa was dead, but he found himself surrounded by friends and admirers. A gracious and sociable man, he loved entertaining callers in the Wanigan, the old white porcelain coffeepot steaming, and the stories unrolling till late into the night. Book dealers sent him their catalogs, and he filled his shelves to overflowing: natural history, travel, exploration—particularly the Arctic—Native

American languages, lore, and history, musicology, literature, biography, and an amazing collection of old cookbooks. Next to his desk he kept the affectionately signed first editions of his old friend Conrad Aiken's books of poems, his schoolmate Samuel Eliot Morrison's histories, the photography of his own island by John Szarkowski of the Museum of Modern Art. They were all his friends now, charmed and delighted by this lively, generous, gregarious old man, so they came to visit, some for a long time: the local Ojibwa, who honored him as friend and scholar, the old rich, the young rebels, writers, artists, but also the local carpenters, fishermen, "characters." He inherited a little money from a rich old friend, Frances Andrews, who loved him, that enabled him to play the patron himself, this man who had little money, no job, no "career," but only a life. He lived on and on, seemingly ageless, despite his start as a frail fellow supposed to have been dead before the First World War. He moved to a little house on the mainland in winter now, and then, in the late '60s, forgetfulness came on him—or as the Ojibwa say, his soul left a few years before his body—and in 1977, at ninety-three, the body took off to join the soul. His last trip to Mallard Island was in 1973 when the Ojibwa and his many admirers among nature lovers conducted a ceremony to install a bronze plaque at the crest of his little kingdom. It praised Ernest Carl Oberholzer: "For fifty years, a friend of the Ojibwa and defender of the wilderness." Ober's body was present that day, still looking alert, but the spirit was checking up on what had become of his younger brother, Frank.

Gene Monahan bagged up her fresh chocolate-chip cookies, made sure we hadn't forgotten any supplies, then guided us the few miles to Bald Rock Point, where we loaded our gear onto her boat, taking off into the autumn sunset for three or four miles to Mallard Island. After we unloaded Gene gave us a tour of the island embroidered with stories and memories. She and her husband were married on the island, Ober serving as best man. As she demonstrated operating the persnickety stove, she remembered Ober standing over it, frying eggs, boiling coffee, telling yarns of his adventures. After we were settled and instructed, we adjourned back to the Wanigan. I made martinis. Gene opened her bag of still-warm cookies. We sat for a couple of hours, listening. Every dish, every book, every antique sat exactly where Ober had left it. His friends—also his legatees—couldn't bear the idea of selling this magical island where Prospero from Iowa had so enchanted them all. Oberholzer's will, in 1965, created a foundation to continue his passions for the environment and Ojibwa culture, to keep the island intact, and to make it available for others to feel its charm, read its books, sleep in its nooks and crannies. She said farewell, "See you in two days." There we were: old friend John, old fat Island, and young Susie from California— alone without a boat—but with eleven thousand books, a stack of music to be played, and a good deal of staring out at the austere beauty of the landscape to accomplish. We lit the fireplace both nights and sat reading aloud to each other out of our book finds of the day, the fire giving our only light. After two days, we wanted to stay, but Gene brought more cookies to tempt us back to the mainland.

An island doesn't have to be very far away from shore or very big to accomplish its true work: to surround you with imminent water, and to unhitch you from the grappling hooks of your own life for a while. Having no electricity helps, as do cold nights with woodstoves and fireplaces, shitting in a honey pot, making coffee

in an old church-basement kettle; even the loons help, yodeling
noisily all night. Eleven thousand books help; there's no pleasure
like literature on a small island—except maybe music on a slightly
out-of-tune decrepit old upright with a cracked ivory or two. It's
amazing how new Bach can sound on an island in the middle of
the night, or maybe just before dawn. The Ojibwa thought these
islands—by whatever name—sacred, but then all islands are sacred in a way, even the prison islands with dark histories. Islands
do not want laptops or cell phones or any ringing or buzzing noise
except the brass bell to summon you to dinner in the Wanigan or
the buzzing of moths around a kerosene lamp or a candle. Islands
want you to read old editions of *Leaves of Grass* or eighteenth-
century travel books or maybe Joseph Conrad's novels. Islands
want you to wash in shallow coves that warm up enough on sunny
days so you can just dip your naked body into them long enough
to scrub off the dust of continents, of offices, of the noise of ringing, buzzing, beeping gadgets, of human foolishness. Even if the
island is small, the imagination grows large to encompass and
comprehend it. Islands want true artists.

When Allan Snowball met me on the dock in front of the
Cedar Bark House in 1986, we were both working for the second
summer as teachers for a little seminar of people interested in
nature and the history of the island. I gave a short guided tour of
the books and what they revealed both about Ober's mind and
about what civilization meant to human beings earlier in this
century. Allan, who knew Ober for the last twenty-five years of
Ober's life, gave a little introduction to Ojibwa culture and language and told stories of his grandfather's friendship with Ober.
Charley Friday, something of a shaman himself, had been Ober's
canoeing pal but also worked for him as a carpenter and stone

mason. Charley built a fireplace for Ober in the houseboat he'd
bought for his old age and moored on the mainland. Charley was
so fond of his stonework in it that he told Ober he'd put his spirit
into one of the rocks to keep Ober company in his dotage. Ober's
senility descended before Charley's death, but Ted Hall, a well-
known local journalist, who was perhaps Ober's best friend and
his long-time neighbor on Gull Island a few hundred yards away,
had insisted that Charley's spirit rock be moved out to the island
to Ober's Big House. Ojibwa elders were consulted. They decided
that, with the proper day-long ceremony, Charley's spirit could
make the trip. Ober's gang of friends gathered for a day of drumming, chanting, ritual burning of herbs, finally the planting of
the spirit stone at the left front end of Ober's island fireplace.
Allan liked being close to his grandfather's soul. He also loved
Ober and thought him his savior.

When Allan was a small boy, his grandfather brought him out
to the island to spend a day with Ober. Ober noticed that the boy
still crawled, couldn't stand upright or walk normally. The boy
has a bad hip, Charley, Ober said. Has he seen a doctor? No money,
no doctor, shrugged Charley. Ober found a doctor, an orthopedic
specialist who diagnosed Allan with a congenital hip defect which,
although repairable immediately, would, if left untreated, leave
him a complete cripple. Ober arranged doctors and financing.
Allan underwent a long series of complicated operations that left
him, though hardly an athlete, capable of walking. His legs were
so shortened by the surgeries that he looked to me like the old
pictures of Toulouse-Lautrec, a man's torso on a boy's wobbly legs.
But legs they were, and they worked to propel Allan through life.
His reverence for Ober was, needless to say, considerable.

Allan inherited, evidently from his grandfather, the gift of

storytelling. He was a handy man with an anecdote. Working together the previous summer, we had taken a fancy to each other's
company and found ourselves, as the only two enthusiastic smok-
ers, often banished together from the company of the squeamish.
We usually ended the day by going up to the bronze plaque on
top of the little hill in front of Ober's house to have a last smoke.
"Ober's soul is right here," said Allan, "next to Grandpa Charley's.
Tobacco is holy—so say the Ojibwa. The dead like a little smoke
too." We fieldstripped our butts, then left the two old spirits a
fresh cigarette for later in the night. Sometimes the cigarettes
were gone in the morning. Never second guess the dead; the spirit
world may be a smoking zone.

Between Gene Monahan's stories, Allan's memories, the
everyday violin hanging on the wall ready to be loaded in the keel
of a canoe, and my chance discovery of Ober's well-thumbed and
practiced old score of Bach's unaccompanied violin partitas, I
began hatching a poem in the summer of 1985. I found a moose
sentence from an Oberholzer essay, but misremembered the real
date of Ober's heroic journey to Hudson Bay. I thought then—
and still think—that World War I was the true divider and initia-
tor of this bloody century, that we continue to live in the shadow
of those monstrous trenches, but that the decade before—when
my own parents were born—was a kind of lost prehistoric age.
The Bach Chaconne is, arguably, the greatest and most profound
piece in the entire history of music, for whatever instrument or
ensemble. It is easy neither to play nor, sometimes, to hear. It
rends the heart. I cannot imagine a fieldstone remaining un-
moved in its presence. I read the poem to the whole group gathered on the island, but Allan liked it best of all. He said he was
honored to have a lively poem dedicated to him, even if, unlike
a proper Ojibwa poem, it didn't rhyme or have much rhythm.

ERNEST OBERHOLZER AND BILLY McGEE
GO CANOEING ON RAINY LAKE

—for Gene Monahan and Allan Snowball

I

In 1913 table feet had claws, men scowled in photographs, world
wars unnumbered yet, your grandmothers and Teddy Roosevelt
still alive. Two, one a Harvard man, the other Ojibwa, paddle
under a fully May moon. Clicks and whispers rise from the just-
broken ice. Otherwise silence. The men say little. One wears
knickers and high boots, a plaid wool shirt, too hot now in
spring. The other wears a skin shirt, face dark under brimmed
hat. A fish leaps. An otter rolls over a few hundred yards ahead.
Ernest Oberholzer spots a moose shadow erect near shore, its
ancient nose pointed somewhere underwater as if music were
rising from that spot. Years later, he writes about moose, saying:

> Sooner or later you will meet one—that ludicrous patch-
> work of snout, hump, bell, and flapping ears that the
> scientists say is one of the oldest animal forms, and more
> than looks it. He not only completes the illusion of the
> past; he makes the Pleistocene a reality.

II

But now it is May, 1913, on Rainy Lake where Canada and
Minnesota come together at the bull's-eye of the continent. The
two canoeists have still not made camp. Billy McGee paddles
while Oberholzer reaches down in the ribs of the canoe, brings
up a violin case. He tightens the bow, rosins its hair, tunes.
Bare fifths ring over splashing fish, moose breathing. He bows
a chord—D minor. Bach's Chaconne. Neither moose, otter, nor
Ojibwa know this music, though they have heard it many times
before. They listen. The violin misses notes in this spiny grandiose

piece, yet sound goes swelling up with that canoe into the night, as if the canoe itself were being bowed by something invisible beside it in the water.

Not just the illusion of the past, this is the past itself, 1913 also a Pleistocene, ice still not quite gone on the cold lake, stone islands only shadows as the moon passes under a cloud, the Chaconne moving into a major key down in the low violin strings, the moose slowly lifting his great heavy nose up from the water into the cold spring night.

The painting that Allan made for me, under Gene's tutelage, will hang on my wall till the day I die. That painting honors history and memory, it honors my old poem, and, best of all, it honors whatever affection, madness, divine afflatus drives us to make works of art, as well as we can make them. After that summer, Allan went back to college, moved to Bemidji, and—too long before his just time—died in 1996. Now he is smoking with Ober and his Grandfather Charley on some well-stocked sardine of an island in the astral ether. I greet him with Walt's words: Salud, Camarado!

Mallard is the island where civilization and wilderness sit down to dine amiably together and drink good wine. Ernest Oberholzer here made a play house—but also a pack-rat collection of the best beauty and intelligence human beings have made for five thousand years. Mallard may be the island where the most generous minds among us choose to spend the afterlife: painting, storytelling, gardening, practicing the Bach Chaconne, maybe even smoking a little between pleasures. It is surely an island of true artists, who give everything—and therefore are able to receive love.

๛ The Necessary Island
The Imagination

THERE YOU HAVE IT—a small tour of a few islands and a few states of consciousness which so resemble islands that they deserve the geographic name. Despite the occasional moralizing and outbursts of advice from the author, the real islands are still real places, separated from other land by water and inhabited by the eccentric characters described. Holm, or "Old Island" himself, still lives in the middle grassland of a large continent, but he has, in the course of scribbling these essays, bought himself a fisherman's cottage called Brimnes, on the northern edge of an island looking farther north to more small islands rising from cold saltwater. He means to die with tide in his ear, salt in his nose, and grass at his back—in fifty years or so.

Meanwhile even the grass grows islands, if you exercise the imagination. Alexander Henry, an eighteenth-century fur trader and explorer (1739–1824) was born in New Jersey, moved first to Montreal, then to Mackinac Island, and in the 1760s to the trackless wastes of interior Canada, now Saskatchewan, where he bought furs from the Assiniboin Indians, traveled over the vast empty flats by dogsled, surviving on boiled buffalo and ox tongue. Traveling in March, still deep winter in Saskatchewan, he says:

At noon we discovered . . . a diminutive wood, or island. . . .

. . . The country was one uninterrupted plain, in many parts
of which no wood, not even the smallest shrub, was to be seen; a
continued level without a single eminence; a frozen sea, of which
the little coppices were the islands. That behind which we had
encamped the night before soon sunk in the horizon, and the
eye had nothing left, save only the sky and snow. The latter was
still four feet in depth . . . [and] drifted into ridges resembling
waves.

Wherever you are, even Saskatchewan, may be your own
island. Listen for surf. John Fowles "always thought of [his] own
novels as islands, or as islanded." He looked for this capacity to
"enisle" (Fowles, too, a shameless verber of nouns!) in other novelists, finding it, of course, in the first modern novel, *Robinson
Crusoe,* and "at the heart of the very first novel of all": the *Odyssey.*
"The island remains where the magic (one's arrival at some truth
or development one could not have logically predicted or expected) takes place; and it rises strangely, out of nothingness, out
of the onward dogwatches, mere journeying transit, in the writing." The island is the domain of the imagination. "Puritans . . .
have always suspected islands," says Fowles. Break the naked
statues off the Yucatán coast. Dam the rivers to drown the islands
full of books and violins. Drive out the Irish monks. Kill the outlaw. Cut down the tree and plow the field. Lock up the lepers and
don't look again. Teach them French, bring them Jesus, and put
a stop to the dancing for the dead. Send Napoleon far away. Send
all the prisoners, the misfits, the revolutionaries, the imaginers
out to their islands, so that order, reason, piety, and capital gains
can flourish. Poor humans! We fear our own imaginations—too
anarchic, too spontaneous, too scornful of the brute reason of

NASDAQ or the Pentagon or the business machine. The imagination leaps to conclusions like a salmon leaping joyfully upstream to spawn. But the imagination is the only divine spark in us—kill it, and you kill any possibility of growing a soul.

Prospero is the great overseer of the imagination in Western literature—and behind him, his own imaginer, Shakespeare, by whatever name you call him. On Prospero's island we are all his puppets, his chess pieces. He moves us at will, with the art of his imagination spirit, Ariel. The practical spirit, Caliban, he finds already living on his island—the lump of dirt that underlies the imagination in all of us. "Thou earth, thou! Speak!" Prospero orders, and since he has tried to civilize his dirt lump by teaching it language: "how / To name the bigger light, and how the less." The lump answers—in English.

> I must eat my dinner.
> This island's mine, by Sycorax my mother,
> Which thou takest from me. When thou camest first,
> Thou strokedst me, and madest much of me . . .
> . . . .
> And then I loved thee,
> And showed thee all the qualities o' th' isle,
> The fresh springs, brine-pits, barren place and fertile.
> Cursed be I that did so! All the charms
> Of Sycorax, toads, beetles, bats, light on you!
> For I am all the subjects that you have,
> Which first was mine own king. And here you sty me
> In this hard rock whiles you do keep from me
> The rest o' th' island.

Prospero chains Caliban because his one urge is to "people this isle with Calibans." Dirt lumps want more of themselves. This

language, like television talk shows, official memoranda, and cy-
berchat goes so far and no further.

> You taught me language, and my profit on't
> Is I know how to curse. The red plague rid you
> For learning me your language!

We carry Caliban with us always onto our islands, and there is
not very much we can do about him. If, as John Fowles maintains,
Prospero "stands for Shakespeare's own power to create magical
islands of the mind", this part "raises very considerable doubts
about the ability of that power to change human nature in any
but very superficial ways." W. H. Auden reminds us that "poetry
makes nothing happen"; it is only "a way of happening, a mouth."
And yet (the two largest English words), without the imagination,
without poetry, what is there? Even the dirt lump at the bottom
of the mind has a few words of language. We must simply teach it
better and not unchain it lightly to go wandering all over the island at will, hatching little broods of more dirt lumps. I'd nominate
the computer on the desk as our newest Caliban. It may show us
a few fertile places if we watch it—very carefully, but it will never
grow up to be Prospero. It is a dirt lump.

The Tempest, says Fowles, "is the first guidebook anyone should
take who is to be an islander; or since we are all islanders of a
kind, perhaps the first guidebook, at least to the self-inquiring.
More and more we lose the ability to think as poets think, across
frontiers and consecrated limits. . . . We are brainwashed into
thinking in terms of verifiable facts, like money, time, personal
pleasure, established knowledge. One reason I love islands so
much is that of their nature they question such lack of imagination; that properly experienced, they make us stop and think a

little: why am I here, what am I about, what is it all about, what has gone wrong?"

Those are the questions I have meant to ask in these essays, and to show answers—not in schemes, plans, projects, recommendations—but in human beings and their grand, unexpected, spontaneous gestures of imagination. For it is only in the actions of human beings that small glimmers of truth—or the soul—can ever be seen. They cannot be told—from pulpit or judge's bench or head office or (God forbid) from an electric screen. You must be in a room—or on an island—when these gestures and inklings come to you. And just as Prospero finally forswears his magic, you cannot quite say them—even in the most magnificent language—except feebly, through a glass darkly. Music, maybe, comes closer than anything else human beings have discovered, but you must sing or play it yourself. You cannot buy imagination at the store. The price is too high—everything you have.

Napoleon, who thought of the whole planet as an island in space to be conquered and made France (or made his own), thought, not surprisingly, that "this island [Saint Helena] is too small for me. The climate is not like ours, it is not our sun, nor does it have our seasons. Everything breathes a mortal boredom here. The situation is disagreeable, unhealthy. There is no water. This part of the island is a desert. It has chased all its inhabitants away." He was still too swollen up in his military Caliban-imagination for this shrunken kingdom in the emptiness of the south Atlantic. Yet after a few years of boredom, languor—a melancholy we non-world conquerors can only begin to imagine—Napoleon turned Prospero in the last year of his life to become a passionate landscape gardener. He ordered a tiny Chinese teahouse built, roofed with a dragon, whose curled tail pointed into the wind. Inside, only a small table and stool—space for one—

and a huge view over the expanse of the Atlantic. He ceased being a slugabed, rising at five in the morning, rushing out to "water the roses and the strawberries, to arrange for trees and bushes to be moved like items of furniture from one place to another until the correct symmetry had been achieved." And then, just as his imagination came to a little more life, he died, and Vignalli, his priest, "managed to remove the Emperor's penis and testicles so that he could keep them as holy and sacred relics." Caliban in a cassock. Still I like the idea of Napoleon's last spurt of interior energy—even on Saint Helena.

To end this tour of islands, I'll play the voice coming out of the cliff face on Drangey when Bishop Guðmundur tries to bless the whole island: "Leave some room for us evil ones." As islands goad and fertilize the imagination, so can they seduce the interior solipsist—the imagination turned inward to feed on itself. One of D. H. Lawrence's best stories (amazingly almost unknown even to lovers of Lawrence) tells the cautionary tale of such psychic cannibalism. "The Man Who Loved Islands" is in three parts—three steadily shrinking islands. He begins:

> There was a man who loved islands. He was born on one, but it didn't suit him, as there were too many other people on it, besides himself. He wanted an island all of his own: not necessarily to be alone on it, but to make it a world of his own.
>
> An island, if it is big enough, is no better than a continent. It has to be really quite small, before it *feels* like an island; and this story will show how tiny it has to be, before you can presume to fill it with your own personality.

Our hero buys his first island at thirty-five, one square mile, close to the coast, a farm—cows, hay, sheep, a few workers: farmhands, housekeepers. No overpopulation, "a horrid thought, for one who loves an island for its insulation. No, an island is a nest which holds one egg, and one only. This egg is the islander himself." He tries to order it as if he were Prospero, but he forgets Caliban. Crops fail, cows fall off cliffs, his yacht runs aground, he is swindled, the servants quarrel, he loses money, more disasters, his image of the pastoral goes to hell. The help like neither each other nor "the Master."

> But then it is doubtful if he really liked any of them, as man to man, or man to woman. He wanted them to be happy, and the little world to be perfect. But anyone who wants the world to be perfect must be careful not to have real likes or dislikes. A general goodwill is all you can afford.

Disillusioned, he sells his island at a great loss to a hotel company who "turn[s] it into a handy honeymoon-and-golf island."

He buys a smaller island, this time "no longer a 'world.' It was a sort of refuge." It is farther from shore. He idles away at his book—but without energy. He tries a love affair—Lawrencean experimental sex in the head. It is a disaster. It was "automatic, an act of will, not of true desire." Humiliated and almost broke, he buys his third island, a few acres of low bare rock plopped in the northern sea, only "sea-turf, a pool of rain-water, a bit of sedge, rock, and sea-birds. Nothing else. Under the weeping wet western sky. . . . This was indeed an island." The final island. Here he shrinks the world; he practices fanatical asceticism. "He didn't want trees or bushes. They stood up like people, too assertive." He doesn't, of course, want people or objects. He comes to hate his few sheep. He drives even the birds away. Once by mistake he speaks aloud, but "rebuke[s] himself for having broken the great silence." He gives up on his "book"—no interest. Finally he comes to hate even the look of printed letters: "so like the depravity of speech." He tears the brass label off his paraffin stove. When the boat comes to take his sheep away, he thinks:

> What repulsive god invented animals and evil-smelling men?
> To his nostrils, the fishermen and the sheep alike smelled foul;
> an uncleanness on the fresh earth.

Even the cat disappears. And now it snows and snows and snows. "'Soon,' he said to himself, 'it will all be gone, and in all these regions nothing will be alive.' He felt a cruel satisfaction in the thought." Then he dies, frozen, starved, silent, alone—in a storm. This last section is worthy to stand with Swift (Gulliver's island of the Houyhnhnms) in its savage dramatization of human misanthropy.

A cheerful story. Loved islands, indeed, did he now? The hero's mistake—the great temptation of islands—was to imagine himself a single egg. The great pounding undertow in Lawrence's work is the passion for organic "connection"—to nature, to human beings, to civilization, to your own body. Just as Donne warned us that we are connected to the promontory of Europe, so Lawrence cries in his loud voice for us to connect connect connect.

We cannot make perfection. If we try to impose it, we become monsters. We are not built for it. We cannot will love. If we will it, it turns to stone. We cannot go "away" to be "alone." There is no "away" and no "alone" except death. If we want not to shrivel up and die like Lawrence's hero, we must trust the imagination to make connection, to give everything away, to sing to the deaf man, to feed the leper, to play impossible counterpoint on the *valiha* with a single hand, to pat Caliban on the head from time to time when he demands money or power or more of himself. You can safely take advice from Old Island. It's all he has to give.

Thanks

SO MANY HAVE HELPED SO MUCH WITH THIS BOOK.
While I mean to praise them for their generosity and wisdom,
they are not to be blamed for the book's faults and foolishness,
which are only mine.

I started to write this book in Arizona, thanks to the hospitality of Doris and Don Wenig of Patagonia, who lent me the "Little
House" as a winter retreat, a desert island of peace, lovely flowers
and good food.

—To my cousins and dear friends, Donna and Les Josephson,
Joan and Chuck and Ken Josephson for cars, pianos, grapefruits,
retreats.

—To Brother Benet Tvedten, Father Guy, Father Augustine,
and all the monks of Blue Cloud Abbey who provided me calm,
hospitality, and wisdom about Father Damien.

—To the children of Snæþór Sigurbjörnsson, and his wife,
Sigurbjörg, farmers at Gilsárteigur: Þórhalla and her children,
Fjóla and Snæþór; Jón Kristjánsson and Gunnþóra and their
daughter, Svandís; and Sigurbjörn Snæþórsson. For twenty years
I have treasured the memory of their generosity and affection.

—To Július Danielsson for finding me the right farm.

—To Valgeir Þórvaldsson, the director of the Immigrant
Museum in Hofsós and my instructor in imagination.

—To Vigdís Esradóttir, manager of the museum and fount of wisdom and song.

—To my cousin Cathy Josephson of Vopnafjörður, a Minneota girl gone right, and to her lovely late husband, Haukur Hreggviðsson.

—To Einar Már Guðmundsson, Einar Kárason, and Friðrik Þór Friðriksson for story upon story late at night and for keeping alive the noble tradition of the imagination in Iceland.

—To Víðar Hreinnsson, Örnólfur Thórsson, and Jóhann Sigurðsson for their grand work with the sagas.

—To Erna Arnar and Þáll Vikunarssón, Séra Bragi Friðriksson and Jón Baldur Sigurdsson, my hosts, my neighbors, my friends in Garðabær, who taught me so much—and fed me so well.

—To Terry Lacy for her long friendship and for her lovely photographs of Iceland. Her own book on Iceland, *Ring of Seasons* (University of Michigan Press, 1997), is full of a quarter century of wisdom and sharp observation.

—To Andrew Elphinstone and Min Dinning, old friends and traveling comrades, through whose eyes I saw Iceland again as if for the first time.

—To President Ólafur Ragnar Grímsson for being an elegant host and history teacher for a large crowd of Minnesota students.

—To Marteinn Hunger Friðriksson and the Cathedral Choir of Iceland for music and metaphor.

—To Howard and Jody Mohr, who have come to enjoy Iceland as much as I do and have shown wry humor where I don't expect it.

—To Paul and Eliana Saxton, old friends from Iceland days and our hosts in Madagascar.

—To Lanto Hariveloniaina, Hanitra Rabetokotany, and Hallie Rabenarivo, guides and teachers in Madagascar.

—To Jean Replinger, who saw to it that I knew Mallard, and to Joe Paddock, biographer of Oberholzer, for facts, stories, and many long years of friendship.

—To my fellow teachers on the SSU Global Studies Iceland tour, Texas Swanjord and Eric Markusen, and to our adventurous students.

—To Chris French, director of the SSU Global Studies program.

—To my colleagues in the SSU English department, who will, I hope, forgive me for one more book.

—To old friends Jan and Dave Lee, who provided a serene cabin high in the Utah mountains for yet another chapter, and for the advice from Mr. Lee, the poet laureate of pain, and of Utah.

—To Gail Perrizo and Tom Guttormsson, who bravely transferred my hen scratchings into the twentieth century, dear friends, neighbors, counselors, partners.

—To John and Lorna Severson Rezmerski, an ever present refuge in time of trouble.

—To Lawrence and Kathleen Owen for showing me a thing or two about Mexico, and Hawaii.

—To M. J. Brekken for almost everything, always.

—To the whole Milkweed gang: Anja, Laurie, Greg, Erik, Susan, Elizabeth, Emily, Beth, Molly, Sid, Hilary, and of course— Emilie! What a lucky man I am to have been a Milkweed writer for so many years.

—Thanks to Wincie Jóhannsdóttir both for her long friendship and hospitality, and for her invaluable advice on Icelandic spelling, grammar, and facts. Where I have gone awry, I have neglected being set on the straight path!

Works Cited

p. 3   John Donne, *The Works of John Donne with a Memoir of His Life,* vol. 3, ed. Henry Alford (London: John W. Parker, 1839), 575.

pp. 7–8   Henry David Thoreau, *Walden* (New York: Modern Library, 1965), 81–82.

pp. 16–17   John Fowles, *Islands* (Boston: Little, Brown and Co., 1978), 17, 28, 30.

pp. 25–26   Gavan Daws, *Holy Man: Father Damien of Molokai* (Honolulu: University of Hawaii Press, 1973), 26.

p. 28   Daws, *Holy Man,* 75.

p. 29   Leviticus 13:45–46. King James Version.

p. 29   John Farrow, *Damien the Leper,* (New York: Doubleday, 1954), 94–95.

p. 29   Quoted in Farrow, *Damien the Leper,* 82.

p. 30   Daws, *Holy Man,* 76.

p. 30   Farrow, *Damien the Leper,* 96, 97.

p. 31   Ibid., 98.

p. 36   *King Lear* 3.4.101–102.

p. 36   Daws, *Holy Man,* 45.

p. 37   Quoted in Daws, *Holy Man,* 63–64.

p. 40   Charles Hyde, quoted in Farrow, *Damien the Leper,* 203.

pp. 40–42   Robert Louis Stevenson, quoted in Farrow, *Damien the Leper,* 207–208, 217–19, 213, 209, 219–20, 220, 221, 210–11, 222.

p. 42   Charles Hyde, quoted in Farrow, *Damien the Leper,* 222.

p. 55   Father Patrick Logan, eulogy for Father Damien, February 3, 1936.

p. 55   William Butler Yeats, *The Celtic Twilight* (New York: New American Library, 1962), 34.

p. 57   Walt Whitman, "When I Heard the Learned Astronomer," in *Leaves of Grass* (New York: New American Library, 1958), 226.

p. 63   J. Humfrey Anger, *A Treatise on Harmony, with Exercises* (Boston: Boston Music Company, 1906), 63.

p. 67   Russell Sherman, *Piano Pieces* (New York: North Point Press, 1997), 7, 9.

p. 67   Philip Dacey, "Thumb," in *How I Escaped from the Labyrinth and Other Poems* (Pittsburgh: Carnegie Mellon University Press, 1977). Copyright © 1977 by Philip Dacey. Reprinted with permission from Carnegie Mellon University Press.

pp. 74–75   Peter Yates, *An Amateur at the Keyboard* (New York: Pantheon, 1964), 3–4.

p. 77   George Bernard Shaw, quoted in David Dubal, *The Art of the Piano* (New York: Summit Books, 1989), 17.

p. 78   Robert Bly, "Listening to Bach," in *Sleepers Joining Hands* (New York: Harper and Row, 1973), 4. Copyright © 1973 by Robert Bly. Reprinted with permission from HarperCollins Publishers, Inc.

p. 80   Milan Kundera, *The Book of Laughter and Forgetting* (New York: Penguin, 1984), 180–81.

p. 81   Sherman, *Piano Pieces,* 6–7.

pp. 97–98   David Quammen, *The Song of the Dodo: Island Biogeography in an Age of Extinctions* (New York: Scribner, 1996), 52, 53, 17–18, 173–74.

p. 102   *Njal's Saga,* translated by Magnus Magnusson and Hermann Pálsson (Harmondsworth, England: Penguin, 1960), 159.

p. 104   *Njal's Saga,* 225–26.

p. 106   William Blake, *The Marriage of Heaven and Hell*, in *The Complete Writings of William Blake* (London: Oxford University Press, 1966), 149.

p. 107   Ralph Waldo Emerson, "Hamatreya," in *Collected Poems and Translations* (New York: Library of America, 1994), 28–29. Reprinted with permission from the Ralph Waldo Emerson Memorial Association and from Houghton Library, Harvard University.

p. 111   Katharine Scherman, *Daughter of Fire: A Portrait of Iceland* (Boston: Little, Brown and Company, 1976), 89.

p. 114   Halldór Laxness, *Christianity at Glacier*, translated by Helgafell (Reykjavík: Helgafell, 1972), 92–93.

p. 119   Brad Leithauser, introduction to *Independent People: An Epic*, by Halldór Laxness, translated by J. A. Thompson (New York: Vintage, 1997), xiii.

pp. 119–21   Halldór Laxness, *Independent People: An Epic*, translated by J. A. Thompson (New York: Vintage, 1997), 196, 374, 377–78.

p. 126   Einar Már Gudmundsson, "Homer the Singer of Tales," translated by Bernard Scudder, in *Brushstrokes of Blue: The Young Poets of Iceland*, selected with a preface by Páll Valsson (London: Shad Thames Books, 1994), 10.

p. 136   *Njal's Saga*, 166.

p. 142   Yeats, "The Circus Animals' Desertion," in *The Collected Poems of W. B. Yeats*, revised second edition ed. Richard J. Finneran (New York: Macmillan, 1983), 348.

p. 171   Yeats, "The Second Coming," in *Collected Poems*, 187.

p. 177   *Common Service Book and Hymnal* (Philadelphia: United Lutheran Press, 1917), 17.

p. 186   Bertolt Brecht, "Concerning Poor B.B.," in *Selected Poems* (New York: Grove Press, 1947), 15.

p. 187   T. S. Eliot, *The Waste Land*, in *Selected Poems* (New York: Harcourt, 1964), 56.

p. 189   W. H. Auden and Louis MacNeice, *Letters from Iceland*
            (New York: Paragon House, 1990), 141, 142.

p. 189   Ibid., 119.

p. 190   W. H. Auden, "Journey to Iceland," in *Letters from Iceland,*
            by W. H. Auden and Louis MacNeice (New York: Paragon
            House, 1990), 25–26. Copyright © 1937 and renewed 1965
            by W. H. Auden. Reprinted with permission from Curtis
            Brown, Ltd.

p. 191   Auden, foreword to *Letters from Iceland,* 8.

pp. 192–93 "The Words of the High One," in *The Elder Edda: A
            Selection,* translated by Paul B. Taylor and W. H. Auden
            (London: Faber and Faber, 1973), 47. Copyright © 1969,
            1973 by Paul B. Taylor and W. H. Auden. Reprinted with
            permission from Curtis Brown, Ltd.

p. 194   *Njal's Saga,* 55.

pp. 194–96 "Audun's Story," in *Hrafnkel's Saga and Other Icelandic
            Stories,* translated by Hermann Pálsson (Harmondsworth,
            England: Penguin, 1972), 123, 124, 126, 128.

pp. 198–99 *The Saga of Grettir the Strong,* translated by Bernard
            Scudder (Reykjavík: Leifur Eiríksson Publishing, 1998),
            16.

pp. 200–201 Ibid., 59, 117, 118.

p. 202   Örnólfur Thorsson, introduction to *The Saga of Grettir
            the Strong,* xxii.

p. 202   W. H. Auden, "Eclogue from Iceland," in *Letters from
            Iceland,* by W. H. Auden and Louis MacNeice (New York:
            Paragon House, 1990), 126. Copyright © 1937 and renewed
            1965 by W. H. Auden. Reprinted with permission from
            Curtis Brown, Ltd.

p. 209   Blake, *The Marriage of Heaven and Hell,* 150, 152.

p. 217   Brenden Kennelly, trans., "The Viking Terror," in *The
            Penguin Book of Irish Verse,* second edition (New York:
            Penguin, 1981), 50. Copyright © 1970, 1981 by Brenden

Kennelly. Reprinted with permission from Penguin
Books Ltd.

pp. 280–81   Etheridge Knight, "Ilu, The Talking Drum," in *The Essential Etheridge Knight* (Pittsburgh: University of Pittsburgh Press, 1986), 75. Copyright © 1986 by Etheridge Knight. Reprinted with permission from University of Pittsburgh Press.

p. 290   Robert Bly, *The Sibling Society* (Reading, Mass.: Addison-Wesley Publishing Company, 1996), 238.

p. 330   Alexander Henry, *Alexander Henry's Travels and Adventures in the Years 1760–1776*, ed. Milo Milton Quaife (Chicago: Lakeside Press, 1921), 270–71.

p. 330   Fowles, *Islands*, 30.

p. 331   *The Tempest* 1.2.312.

p. 331   Ibid., 1.2.335.

pp. 331–32   Ibid., 1.2.330–33, 336–43, 350, 363–65.

p. 332   Fowles, *Islands*, 100.

p. 332   W. H. Auden, "In Memory of W. B. Yeats," in *Selected Poems*, new edition ed. Edward Mendelson (New York: Vintage, 1979), 82.

pp. 332–33   Fowles, *Islands*, 105.

p. 333   Napolean Bonaparte, quoted in Julia Blackburn, *The Emperor's Last Island: A Journey to St. Helena* (London: Vintage, 1997), 97.

p. 334   Blackburn, *The Emperor's Last Island*, 129, 135.

pp. 334–36   D. H. Lawrence, "The Man Who Loved Islands," in *The Complete Short Stories*, vol. 3 (New York: Penguin, 1986), 722, 727, 733, 734, 738, 740, 743, 742, 744. Copyright © 1922 by Thomas Seltzer, Inc. Renewal copyright © 1950 by Frieda Lawrence. Reprinted with permission from Viking Penguin, a division of Penguin Putnam Inc. Laurence Pollinger Limited, and the Estate of Frieda Lawrence Ravagli.

BILL HOLM is both a poet and essayist. He lives in Minneota, Minnesota, close to where he was born on a farm on the tall-grass prairie. He makes most of his living as a professor of English at Southwest State University in Marshall, Minnesota, a curious hotbed of lively literary activity in an unlikely geographical place. He has often taught abroad, twice in China, in Iceland, and in Madagascar, and these adventures and his other travels in Europe, Asia, and North America have fertilized his imagination and often have been the subject of his work. He has published eight books of various kinds—poetry, essays, travel, memoir—most recently *The Heart Can Be Filled Anywhere on Earth: Minneota, Minnesota* (Milkweed Editions, 1996), *Playing Haydn for the Angel of Death* (Minnesota Center for the Book Arts, 1997), and *Faces of Christmas Past* (Afton Press, 1997).

Holm is a winner of several awards, including a Fulbright scholarship, a Bush Foundation arts fellowship, and a National Endowment for the Arts grant. He has been a lecturer for the USIS in Madagascar, and was a visiting lecturer for the Alaska Arts Council in 1999. Last year, he bought an old fisherman's cottage in Iceland that he intends to use for writing and fjord watching. Along with travel, his greatest love and most frequent metaphor is music—particularly the piano. His current project is to master the repertoire of marvelous pieces written for the left hand alone. What is inside music is what language aspires to say, but can never quite get right. He also is attempting to persuade more Americans to read Shakespeare's plays and the King James Bible. That way, he says, "We'll all be as smart as Lincoln, and might start writing as well as Whitman."

Brown Dog of the Yaak:
Essays on Art and Activism
Rick Bass

Changing the Bully Who Rules the World:
Reading and Thinking about Ethics
Carol Bly

The Passionate, Accurate Story:
Making Your Heart's Truth into Literature
Carol Bly

Transforming a Rape Culture
Edited by Emilie Buchwald, Pamela Fletcher, and Martha Roth

Swimming with Giants:
My Encounters with Whales, Dolphins, and Seals
Anne Collet

Writing the Sacred into the Real
Alison Hawthorne Deming

Rooms in the House of Stone
Michael Dorris

The Most Wonderful Books:
Writers on Discovering the Pleasures of Reading
Edited by Michael Dorris and Emilie Buchwald

Boundary Waters:
The Grace of the Wild
Paul Gruchow

Grass Roots:
The Universe of Home
Paul Gruchow

The Necessity of Empty Places
Paul Gruchow

The Mythic Family
Judith Guest

The Art of Writing:
Lu Chi's Wen Fu
Translated from the Chinese by Sam Hamill

Chasing Hellhounds:
A Teacher Learns from His Students
Marvin Hoffman

Coming Home Crazy:
An Alphabet of China Essays
Bill Holm

The Heart Can Be Filled Anywhere on Earth:
Minneota, Minnesota
Bill Holm

Shedding Life:
Disease, Politics, and Other Human Conditions
Miroslav Holub

A Sense of the Morning:
Field Notes of a Born Observer
David Brendan Hopes

Rescuing Little Roundhead
Syl Jones

Taking Care:
Thoughts on Storytelling and Belief
William Kittredge

I Won't Learn from You!
The Role of Assent in Learning
Herbert Kohl

Basic Needs:
A Year with Street Kids in a City School
Julie Landsman

Tips for Creating a Manageable Classroom:
Understanding Your Students' Basic Needs
Julie Landsman

Of Landscape and Longing:
Finding a Home at the Water's Edge
Carolyn Servid

The Book of the Tongass
Edited by Carolyn Servid and Donald Snow

Homestead
Annick Smith

What Makes Pornography "Sexy"?
John Stoltenberg

Testimony:
Writers of the West Speak On Behalf of Utah Wilderness
Compiled by Stephen Trimble and Terry Tempest Williams

Shaped by Wind and Water:
Reflections of a Naturalist
Ann Haymond Zwinger

Interior design by Elizabeth Cleveland
Typeset in Chaparral 11.5/15
by Stanton Publication Services, Inc.
Printed on acid-free 55# Perfection Antique Recycled paper
by Maple-Vail Book Manufacturing